The Jazz Tradition

The Jazz Tradition

NEW AND REVISED EDITION

Martin Williams

OXFORD UNIVERSITY PRESS
Oxford   New York   Toronto   Melbourne
1983

OXFORD UNIVERSITY PRESS
Oxford London Glasgow
New York Toronto Melbourne Auckland
Delhi Bombay Calcutta Madras Karachi
Kuala Lumpur Singapore Hong Kong Tokyo
Nairobi Dar es Salaam Cape Town

and associate companies in
Beirut Berlin Ibadan Mexico City Nicosia

Library of Congress Cataloging in Publication Data

Williams, Martin
 The jazz tradition.

 Includes index.
 1. Jazz music—History and criticism. 2. Jazz
musicians. I. Title.
ML3506.W545 1983   785.42   82-18971
ISBN 0-19-503290-X
ISBN 0-19-503291-8 (pbk.)

Printing (last digit):   9 8 7 6 5 4 3 2 1

Printed in the United States of America

5562

ACKNOWLEDGMENTS

My first debts are to Donald Allen and Barney Rosset who started this when Allen asked me to write about Thelonious Monk in *Evergreen Review* No. 7. From that beginning, *The Jazz Tradition* and some of its theories evolved. My second debt is to Sheldon Meyer who saw what sort of book this could be and encouraged me to revise the material and make it that sort of book.

It may be that I am indebted to every writer on jazz I have ever read and to every musician I have ever heard and spoken with. Specifically, I am indebted to those writers whose names are included herein. The theoretical aspect of my work owes a debt to André Hodeir, particularly to his exposition of the role of Louis Armstrong in jazz history.

Some of the chapters in this book have appeared previously in different form. As included here, they have all been somewhat revised. Some have been thoroughly rewritten and expanded. Also, I have sometimes deleted repetition of basic ideas from one piece to the next except when the repetition seemed to me to serve the purpose of emphasis. I have previously had something to say between hardcovers on several of the artists discussed in these pages. I hope anyone acquainted with those earlier comments will agree that I have things to add here.

The essays on Louis Armstrong, Bix Beiderbecke, Billie Holiday, Count Basie and Lester Young, John Lewis and the Modern Jazz Quartet, Sonny Rollins, Horace Silver, Coleman Hawkins, and Ornette Coleman originally appeared, in different form, in the *Evergreen Review*. The section on Jelly Roll Morton includes several paragraphs from an essay in the *Evergreen Review* but its major portions, here somewhat revised, come from a study written for *Jazz,* edited by Nat Hentoff and Albert J. McCarthy and published by Rinehart in the United States and Cassell in Great Britain.

The chapters on Thelonious Monk and Miles Davis combine material which appeared in the *Evergreen Review* and in the *Saturday Review* in editor Irving Kolodin's "Recordings" section.

The chapter on Charlie Parker combines material which appeared in the *Evergreen Review* and in *Down Beat*. My comments on John Coltrane first appeared in slightly shorter form in *Down Beat*.

In this edition of *The Jazz Tradition,* there are new essays on King Oliver, Sidney Bechet, Art Tatum, Charlie Mingus, and Sarah Vaughan, and I have extensively revised the essay on Duke Ellington. Also, I have added some new comments on those artists whose continuing careers seemed to call for such comment. I have otherwise not restrained an impulse, which any writer must feel, to modify or improve my comments of a decade ago.

I have sought advice and suggestions this time from several colleagues and friends. John Eaton was helpful and encouraging with Art Tatum, and Arnold Laubich, Wiley Hitchcock, and Rick Woodward each offered comment on that same essay. Bob Wilber read and commented on my Sidney Bechet essay. Lawrence Koch saved me from repeating a blunder in the Ellington chapter. Julian Euell offered suggestions on Charles Mingus and Sonny Rollins, as did J. R. Taylor on Mingus.

On Duke Ellington's music, I am much indebted to several writings of Gunther Schuller's—as I believe all future comment on that remarkable musician should be.

Larry Kart read all the essays in the first edition of *The Jazz Tradition* and made valuable suggestions. Mark Tucker has read most of the essays herein, old and new, offered many valuable comments, and on King Oliver in particular, he encouraged me to do better than I would otherwise have done.

I am grateful to them all.

M. W.

Alexandria, Virginia
October 1982

CONTENTS

The Jazz Tradition

1

INTRODUCTION

A Matter of Fundamentals

One observer has suggested that jazz music—or all jazz music but the most recent—represents a kind of cultural lag in which the devices of nineteenth-century European music have been domesticated and popularized in the United States, adding that at the same time these devices were inevitably influenced by an African-derived rhythmic idiom.

I am sure that proposition is untrue. It assumes that European ideas of harmony and melody are fundamental to jazz and used in jazz in the same way that they were in Europe, whereas the truth may be that in jazz, rhythm is fundamental.

Jazz did not exist until the twentieth century. It has elements which were not present either in Europe or in Africa before this century. And at any of its stages it represents, unarguably it seems to me, a relationship among rhythm, harmony, and melody that did not exist before. Whatever did not exist before the twentieth century is likely to express that century.

If we undertake a definition of jazz, we would begin with the fact that it is an Afro-American musical idiom, and we would already be in trouble, for almost all our music is in an Afro-American or Afro-influenced idiom.

And so, to digress for a moment, is much of our culture Afro-influenced. Most of our slang comes from the gallion

3

(as the black ghetto was once called), although numbers of our population continue to believe it is the invention of the teenagers in the corridors of our largely white high schools. So does most of our dancing. And how many Americans realize the origins of the strutting and baton twirling of our drum majorettes—and how would they react if they did know? More than one foreigner has observed that Americans do not walk like their European and Asian relatives, and one observer has gone far enough to declare that they walk more like Africans. Modes of comedy in America have been deeply influenced by our minstrelsy, which, however much it was distorted by white blackface, was still black in origin and, more important in device, in attitude, and in outlook.

To return to our music, it might surprise the patrons at the Nashville Grand Old Opry to learn how deeply their so-called "Country and Western" idiom has been influenced by an Afro-American one, but their reaction would not change the facts. And it should be widely acknowledged that no one in any musical idiom any longer writes for (let us say) the trumpet as he once did because of what jazzmen have shown that instrument can do. Most of our musicians also know that American symphonic brassmen generally have an unorthodox vibrato because of the pervasiveness of the jazzman's vibrato.

It should be acknowledged that today jazz is not *the* popular idiom of American black men. And jazz shares such contributions as its "blues scale" and its unique musical form, the twelve-bar blues, with other popular idioms. But jazz is the most respected Afro-American idiom, the most highly developed one, and the idiom to which improvisation is crucially important.

I hope that from the chapters that follow two ideas will emerge of how jazz has evolved. One has to do with the position of certain major figures and what they have contributed to jazz. The other has to do with rhythm.

I should say at this point that I did not begin with these ideas as preassumptions. They emerged in my own mind and related themselves to the theories of other commentators only as I undertook to write the chapters themselves. They offer, I hope, a more comprehensive and perhaps more musical view of the way jazz has developed than has previously been available.

If we take the most generally agreed-upon aesthetic judgments about jazz music, the first would undoubtedly be the dominant position and influence of Louis Armstrong—and that influence is not only agreed upon, it is easily demonstrable from recordings.

If we take a second generally agreed-upon opinion, it would concern the importance of Duke Ellington, and most particularly Ellington in the maturity of 1939–42.

And a third opinion? Surely the importance of the arrival of Charlie Parker. And after Parker, what made jazz history was the rediscovery of Thelonious Monk. And after that, the emergence of Ornette Coleman—or so it would be if one were looking for evidence of originality after Parker and Monk.

The pattern that emerges from those judgments would be a kind of Hegelian pendulum swing from the contributions of an innovative, intuitive improviser (Armstrong, Parker), who reassessed the music's past, gave it a new vocabulary, or at least repronounced its old one, and of an opposite swing to the contributions of a composer (Ellington, Monk), who gave the music a synthesis and larger form—larger, but not longer.

And before Armstrong? As I hope my essay demonstrates, Jelly Roll Morton's music represented a synthesis and summary of what jazz, and Afro-American music in general, had accomplished up to the moment of his arrival.

There remain the matter of the direct influence of the great figures on some of their immediate followers, and the matter of the few players whom one might call dissenters.

Following Armstrong I have written of Bix Beiderbecke, whose ends were comparable with Armstrong's but whose means and origins were somewhat different. I have spoken of the direct but very different effect of Armstrong on Coleman Hawkins and on Billie Holiday, and of the somewhat less direct effect of his work on the Count Basie orchestra. Similarly, I have tried to discuss Charlie Parker's effect on Miles Davis and on Horace Silver, and to discuss their own contributions. I have endeavored to point out the things that Monk, John Lewis, and Sonny Rollins have in common, along with the things they do not.

The question of where a study like this stops becomes fairly arbitrary at some point. One's final word on where it stops must be that it had to stop somewhere, and it stopped where I stopped it. I have here added chapters on King Oliver, Sidney Bechet, Art Tatum, Charlie Mingus, and Sarah Vaughan. Were I to continue, my next choices might include Earl Hines, Fletcher Henderson, Roy Eldridge. . . . But, as I say, my book stops where it stops.

If we examine the innovations of Armstrong and Parker, I thing we see that each of them sprang from a rhythmic impetus. Similarly, if we look at pre-New Orleans music—cakewalk tunes, then ragtime—we can again identify a definite and almost logical rhythmic change. Similarly, looking beyond Parker to more recent developments we see important changes in rhythm.

Dizzy Gillespie has said that when he is improvising he thinks of a rhythmic figure or pattern and then of the notes to go with it, and I am sure that any important jazz musician from any style or period would give us a similar statement. Indeed, the musicians and fans give us the key to the changes in the music in the style-names themselves: cakewalk, ragtime, jazz, swing, bebop. Casual as they are, regrettable as they sometimes may seem, these words do not indicate melodies or harmonies. They indicate rhythms.

In all the stylistic developments of jazz a capacity for rhythmic growth has been fundamental. And in saying that, I believe we are saying more than we may seem to be saying. There is nothing in the outer environment of the music, nor in the "cultural influences" upon its players, to guarantee such growth. Quite the contrary. One might say that during the past hundred years of jazz and the African-American music that preceded it, American black men have relearned a rhythmic complexity (in different form) which was commonplace to their African ancestors.

And here we find ourselves up against the "liberal" bugaboo of "natural rhythm" and whether Negroes have it or not—up against the position which holds that Negroes do not and could not have something called "natural rhythm," and that it is insulting and even racist to say that they do.

Negroes certainly could not have *un*natural rhythm. The music ultimately comes from people, not alone from their environment or their cultural influences. Certainly blacks must have a rhythm natural to their own music and their own dances (which does not of course mean that "all" Negroes have such a thing, nor that others may not acquire it). Nor is the rhythm simply personal to certain musicians, otherwise there would not be such a wide response to it on the part of others—other musicians, dancers, listeners.

My sense of human justice is not, I hope, dependent on the assumption that black men *could* not have a natural rhythm. Differences among peoples do not make for moral

inequality or unworthiness, and a particular sense of rhythm
may be as natural as a particular color of skin and texture
of hair. No, it does no damage to my sense of good will
toward men or my belief in the equality of men, I trust, to
conclude that Negroes as a race have a rhythmic genius that
is not like that of other races, and to concede that this genius
has found a unique expression in the United States.

It is worth pointing out that the rhythmic capacities of a
jazz musician are not directly dependent on other aspects
of technique in the traditional sense. Players either *think*
rhythmically in a particular style, or they do not. Oscar
Peterson has prodigious facility as a pianist but rhythmically
he does not think in the manner of "modern" jazz, and when
he undertakes a Parker-esque run we may hear an incon-
gruous fumbling in the fingers. Similarly, Buddy Rich, an
astonishingly accomplished drummer technically, still plays
swing-era drums rhythmically.

I think that a rhythmic view of jazz history provides the
most valuable insight into its evolution. But I do not mean
to set up absolute standards in pointing it out, and there
are contradictions when one comes down to individual players, particularly white players. Thus, such harmonic and
linear modernists as Stan Getz, Gerry Mulligan, and even
Art Pepper think in an older rhythmic idiom of alternate
strong and weak accents or heavy and light beats, within a
4/4 time context. Still, pianist Al Haig, for example, who is
white, grasped quite early the rhythmic idiom of Gillespie
and Parker. Coleman Hawkins, on the other hand, once he
had absorbed early Armstrong and begun to develop his own
style, became almost European in his emphasis of the
"weak" and "strong" beats. (I expect, by the way, that this
is because Hawkins is not a blues man.)

Any theory of how an art has evolved holds its dangers.

The life of an art, like the life of an individual, resists schematic interpretations, and the interpreter who proposes one risks distorting his subject to suit his theories. It should go without saying that I hope that my view of jazz history does not involve distortions. But it is my further hope that, the theoretical aspects aside, the individual essays herein may stand on their own as tributes to their subjects.

2

KING OLIVER

Father Figure

King Oliver's Creole Jazz Band has been called one of the legends of early jazz, and perhaps *legend* is the right word for, although there were records made in 1923—thirty-seven selections in all, counting the alternate versions and alternate takes—one needs to hear those records with a sympathetic and even creative ear, so badly were some of the selections recorded, on equipment primitive even for their time. And what one hears is a group of improvising, blues-oriented players, acutely, reflexively attuned both to one another and to the collective power and thrust of their fine ensemble style. That style was at once spontaneous and deliberate, passionate and controlled, controlled in ways that make its passion all the more convincing.

The style and the power of the music were celebrated among the Creole Band's Midwest following and among musicians alike, even before Louis Armstrong had joined them in 1923. And Armstrong aside, it would not be unfair to describe them as a musical whole greater than the sum talents of the individual members. For the lesser members, trombonist Honoré Dutray, banjoist Bill Johnson—even pianist Lil Hardin, mistakes and all—sympathy, thrust, and nuance counted for everything, for none of them played anything otherwise much above the ordinary and the simplicity and repetitiousness of their work was contained by their abilities as interpretive rather than creative musicians. And as exceptional as the Dodds Brothers were, Johnny on clarinet and "Baby" on drums, they were ensemble players foremost.

Johnny Dodds's idol, Sidney Bechet, had already become a solo star in front of the Will Marion Cook orchestra several years before. And yet, and yet. Dodds had some techniques which might still challenge a jazz clarinetist (those in doubt should hear *Snake Rag* and *Alligator Hop*). And Dodds, with so strong and unforgettable a musical personality, could also adapt and integrate himself spontaneously with the others. Still, it is probably accurate to say that the subsequent course of jazz might have been much the same without Johnny Dodds. But not so for the leader, not so for Joe Oliver.

Evidence that the earlier life of the group must have been exceptional can be gained from any of its recordings, for such quick, mutual sympathy among a group of improvisers cannot be brought about by the addition of one musician, no matter how brilliant he is. But it can probably best be heard on a selection like *I Ain't Gonna Tell Nobody*, where Armstrong does not shine but where the ensemble is sublime and its sublimity is sustained. Or it can be heard in the poised, relaxed power of *Chimes Blues*. And *Krooked Blues* tells us a lot about how the joys and the anguish of its music prevail in a performance where the more complex textures, breaks, and other arranged effects might have dominated.

The Oliver band's virtues are well indicated on its first seven titles recorded for Gennett in April 1923: *Canal Street Blues, Mandy Lee Blues, Chimes Blues, Weather Bird Rag,* and *Dippermouth Blues,* to pick the best of them. And thus the New Orleans polyphonic style received one of its best statements on records in one of its earliest. *Weather Bird Rag* is all communion and all momentum and grace, with beautifully timed accents, and sly, superbly timed breaks. Faced with such perfection of style, there was nothing for jazz to do but try for something else—which is precisely what Armstrong and Earl Hines did, within only five years and on the very same piece.

Lawrence Gushee has remarked on the Creole Band's "affirmation of integrity" in almost all it plays, and on "the somber stride of *Riverside Blues,* the steady roll of *Southern Stomps,* the rock of *Canal Street Blues,* the headlong spirit of *Weather Bird.*" But we probably should not pick master-pieces from the Creole Band's recordings, although we can say that *Sweet Baby Doll* and *Where Did You Stay Last Night?* are relative failures and that *Tears* is rather stolid except for Armstrong's breaks.

Despite the fact that King Oliver led an integrated, total ensemble, we can still delight in details: the fine interplay of Oliver and Armstrong on the Paramount version of *River-side Blues;* Dodds's firm, purposeful continuity on *Canal Street Blues;* the sedate trio on *New Orleans Stomp;* the momentary tango-charleston effects from the rhythm and Dutray on *Weather Bird* and *Mandy Lee Blues;* the swirling trio on *Chattanooga Stomp* (from theme statement in har-mony by Oliver and Jimmy Noone, substituting for Johnny Dodds, which gradually loosens to prepare for the increas-ingly jubilant polyphonic variations that follow); the differ-ing two-cornet breaks on the two takes of *Southern Stomps;* Oliver's splendid finale on *Alligator Hop,* or his solo on *Jazzin' Babies Blues* (which Armstrong later developed into his second solo chorus on *Muggles*). And there are Oliver's three celebrated choruses on *Dippermouth Blues,* that ma-jestic structure built only of one- and two-measure fragments.

The alternate takes and alternate versions that we have are revealing. There are two takes of *Mabel's Dream* from Para-mount, and if the second and better-known take is superior, the availability of the first at least lets us hear how differently the leader might treat his material from performance to performance. He not only introduces a different approach in each version of the trio, his effort is clearly to follow through on each approach logically. And Oliver has ingeniously recast the simple two-bar phrases of the piece, placing his accents, his pauses, and rests unexpectedly, but with confidence and ease. On the faster Okeh version, the trio to *Mabel's Dream* is a dazzling cornet duet, with Oliver still in the lead.

Within the limits of the style, the members of the Creole Band are constantly making choices, choices of notes, choices of phrases. And the essential paradox of the Creole Band's music is that although spontaneous choice on everyone's part is constant, choice that is at once personal and collaborative, the ensemble result flows with the inevitability of fate—no, with the passionate inevitability of life itself.

King Oliver's next group, called (for some reason) the Savannah Syncopators, is evidence of change. The leader, whose earlier ensemble seemed to carry each of its tempos with such graceful momentum, repeatedly picked wrong ones. There was an effort, probably following Fletcher Henderson's example, to preserve the sound of the New Orleans ensemble so that the Syncopators' two, sometimes three, saxophones often doubled on clarinets in the ensembles. But if I tell you that the Syncopators' few successes include *Snag It* and *Wa Wa Wa* and *Deep Henderson*, I will be telling you that spontaneous polyphony had given way to spirited but arranged, antiphonal riffing. *Deep Henderson's* chief moment comes when Oliver's strong horn cuts through the ensemble, and he sounds marvelously like the Armstrong of 1923–36.

Oliver's final recordings made for Victor in New York in 1929–30 are largely by studio-assembled groups and they show an extreme unevenness in the leader's own playing.

Oliver could be hesitant (*You're Just My Type*); or simple
but effective (his opening obbligato on *What Do You Want
Me to Do?*, almost the equal to his superb accompaniment to
singer Sippie Wallace on *Morning Dove Blues*); or shiningly
assertive (*Too Late, New Orleans Shout*).

I have said that jazz would not have been the same without
Oliver. His *Dippermouth Blues* choruses became the unin-
spired trumpeter's emergency solo on the medium blues in
C or B-flat well into the 1940s, but mere imitation is of course
not the same thing as influence. Perhaps the best way to
express his effect is to say, in Gunther Schuller's phrase, that
Oliver began to hear and play the "singing quality" between
the four evenly-accented beats-to-the-measure of the New
Orleans style. And his effect on Armstrong made Oliver, at
second hand, an influence on everyone.

Oliver was a seminal artist, but it would, of course, be foolish to contend that he was an excellent cornetist-trumpeter.
He had limited range. And (unlike Armstrong) he may early
have acquired an improper horn placement, embouchure,
and attack that account for the decline and unevenness in
his later work.

Oliver's muted sound and gradations of muted sound are
the crux of the matter surely. And these resources were not
matters of simple, spontaneous impulse. They were carefully
worked out and carefully crafted, like all jazz men's resources,
to be used in performance spontaneously.

Oliver's effect on Bubber Miley carried to the Ellington
ensemble, and as developed by Miley and then refined so
flexibly and sublimely by Cootie Williams, the plunger-
muted growls and cries became a major resource, and hall-
mark, to Ellington and the textures of his brass.

But Oliver's art and his position cannot be accounted for
only by such overt effects, crucial though they were, nor even
by the lasting ensemble pleasures of his earliest recordings.

I think that Oliver lacked humor or, at any rate, that the wry, self-effacing humor of the blues was not quite a part of *his* blues. He did not have the optimistic good spirits and *joie de vivre* of Armstrong. But he had dignity, a dignity which allowed him to speak uncompromisingly, unapologetically of the deepest sorrow and anguish and the most sublime joy and communal jubilation. And he gave jazz the voice of humanity, generous and unashamed.

3

JELLY ROLL MORTON

Three-Minute Form

One thing that leads us to believe that we should call jazz an art, and not just acknowledge it as a remarkable expressive musical culture, is that its best works survive the moment. In doing that they defy all, for not only are they intended for the moment (as is much of our culture), they are often improvised on the spur of the moment.

Much jazz does survive but, to hear that it does, we must be willing to forget what is merely stylish and what is merely nostalgic. Probably no man in jazz was ever more the victim of both stylishness and nostalgia than Ferdinand "Jelly Roll" Morton. Because of the innovations of Louis Armstrong, he was already going out of style before his major work had been recorded. The colorful character of Jelly Roll Morton seems to be one of the abiding clichés of jazz history. The attitude may come from writers' efforts to get people interested in Morton by hooking them on the "character," and it is certainly encouraged by one kind of look at a life that was full of wandering, pimping, bragging, and wild ostentation in dress and possessions. And the braggart, the blowhard, the exaggerator, the liar (often just the audacious kind of liar who does not really expect to be believed)—they were Morton too, and these images encourage one to make a cozy, implicitly patronizing account of him. But in his life and his wanderings, amid all the delusions and painful paranoid railings, was a kind of larger integrity: the music in him always seemed to triumph and led him on.

Morton was an exasperatingly complex and even contradictory man, and he had a large and fragile ego that hardly encourages one to try to understand the man and, what is more important, his music. From his life one grasps what seems enlightening. But the ultimate point is the music. Our knowledge of his life and his world is important only insofar as it enlightens us about his music. And, hearing his music, we know that it expresses more of the man and his deeper feelings than his public masks, his pride, his snobbery, his pontifications, and his prejudices can show us.

One of Morton's best recordings is of a piece he called *Dead Man Blues*. Like W. C. Handy's blues, and like ragtime pieces before them, *Dead Man* is built on several themes—specifically three. The themes obviously need to work well together. And they need to be put into an order that gives the piece as a whole a sense of musical and emotional development.

In planning a performance, one concern of a jazz composer-arranger is to decide who plays what, who improvises when and how much: how to bring out the best in each player without letting him overpower the total performance. The whole, in an ideal performance of a great jazz composition, has to be greater than the sum of its parts.

Musically, Morton's recording of *Dead Man* begins with an echo of a funeral procession, an introductory strain from the familiar Chopin *Funeral March,* the lead played on trombone with a hint of humor. From this point on, *Dead Man* attempts the difficult task of being sober without being stodgy.

The first theme in *Dead Man* is stated in a dancing polyphony[1] by the trumpet's lead, with the clarinet in a quietly simple second part behind it, and a trombone in a rhythmic-melodic bass line. There is a buoyancy of melody and rhythm in this chorus; it is quite unlike the heavy, plodding, and strident Dixieland of earlier and later years, and such masterful ensemble playing in this style is perhaps a lost art.

The second section of *Dead Man* is a series of variations, overlapping two of its themes. The first is a chorus by Omer Simeon's clarinet, a variation on the first theme. The second is a two-chorus solo by cornetist George Mitchell, comprising the second theme plus one variation on it. Mitchell shapes lovely, logically-developed, simple melodies. They hang together but his second chorus develops his first, and it further prepares for the entrance of the third *Dead Man* theme. It is rare that a solo can have such structural uses and still be beautiful in itself, but the great jazz composers can always encourage such playing.

Dead Man's third section begins simply, with a trio of clarinets playing a lovely, riff-like blues line in harmony.[2] As they repeat the chorus, Kid Ory's trombone enters behind them with a deep, moaning countermelody.

In the final section, as if encouraged by Ory, Mitchell and Simeon join the trombonist, the other two clarinets drop out, and the three horns play a lovely, three-part polyphonic variation on the opening theme. Thus the closing polyphony

1. I have here again followed the general practice of calling the New Orleans style polyphonic. However, polyphony implies several melodic lines of equal importance, but in New Orleans jazz the trumpet (cornet) or trumpets obviously carry a lead melody to which the lines of the clarinet, trombone, and rhythm are secondary.
2. This theme was not used in Morton's other versions of *Dead Man;* it does not appear in the sheet music nor in the piano roll version of the piece. However, King Oliver had recorded the strain as *Camp Meeting Blues* in 1923.

balances the opening. The three clarinets then tag the performance with a brief echo of the third theme. The overall
scheme of *Dead Man Blues* is therefore intro/A/A1 (clarinet
solo)/B and B1 (cornet solo)/C/C1/A2/tag.

In some accounts, Morton's music is placed in a neat category called "New Orleans style," and there the explanations
stop and the enthusiasm starts.

That category is not so neat. The usual explanation is
that New Orleans style is something the Original Dixieland
Jazz Band first popularized, the style Kid Ory put on records
in 1921, the style King Oliver's Creole Jazz Band recorded in
1923, the style certain of Johnny Dodds's groups (The Wan-
derers, The Boot Blacks, The Black Bottom Stompers) recorded later, and that the early Armstrong Hot Fives reflected. Such an effort to place Morton historically is far too
general to be very enlightening. There were many kinds of
music played in New Orleans and a number of these, from
the propriety of A. J. Piron to the crudeness of Sam Morgan,
we would be willing to call New Orleans jazz or something
near it. They were not all alike. Furthermore, despite the
similarities, it should be obvious that there are some musical
differences in conception between Morton's orchestral music
and Oliver's. Oliver's music was improvisational, blues-
oriented and played by musically integrated instrumentalists,
whose greatest virtue came from the individuals involved
and the way they blew together. Morton's is the leader's
compositionally conceived music with careful orchestra-
tional form. Rhythmically, Morton's music represents an
earlier stage in jazz than Oliver's. But for the moment he
does represent, Morton was a modernist, as far as we can
tell. He was also perhaps something of an innovator, but
his music showed more sophistication, consciousness, and
formal musical knowledge than Oliver's, and he had defi-

nite theories about what he was doing. At the same time, Morton never abandoned the expressive and earthy realities of jazz and the blues.

As far as we can tell—as far as written documents, published scores, and recordings enable us to tell—Morton was the first great master of form in jazz. In this respect, he belongs with Duke Ellington, John Lewis, and Thelonious Monk. By the late 1930s, Ellington had absorbed into his music the innovations which Louis Armstrong, as an improviser, had announced. Lewis (partly by assimilating and transforming form from Europe) and Monk (by working more directly with the implicit resources of jazz itself) found form within the innovations represented by Parker, Gillespie, and Monk himself.

With what resources at hand did Morton work? Buddy Bolden's? If we accept Bunk Johnson's re-creations of Bolden's style, Bolden's sense of form as an improviser was a strong one and strikingly like Morton's as an orchestrator (and, incidentally, like Monk's). We can say that despite his exemplary handling of single-theme compositions, Morton's conception represents an extension of the form established by the great ragtime composers, but it also incorporates rhythmic, harmonic, and variational elements of the jazz movement and the blues. Morton's conception was later than Scott Joplin's or perhaps Bolden's, earlier but more sophisticated than Oliver's. In effect, Morton's music represents a summary of all that jazz had achieved before Armstrong's innovations reinterpreted its basic language.

There are some curious likenesses among these leaders of form: Morton, Ellington, Lewis, Monk. All are pianists (or at least they all play piano) and all have been called poor pianists which in some, usually irrelevant, senses, several are. All are major composers, of course—among *the* major composers in jazz. All may show, at least part of the time, an orchestral (rather than horn-like) conception of the piano, which can make them all sometimes unorthodox but extremely effective accompanists. All have taken strikingly similar approaches to the problem of improvisation vs. form, freedom vs. discipline, individuality vs. total effect. And for Morton and Ellington at least, as their messages of form began to take effect, revolutionary improvisers arrived. The maturing of Ellington's sense of form was followed by Parker's innovations, but Ellington had a lot to do with planting the seeds. There were signs of another revolution as Monk's sense of form began to be recognized, and Monk planted the seeds. Morton was the unluckiest of the four, for he had hardly begun recording and regular publication before Armstrong's revolution had already taken effect. He began almost as an anachronism, a leader of a style already becoming unstylish. But perhaps hints of Armstrong's innovations are to be heard in his music. And obviously it is not against Armstrong that Morton should be judged artistically.

One other thing that all these men (Morton, Ellington, Lewis, and Monk) share is a crucially important movement —ragtime. Ellington was steeped in its Eastern, later "stride" branch. Monk got it indirectly from Ellington and somewhat more directly from James P. Johnson and Fats Waller. Lewis got it indirectly and largely from Ellington, but he has professed an admiration for James P. Johnson, whose relationship to ragtime was direct, and was based on the Midwestern-Sedalia-St. Louis version.

In itself, ragtime proved to be a kind of blind alley, but its contribution to jazz, and to form in jazz, is probably immeasurable. From one viewpoint, it was the most formal, most "European," even most "highbrow" movement associated with jazz. It is incredible that in so short a time its folk themes, ring shouts, church themes, European dances, and military strains could be so transformed and formalized as to create a unique, identifiable body of pianistic music. Within a decade after the emergence of ragtime (beginning in about 1899) exploitation, excess, popularization, decadence, and its own implicit limitations had overtaken it. Meanwhile, for the greater jazz movement, its work had been done and would abide for fifty years.

Although Morton respected the best ragtime men and said so, he apparently saw what was happening and what was missing. The music had become, in the hands of pseudo-ragmen, a kind of showman's piano for vapid displays of fingering; and in the hands of publishing-house hacks, it was a style in which to compose banalities. Joplin's work aside, by about 1905 the style had become rigid, and even some of the more legitimate rag composers simply decorated or reworked ragtime commonplaces. Morton was part of a movement which saved things from decadence. Ragtime was structurally, rhythmically, and emotionally limited, and Morton seems to have known it.

The printed scores of Morton's typical multithematic pieces—*Wolverines, King Porter Stomp, The Pearls, Kansas City Stomps, Grandpa's Spells,* etc.—show three themes, a developing or contrasting melodic and tonal relationship among them (often as ABC or ABAC), plus one or two choruses of variation on the third theme. A very few ragtime scores survive which include written variations. In performance, spontaneous variations, or at least decorative embellishments and fills, were sometimes made, but variation is not essential to this music. Written variation is obviously essential to Morton's music, and we know that in performance, improvised melodic variation is a part of its substance.

There are other differences: in rhythm, harmony, and emotional range.

One could describe Morton's smoothing out of ragtime rhythms as the result of the addition, to the clipped 2/4 and

simple syncopations of ragtime, of more complex tango-
derived syncopations and of polyphonic bass melodies borrowed and transformed from certain marches and European
dance music. One could also describe his harmonic progress
as based on his knowledge of European music and the intuitive freedom with which he could relate tonalities and
arrive at simple substitute chords—something which neither
King Oliver nor James Scott knew as much about. And his
emotional range was perhaps the result of his feeling for the
blues. But these categories make very arbitrary separations,
they overlap in practice, and they do not give a complete
picture even of Morton's "sources."

Many of the ragtime composers were well-schooled, some
undoubtedly better schooled than Morton. Most of the
resources that Morton used were there in the European
music to which he was exposed—ready and waiting to be
used, as it were, for a long time. But, as the history of jazz
has shown repeatedly, the Promethean task is always a matter
of showing that such European-derived techniques will
work as jazz, how they will work, and assimilating them
into the jazz idiom. Making a musical resource work into
jazz is never easy, never the result of only formal musical
knowledge nor of will. It takes what we can only describe
as an intuitive genius and insight into the nature of jazz.

A fundamental aspect of Morton's music came from the
way that his bass lines and his other melodic phrases inter-
acted to produce polyphonic and polyrhythmic patterns, anticipated downbeats, delayed accents, syncopated Spanish
rhythms, and trombone-like melodies.

In *Mr. Jelly Roll,* Alan Lomax invited us to see Morton's
music as an ingenious combination of "Downtown" and
"Uptown" New Orleans elements: the largely European
(but "folk" and therefore rhythmic) music of the colored
Creoles, plus the earthier music—blues, work songs, spir-

ituals—of the uptown Negroes and ex-slaves, some of whom had migrated from nearby plantations.

Similarly, one might see it as an alliance between rag-time and the blues, with importations from French and Spanish folk musics, Baptist hymns, and martial music—the last at least analogous to rags.

Unfortunately, most discussions of the constant flirting of jazz with "Latin" music soon bog down into a listing of compositions, beginning with Joplin's *Solace* and including Horace Silver's *Señor Blues* or Ornette Coleman's *Una Muy Bonita*. The source of the syncopated 2/4 (which led to-wards 4/4) of jazz may well be the tango. The source of the behind-the-beat delays and "around-the-beat" accents which are so important to Morton's *New Orleans Blues, New Or-leans Joys, The Crave,* or *Mamanita* could also be the tango. The very placement of the melodic phrases in, for example, the third theme of Morton's *Wolverine Blues* corresponds with the placement of the heavy beats in a tango—but *Wolverines* is not a jazz tango. Clearly, "the Spanish tinge" (Morton's name for this Latin influence) goes deeper than certain compositions, than an occasionally brilliant effect which one hears not only in Morton's but in Oliver's rhythm section, and than Morton's own comments might lead one to believe.

And from the blues the music gained further rhythmic character and variety, depth, honest passion, and spontane-ous variation and improvisation.

Between the waning of ragtime and the ascendancy of New Orleans jazz music, there was an overlapping popular movement in American music called "the blues craze," which was announced by the song publications of W. C. Handy, pieces like *St. Louis Blues* and *Beale Street Blues.* In some ways, Handy's approach was more formal even than ragtime's. It was also perhaps a bit arty. He took indigenous

blues melodies, made them regular, harmonized them, and
evolved a system in which the "bent" tones of the blues
"scale"—notes found in every music in the world except
Western concert music, by the way—could be imitated by
putting the third and seventh notes of the scale in minor.
He built several of these melodies into often splendidly
organized multithematic compositions on the model of rags.
Even in Handy's somewhat fussy approach, rhythmic variety,
"breaks" (suspensions of a stated pulse), and passion were
captured.

As is evident from Morton's re-creations on his Library
of Congress recordings of the kinds of blues that were played
in the lowest dives in New Orleans, there was a lot of structural and, more important for the moment, rhythmic diver-
sity in this music. There were blues in the clipped 2/4 of
ragtime, in the smoother and syncopated 2/4 of Creole jazz,
in a 4/4 swing suggesting the rhythm of Armstrong, and
even in the eight-to-the-bar of boogie woogie (which, by the
way, suggests the rhythmic patterns of modern jazz). Handy's
records of his own blues used a mechanical version of rag
rhythm and a rather arty dance band approach. When others
played Handy's blues, a rhythm almost like New Orleans
Creole jazz often emerged.

Even in the most formally compositional blues, there can
be emotion unknown to ragtime. There would be no jazz
without the blues or, to put it a bit differently, without the
blues jazz would be a sterile music. But without ragtime,
what a melodically limited kind of rhythm-making jazz
might be! The European tradition of form, discipline, and
order probably affects jazz more *directly* today than before,
but these ideals crucially affected it indirectly through ragtime long ago.

The blues had rhythmic variety, passion, and, chiefly because of Handy's work, a certain public respectability. Like

most folk music, the blues were performed with improvisation. Combining the melodic-compositional emphasis of rags and the improvisational-variational emphasis of blues, we have the basis for Morton's principle of thematic variation. Inevitable or not, simple or not, it was an almost brilliant stroke, for it combined and developed the virtues of both forms but the dangers of neither. It made variation meaningful, but channeled and controlled it. It kept the music fresh and alive, but gave it order and purpose. It also opened up many possibilities for future developments. Later conceptions might have allowed more freedom, but at this stage, and with polyphonic structures, it was precisely this discipline of Morton's that helped immeasurably to transform emotional impulse and musical craft into art.

Morton's "theory of jazz" which he gave to Alan Lomax is not so much a theory as it is a specific response to the definition of jazz which used to be in certain American dictionaries (something about loud, fast, blatant, cacophonous noises) and similar "Aunt Sallies." But it does give certain principles that were important to him and, perhaps more to the point, does affirm that his mind was the kind which thought about practice and arrived at principles. The fact that he acknowledges that he worked out his style at medium tempos (which permitted him to work on note-doublings, embellishment, and accentual displacements) not only indicates a fundamentally rhythmic approach to jazz but coincidentally indicates the basis on which most subsequent innovations were also worked out. Hear the recordings made at Minton's in the early 1940s; hear the Armstrong of the late 1920s and early 1930s. Much has been made of Morton's remark, "Always keep the melody going some way." It does acknowledge that thematic variation is Morton's way, but it is actually an afterthought to his insistence on proper and interesting harmonization.

Much has been made of Morton's insistence that riffs (simple, rhythmically pronounced melodic phrases repeated over and over) are for background, not for themes. No one could doubt that the great effectiveness of riff melodies is often bought cheap, but Morton himself wrote some riff melodies, and the very riff he used to demonstrate his point was the final theme of his rewriting of Santo Pecora's *She's Crying for Me* into *Georgia Swing*. Many of his other themes, like many rag themes, are simple and brief enough in their basic ideas to amount to riffs. At any rate, one could hardly doubt the effectiveness of riffs behind soloists. Nor could one question that his principle that a jazz pianist should imitate an orchestra has the confirmation of time; from Morton through Bud Powell, Earl Hines through Erroll Garner, pianists follow either band or horn styles.

As Morton put it, using "breaks"—brief two-bar, suspensions of a stated rhythmic pulse—is "one of the most effective things you can do in jazz." In a sense they are a culmination of the rhythmic resources of the music (unless "stop time," two-bar breaks in series, carries things a step further) but Morton is probably the only man, musician or critic, who made them a principle. They continue to be used today (often at the beginning of choruses instead of as a climactic device), and the subtle sense of time and suspense they require is the bane of many a "revivalist" dixielander and an excellent test of a musician's swing.

Morton's assertion that jazz can be played soft, sweet, slow, with plenty of rhythm (or, as André Hodeir later put the same principle, "swing is not the same as getting hot") is, of course, crucial. The problem of swing at slow tempos plagues jazzmen periodically.

Morton was, as I say, something of a modernist. That is why he so frequently ridiculed "ragtime men." He was part of a movement which saved Afro-American music from degeneration at the hands of pseudo and second-rate ragtimers and continued its development. He obviously respected the *best* ragtime and its composers, however. And that is also why he frequently scorned blues instrumentalists ("one tune piano players"). His work was more sophisticated, formal, knowledgeable, resourceful, and varied than theirs. It was a product of intelligence and theory as well as emotion and intuition.

Morton's real reputation depends on a brilliant series of orchestral recordings he made for the Victor company between September 15, 1926 and June 11, 1928—a short enough period, but greater reputations in jazz have been made on less finished work.

These recordings are the real successors to the striking series of piano solos he made for Gennett, Paramount, Rialto, and Vocalion between 1924 and 1926. He had made other orchestral records before the Victors, none of them really worthy of him as a pianist nor anticipating the orchestrator and leader he was to become. But in those early band records he did try out some of the devices and effects he was later to perfect.

The exception among the early band recordings, and a real success, are the simplest in scoring, the pair of titles on Paramount, *Big Fat Ham* and *Muddy Water*—polyphony plus solos. Jasper Taylor's excellent (if overrecorded) woodblock drumming falls into just the right rhythmic role for Morton's music. There is fine group swing, the right balance between discipline and expressiveness in the playing, with the Keppard-Oliver-like trumpet and the clarinet understanding and displaying this relationship excellently. But Morton's attempt to use a saxophone as an extra polyphonic voice is a failure; it was something he would try again and something he seldom made much of, partly because few of these saxophonists ever got any swing.

Otherwise, an inept clarinetist, an amateurish trumpeter, or a rhythmically awkward ensemble usually spoils these early recordings. The Morton-directed version of *London Blues* by the New Orleans Rhythm Kings ably alternates passages in harmony, counterpoint, solos, and breaks, along the lines he later perfected. The later Okeh *London Blues,* reorchestrated in polyphony and spoiled only by bad clarinet, shows for the first time on records the effective variety and thoughtfulness of Morton as an accompanist. Among the remaining records, the Gennett version of *Mr. Jelly Lord* (1926) features a three-man reed section which plays, and swings, in harmony.

As I have said, Morton's achievement, before the Victor orchestral recordings were made, was his piano, and we should take a closer look at that style.

In 1944 William Russell wrote an analytical review of Morton's rediscovered *Frog-i-More Rag* solo for the magazine *The Needle,* which, I think, offers a definitive statement of Morton's style:

> Jelly Roll's piano style and musical greatness are nowhere better demonstrated. . . . All the most typical features . . . are abundantly evident: his wealth of melodic invention and skill in variation; the tremendous swing . . . his feeling for formal design and attention to detail; his effective use of pianistic resources; the contrasts of subtle elegance with hard hitting drive; the variety of harmony, and yet freedom from complication and superficial display. . . .

> Jelly Roll had a more formal musical training and background than many New Orleans musicians. . . . At times the close-knit design is marked by an economy of means

that amounts to understatement. *Frog-i-More* follows the usual form of Morton's stomps—introduction, a short three-part song form, and a trio section. A definite musical idea is used for each new part. Since the opening idea for the first strain, an ascending succession of 7th chords, does not immediately establish the tonality, a curious effect of an extension of the introduction is created. The contrasting second strain is unusually forceful, employing a repeated-note motive and powerful left hand bass figures in Jelly's full *two-handed* style. After a modified return of the first strain a characteristic Morton trill bridges over to the trio. . . .

Jelly took great pride in his "improvisations" (on theme) . . . listen to the trio section to discover Jelly's phenomenal skill in variation. And if one were to study the four different versions of *The Pearls* or the half-dozen recordings of *Mr. Jelly Lord,* and perhaps also take time to compare some of these variations with the published versions, he would begin to get an idea of Jelly's unlimited imagination and mastery of motival variation. . . . The beautiful chorale-like melody of the *Frog-i-More* trio is first played very simply, in a style reminiscent of the sustained trio of *Wolverine Blues.* . . . On paper the tune, with its constantly repeated motive, presents a singularly four-square appearance, but Jelly's performance is a revelation of rhythmic variety by means of such devices as shifted accents, slight delays, and anticipations. . . . As raggy as Jelly's performance of this chorale is, it nevertheless is in perfect *time;* the regular pulse can be felt throughout with no loss at all in momentum. . . . The melodic invention of this finale is as notable as its immense rhythmic vitality. . . . Jelly's rhythmic impetus and melodic embellishment give the effect of a fantastic and frenzied variation. Actually, each bar is directly related to its counterpart in the first simple statement and all of Jelly's characteristic and fanciful "figurations" are fused with the basic idea as though they belonged there originally . . .

with Jelly Roll, no matter how exuberant rhythmically or
varied melodically the final choruses become, there is never
any doubt of their musical logic and each note grows out of
the original motive. Nor is the typical flavor of the unique
Morton style ever . . . lost.

When Morton recorded his music, reminiscences, and
fabrications for the Library of Congress, beginning May 21,
1938, he gave us documents that are revealing, exasperating,
and delightful. His piano invention is extended, unham-
pered by such things as the time limits of recording for a
ten-inch 78 r.p.m. There are unique revelations of his resources and fine inventiveness on the extended versions of
Wolverines, The Pearls, Creepy Feeling. But this man,
aging, sick, inwardly discouraged behind the pride and
bravado, sometimes faltered in fingering and time.

One of his most revealing performances is of Joplin's
Maple Leaf Rag, first in St. Louis-ragtime style, then in his
own. The performance speaks for itself of his innovations in
rhythm, tempo, polyphonic effect, improvised variation. Guy
Waterman has said of Morton's reorganization of Joplin's
Original Rags:

> The most obvious indications of Jelly's jazz approach stem,
> in the right hand, from the improvisation and, in the left
> hand, from the anticipated downbeats and the octave runs
> of four sixteenth-notes, Jelly's trademark. Actually, however,
> these devices do not explain the full transformation which
> Jelly brings about. There is a gulf which separates ragtime,
> as the early rag composers understood it, from jazz as Jelly
> epitomized it. This gulf has more to do with the type of beat
> which the two develop and the nature of the momentum
> which builds up. The difference is reflected in the entire
> organization of the performance.[3]

3. *The Jazz Review,* December 1958.

Two other performances on the Library of Congress series are worth examining for what they show us about Morton's ideas of structure. The first is an extended version of *Kansas City Stomps*. As published, *Kansas City Stomps* consists of an introduction (a "tune-up" motif) and three themes: A (*e* flat), A (an exact repeat), B (*e* flat), B (an exact repeat), C (*a* flat), C' (a melodic variation). Both A and B are sixteen-bar themes (out of ragtime, polkas, and marches) and C is an unusual twelve-bar melody with a double break at bar one and at bar seven, making two six-bar units.

In this performance Morton plays: introduction, A, A' (a variation), B, B' (a variation), A" (another variation), C, C' (a variation), introduction (a modulational interlude), A"' (a third variation). Thus an implicit rondo is completed, with each return to each theme a variation on that theme.

Then there is the challenge of a single theme. *Hyena Stomp* is a simple sixteen-bar melody of pronounced rhythmic character—an extended two-bar riff, if you will, on one of Morton's favorite chord structures. As a comparison of the shortened printed score and the orchestral version he did for Victor records will show, the basic outlines of the way Morton handled variations on it were compositionally preset—but that is true of much jazz. As is also true in jazz, the way the outlines are *used* in performance can be another matter.

The basic motive of the theme is stated in the first two measures, then moved through a chorus of sixteen bars which serves as an introduction. There follows a second sixteen-bar chorus in which the melody is again stated in bare form. In these first two statements the harmony is deliberately rung clear so that an almost lyric mood is set with that riff, but there are hints of the kind of rhythmic variation to come. There follows a series of six variations. Each is based on a musical idea which Morton works out; each is related to what immediately precedes and follows it, either as contrast or complement; each is also part of the total pattern of the performance; and each is orchestrally or instrumentally conceived.

Chorus three is primarily rhythmic, an appropriate contrast to the careful harmonic-lyric emphasis of the first two. Morton simplified the melody and harmony drastically in a kind of "barrelhouse" destruction of the piece, in which the swinging momentum and a partly polyphonic bass line are first introduced. From this simplification, Morton rebuilds *Hyena Stomp* in various ways. The fourth chorus is an elaborate lyric transformation—melodically the most complex—of the theme, dancing lightly after the heavier motion of what has preceded it. From this point on, as we gradually return to and build on the pronounced rhythmic momentum introduced in the third chorus, we hear a melodic simplification from this peak, and dynamic building. The fifth chorus is an excellent stroke. It still refers to the melody but it also transforms (by simplification) the fourth, forming a kind of two-chorus unit with it. The sixth chorus is a contrast, but one which had been subtly prepared for. It is a variation in the bass (a rather complicated one for the time) under a simple treble statement, and in the preceding chorus there has been much activity in his left hand, readying our ears for this one. In the seventh chorus we are reminded of trumpet figures, and these gradually build into an ensemble variation in the eighth. Morton leads into and makes his climax. The dynamic-rhythmic ideas continue to build excitement and the rhythm swings freely and simply.

Assigning the styles of the variations to instruments, we would have:

Chorus 1   ensemble in harmony
Chorus 2   ensemble, hints of polyphony
Chorus 3   polyphony
Chorus 4   clarinet solo, lower register
Chorus 5   clarinet, upper register, trombone in polyphony
Chorus 6   trombone solo, broken polyrhythms behind
Chorus 7   trumpet into riffs, hints of polyphony
Chorus 8   unison brass-like riffs, still on theme

On the basis of the various ways that Morton handles his simple theme, we have heard some remarkable things, but there is even more in some of the details.

As we have seen, our chorus unit is sixteen measures. But Morton used variations which joined two groups of choruses (four and five, seven and eight). At the same time, each chorus, by the nature of the theme, may fall into two eight-bar units. These, in turn, may fall into units of four bars. Then there is the fact we began with: the basic melodic motive can be stated in two bars. To some, such a thing is evidence of melodic crudeness. Morton, apparently aware of these limitations, took interesting advantage of them and made them principles of his structures. The final chorus, for example, consists of an unbroken eight-bar line followed by two four-bar units, held together emotionally. Also, the first melodic fragment in chorus one is not exact; an improvised shift of meter is then corrected in bars three and four. And in the two clarinet choruses Morton handles bar lines with further ingenuity: the first is based on a parallel repetition of two-bar units; the second begins with contrasting two-bar units. Thus Morton builds variations in continuity within choruses, combines some of these into double choruses and, within this, works out small structures of two, four, and eight bars, all of which contribute by contrast, parallel, and echo to a total development and unity.

Any such an attempt at scrutiny as the foregoing is bound

to make a music that is warm, passionate, and spontaneous seem a contrived and pat set of devices. The point of it, of course, is to illustrate general and subtle principles of style. In any given performance, the application of Morton's ideas will be different. But once one grasps the nature of these ideas and their relationships, the excitement, beauty, and uniqueness of Morton's work will, I think, possess him even more strongly and lastingly.

Behind the success of the Victor recordings are a maturity in Morton's conception, the availability of a group of musicians equipped both to play well and to follow Morton's exacting instructions and leadership, careful rehearsal, and a series of exceptional orchestrations.

Like the question of how many of his compositions Morton borrowed or otherwise got from others (a question hardly confined to him—it might be raised about many major jazzmen), the question of how much musical knowledge he actually had and how much help he had with scoring is perpetually unresolved. One can get testimony, often from excellent jazzmen, that Morton knew little about music and played badly. One can get just as much reputable testimony that he was an excellent musician, ahead of his time in several respects, and could play extremely well. The only answer, of course, is his playing—*with* its faults and with its evident evolution and refinement. The answer to the complaint that Morton did not make his own orchestrations is the obvious fact that a single musical intelligence and taste is behind them. Doc Cook, Tiny Parham, Mel Stitzel, and others have been mentioned as helpers with scoring. The answer undoubtedly is that, even if Morton needed help, the conception was nevertheless his.

The ensembles for the Victor recordings were sometimes written—always at least sketched—in advance. Obviously those with harmonized parts were written or at least carefully rehearsed, but so were some of the polyphonic ensembles. They are the disciplined perfection of integrated, interwoven, early New Orleans polyphonic improvising, surpassing all others we have on records. The release of alternate "takes" of the recordings confirms that in ensemble nearly everyone except Morton played ad lib upon a presketched outline of his part.

The solos, more often than not, were improvised. There are exceptions: Johnny Dodds obviously plays (or plays from) two written choruses on *Hyena Stomp,* and Omer Simeon obviously allows himself little freedom on *Shreveport Stomp.* On the other hand, the release of a very different and superior take of the excellent trio recording of *Wolverine Blues* confirms that, for that performance, Johnny Dodds improvised entirely, using the chord structure alone, while Morton varied the trio theme behind him. And, as several of Omer Simeon's and George Mitchell's solos on the alternate takes demonstrate, Morton would often work out with the instrumentalist a sketch or plan which the latter, in turn, was free to fill in or ad lib. Surely the similarities between Morton's way of working with his musicians and that of both Ellington and the Modern Jazz Quartet confirm that there has been only one really successful, variously arrived at solution to the problem of improvisation and total form, of spontaneity and group discipline, in jazz.

One thing that immediately strikes one about the Victor recordings is the extraordinary way in which the players in the various groups work together. Such unity (and it is beautifully recorded) would be rare even for a group that had been playing together for many months, regardless of the stylistic sympathy of its members with one another. For pick-up groups, even ones so carefully selected and rehearsed as these were, it is almost unthinkable. And one should remember that such discipline as Morton exacted may easily produce negative results in the playing of jazzmen of any school.

Smokehouse Blues, from the first recording date, is exceptional if only for the polyphony of its last chorus and because it is so movingly and passionately played. One must wait almost until Morton's last years for so moving a blues.[4] The orchestration is largely soloistic, however, and the soloists were equipped for it. They were equipped not only to play expressively but also to let emotional subjectivity contribute to the performance as a whole rather than detract from its development—a task few jazzmen have been able to fulfill unless they were willing to submit their talents to the direction of a Morton or an Ellington. One brief break in the clarinet chorus has Simeon double-timing while Morton's piano and Johnny St. Cyr's banjo quadruple-time beneath him! Yet the effect of this sudden contrast is to enhance the mood of the piece, not to interrupt it. Morton's own unaccompanied solo does not seem to fit rhythmically with the rest of the recording, but before one decides that his sense of rhythm was failing him (as it sometimes did), one should be aware of the deliberate rhythmic variety that is a part of so many of these recordings, and be aware that the successful use of it is a crucial part of Morton's achievement. *Black Bottom Stomp,* an excellent case in point, was also made at this first Victor date.

Black Bottom, one of Morton's best compositions, is built on two themes: one of sixteen measures, and a second of twenty. The version by the Red Hot Peppers is easily one of Morton's best recordings.

The ensemble included cornet, George Mitchell; trom-

---

4. Charles Luke's *Smokehouse* is not a twelve-bar blues, of course, but a sixteen-bar piece in the slow blues mood. However, Morton's *Wolverine Blues* is not a blues but is in post-ragtime "stomp" style.

bone, Kid Ory; clarinet, Omer Simeon; piano, Morton; banjo, Johnny St. Cyr; bass, John Lindsay; and drums, Andrew Hilaire. In the brief performance, these men interpret the themes of *Black Bottom* and make solo variations on them. Some of their variations are thematic and some are fresh inventions on their chord patterns. They offer passages in harmony, polyphony, and patterns broken four bars at a time between soloist and group. Morton's piano solo is unaccompanied, but the other soloists play with the rhythm section, sometimes with banjo, sometimes without, and one clarinet solo is accompanied only by the banjo. Sometimes the beat is a pronounced heavy/light/heavy/light; at other times it is an even 4 and there is one climactic chorus with a pronounced back beat. There is the "black bottom" variant of the Charleston rhythm: there are two-bar breaks, sometimes by one instrument, but once split between two of them. There is a wide variety of combinations of instruments and textures. Morton had the audacity to try something which is still highly unusual: his strongest climaxes are made, not simply by increasing dynamics or by accumulating masses of instruments, but by holding back Lindsay's string bass and Hilaire's tom-tom and bass drum until key moments.

My brief description makes the performance sound absurdly cluttered and pretentious. But it is neither. *Black Bottom Stomp* flows with such apparent simplicity and almost fated logic that one barely notices its astonishing variety. One thing that holds it together is its patterns of echo as various effects appear and reappear: this polyphonic passage is balanced by that one later on; this rhythmic pattern is echoed in a later one; the clarinet lead here is balanced by the clarinet solo there—the very variety is given in an orderly manner.

To be a bit more detailed, *Black Bottom* begins with an eight-bar, written introduction for the ensemble given as

four bars plus an exact repeat. The first chorus of the first A
theme is offered in written harmony, but at a couple of
points the clarinet and the trombone momentarily break
away into a kind of polyphony. In A1, we are given four
bars ad lib by cornet in solo, followed by four bars written
for ensemble, four more for cornet, four more for ensemble.
Mitchell's second four bars are a sprightly variant of his first.
In A2, the third appearance of the first theme, the clarinet
plays a paraphrase over a lightly sketched "black bottom"
rhythm by the banjo alone.

A four-bar interlude introduces the stomping B theme
which we hear in improvised polyphony, and in this opening
chorus a two-bar break is shared by cornet and trombone.
Also evident in this chorus is the important role that bassist
John Lindsay plays, and is to play, in the arrangement. B1,
the second appearance of the second theme, is a nonthematic
clarinet invention of eighteen bars, and an ensemble figure
of two bars. B2 is an unaccompanied piano solo by Morton,
also nonthematic and followed by the same two-bar ensemble figure that ended the previous chorus. B3 is a cornet solo,
a thematic paraphrase over a stop-time variant of the black
bottom rhythm. B4 is a nonthematic banjo solo, under
which Lindsay varies his pattern ingeniously between 2/4
and 4/4. Some of the banjo's figures may be familiar, but
the playing is wonderfully spirited. B5, due to be an all-out
ensemble climax, has the cornet, clarinet, and trombone
delicately interweaving in polyphony over a very lightly
played, understated rhythm, with a superbly placed break
by Hilaire's cymbal. B6, the final ensemble, is the true
"stomp" chorus, with Lindsay and Hilaire in strong, the
latter with emphatic bass drum plus the aforementioned
tom-tom back-beat, with an unexpected trombone break.

Morton's music reflects a deep understanding of the value
and purpose behind a device or an effect, and all parts of

Black Bottom Stomp are intrinsic to a knowingly paced whole. Could anyone else in jazz history—even Ellington—put so much into a brief performance with such success? The Red Nichols-Miff Mole version of *Black Bottom,* made a few months after this one and apparently using the same orchestration as its point of departure, is a rhythmically unsure, superficial, ineptly played sequence of lumbering effects.

The strongest contrast to the complexity of stomps like *Black Bottom* is a recording like *Jungle Blues.* It is a deliberately archaic piece, whose basic ingredients are a primitive blues bass line and a simple riff. Before he has finished, Morton has in effect formed the riff into three themes (and they are good ones), handled the heavy "four" of the bass with some variation, occasionally relieved it briefly and, as he usually could, spun the performance to the brink of monotony, ending it at exactly the moment-too-soon.

Between the complexity of *Black Bottom Stomp* or *Grandpa's Spells* and the comparative simplicity of *Jungle Blues* or *Hyena Stomp* lies the range of an artist.

Dead Man Blues is probably the masterpiece of the Victor series for its superior themes, its orchestration, and its performance.[5] There are wonderful details in *Dead Man Blues:* the easy swing of Mitchell's never-obvious lead, the strength of Omer Simeon in both his ensemble and solo melodies, the beautiful outward simplicity of the two trio choruses. The opening and closing ensembles seem the fruition of the years of New Orleans ensemble playing, of its simultaneous improvisation. They are choruses which in themselves might

5. I have not mentioned the verbal exchanges between Morton and Johnny St. Cyr, the lame jokes, that begin the record. Such things are apt to seem either pointless or annoying to us in Morton's records even when they are used sparsely and intended humorously. Perhaps more important, they indicate an approach to one's audience that is more real than arty.

make reputations for an orchestrator and his players and which, as part of a whole performance, are among the most effective understatements in jazz recording.

Dead Man redeems *Sidewalk Blues* wherein Morton was perhaps a bit too preoccupied with the excellence of his ensemble's swing and a bit careless with the quality of his melodies in the introduction and trio, and with some of his trombone lines.

Some kinds of failure are necessary to an artist, particularly if they show him by contrast just what he does best. To have followed *Dead Man* by the excessively corny and banal added parts for two violins on *Someday Sweetheart* is perhaps a bit like John Lewis's having followed *Sait-on Jamais* with *European Windows;* because if Morton's intentions were more "dance band" and Lewis's more "concert hall," both tended, perhaps equally, toward "acceptability." Morton's other "experiment" in the Chicago recordings—that of again adding the extra voice of an alto saxophone—cannot be called a failure. Stump Evans swings more than the saxophonists on Morton's earlier records and, for all the modified slap-tonguing in his solos, his part interferes far less in the polyphonic sections. Indeed, particularly on the trio of *The Pearls* he seems to contribute to an interesting texture and ensemble swing.

If *Black Bottom Stomp* has a serious rival among the fast stomps, it is the marvelously titled *Grandpa's Spells. Grandpa's* is better written. Its orchestration is exceptional, lacking only the touches of brilliance one hears in *Black Bottom,* and it is very well played. Its plan is ingenious but, again, an outline is only an introduction. There is the same variety among polyphony, harmony and solo, rhythmic emphasis, breaks, etc. There is also an ingenious use of rhythm instruments, this time an apparently innovative conversation of breaks among string bass, trombone, and ensemble. Is there anything comparable in jazz recording until Ellington's *Jack the Bear*?

Grandpa's Spells illustrates a further point about Morton's instrumental music. New Orleans jazz, like all jazz, retains highly "vocal" elements, but in it we hear a relatively developed instrumental style, not simply a vocal style transferred to instrument. Morton was a pianist, and his piano imitated a jazz orchestra, but he knew that some of his ideas were too directly pianistic to be simply transferred to the horns and rhythm. When working with the Peppers he did not simply rescore his conception back to its orchestral source; sometimes he needed to recompose and he knew it. *Grandpa's Spells* in the Hot Peppers version opens with a recomposed first theme played on St. Cyr's banjo.

The more one hears Chicago-made Hot Peppers recordings, the more one is impressed with Morton's remarkable ability in choosing and rehearsing his musicians, particularly George Mitchell and Omer Simeon. Both men understood Morton rhythmically. Simeon's strength was his ability to improvise from a sketch or outline, and particularly to make responsive countermelodies in ensemble passages. Mitchell's elusive rhythmic sense was perfectly suited to Morton's, lying between the staccato 2/4 accents of an earlier day and the even 4/4 accents to come. Most important, Mitchell's cornet melodies were probably as complex as they could be and still remain an integrated lead voice in the polyphonic ensembles. A little more of the virtuoso cornet soloist and the ensemble begins to collapse, as Louis Armstrong's work of this period made increasingly evident.

To single out moments from these recordings is obviously unfair since I am claiming such unity of conception for the best of them. But, with that in mind, there are some things that could be mentioned: the chorus on the trio of *Cannonball Blues* when the banjo carries the theme against the double-time piano comments of the leader; the conversation in "twos" on *Wild Man* between clarinet and piano, then clarinet and alto, in which one will intermittently egg the other into double-time; the announcement which *Steamboat Stomp* makes that Morton's orchestral style has dealt with the problem of faster tempos; and the entirely infectious movement and swing of *Doctor Jazz,* a jazz composer's version of a single-theme pop tune.

On June 11, 1928, Morton held his first Hot Peppers recording session in New York. I think that the location probably accounts for the final fulfillment of Morton's rhythmic conception which we hear on *Georgia Swing, Kansas City Stomps, Shoe Shiner's Drag,* and *Boogaboo.* Some Northeastern players were using, and continued to use, an older rhythm that was rather closer to ragtime, and Morton could take direct advantage of that fact. It was easier to get these players to swing *his* way than it would be for Red Allen or J. C. Higginbotham on later records. *Shoe Shiner's Drag (London Blues)* was apparently impressive enough to be remembered and recorded by Lionel Hampton and it is a blues on a sophisticated, substitute chord structure. But the best work from this recording date is *Kansas City Stomps.* At a medium tempo, it features excellent polyphonic writing and playing on several themes, and it sustains throughout the swing of some of the Chicago recordings which have slower tempos, with their same easy understatements in climaxes. *Georgia Swing* is almost as good. Ward Pinkett is a fine trumpeter for Morton to have chosen: his sense of time and accent is almost equal to George Mitchell's, and Morton knew how to use the variety of effects he could produce with mutes.

The last of the great Victors—in 1928—is a quartet based on Oliver's *Chimes Blues,* which Morton called *Mournful*

Serenade. None of his subsequent recordings is supposed to be as good as the earlier ones. But the point is that he had too much taste and insight merely to repeat and decorate, to reiterate and complicate what he had already done. Twenty-five sides had displayed his music, as complete and close to perfection as an artist can ask. It was time to try other things, and among those other things are some real successes.

The first date announced the things he would work on. *Red Hot Pepper* successfully modifies the earlier manner towards big-band scoring. The blues, *Deep Creek,* is a string of solos on more than one theme with opening and closing ensembles. Certainly many of Morton's big-band arrangements suffer by comparison with what Don Redman, Fletcher Henderson, and Ellington did, but Morton's best were done in 1928 and 1929, and their best a bit later. *New Orleans Bump* is a successful example of the same kind of thing his successors were to do, and it is another excellent example of pushing simplicity to the brink of monotony, then saving it by a hint of variety and by knowing exactly when to stop.

In others of these later records there are fine moments: the clean swing and passion of the last chorus of *Pontchartrain*; the well-paced and varied textures of *Burning the Iceberg* (the familiar integration of section harmony, polyphony, and solo now being used in the new conception for a larger group) despite its rather anachronistic basic rhythm; and the handling of the first theme in its various appearances on *Pretty Lil* (by an immediate reduction in the second chorus, later by solo variation, etc.). If the scoring or the handling of elements on a later record is not quite on that level, there may well be other things: the superb interplay of piano and guitar on *Little Lawrence* or the very effective piano breaks and solo on *Tank Town*

Bump. When one of these records fails, it does not fail because the music on it is pedestrian or banal. Even when the arrangements are based on familiar chord structures or melodic patterns, Morton may handle them with a freshness that will discover in them something alive and unhackneyed, if not always artistically satisfying.

Finally, a performance like *Blue Blood Blues* shows that Morton knew exactly what the theme/string-of-solos/theme approach might achieve, and that recording is still one of the best of its genre—possibly *the* best before some of the small-group recordings of the late 1930s.

A decidedly minor artist (or minor craftsman) may be a major influence—even on a major artist. But it is also quite possible for a major artist to have little influence on his immediate successors. The kind of after-the-fact argument which elevates a man on the basis of influence often avoids a crucial evaluation.

I would like to present Morton on his own terms. If one cannot quite see his achievement on those terms, if one needs comparisons with the work of those around him to help, there is the evidence of: the inept, unswinging, monotonous recordings of his own pieces made by Red Nichols and Miff Mole, The Original Memphis Five, or the California Ramblers; King Oliver's pedestrian *Dead Man Blues*; the Fletcher Henderson version of *The Chant*; or the more recent versions of Morton's compositions made by Turk Murphy and Pee Wee Erwin. One can also learn much by comparing the hesitant versions which some of the Southwestern bands made of his things in the 1920s—the Benny Moten version of *Midnight Mama,* for example.

It is among Southwest musicians that one can gather the verbal evidence of Morton's influence. Interviews bring testimony that Morton, his compositions, his musical training,

or his scores were an inspiration. Andy Kirk, Jimmy Rushing, Don Redman, and Ben Smith have all attested to it.

In *King Porter,* we can see one specific and clearly identifiable influence of Morton's work on jazz. In the variations
on the trio, we hear figures which are typical of Morton,
which Henderson's arrangement used and passed on to
Benny Goodman—a kind of scoring for brass (and Morton
clearly had brass in mind in such sections) which set a pattern used by almost everyone during the swing period, even
Ellington. Hear *Bojangles* for the clearest instance. One can
hear it still in everyone who writes big-band jazz scores.

But the real challenge of Morton's work is not a simple
result of Morton the composer, the orchestrator, the theorist,
the master of form; it is the more complex challenge that
in him jazz, by the mid-1920s, had produced an artist.

One can find a lot of reasons for finding this man with the
clown's nickname still important in the jazzman's heritage.
In him jazz did produce one of its best composers, best leaders, and one of its first theorists. More important, he first
demonstrated the only way jazz has ever found to free its
larger structures and groups from the tyranny and subjectivity of the moment.

4

SIDNEY BECHET

First and Last

Sidney Bechet's earliest recordings come from mid-1923, and they offer a fully developed musician. Fully developed not only because he played with power and authority, but also because we know from his biography that by then he had been a star soloist for some years, and because the elements and resources of his style can be heard on those records, elements that changed very little over the years. Yet Bechet did some of his most challenging recording work in 1957, the year before his death, collaborating with French pianist Martial Solal, effectively interpreting, ornamenting, and improvising on a repertory of standard songs which few of his New Orleans contemporaries would have undertaken in the first place, and which none of them, not even Jimmy Noone, could have handled so confidently.

By the time of those 1923 records, Bechet had taken up the soprano saxophone, had mastered that difficult instrument, and had come to prefer it to the clarinet. At a time when jazz saxophonists were apt to be shallow, fleet-fingered, slap-tongued virtuosi, Bechet's work must have come as a revelation of eloquence, depth, and elegance of musical phrase. On *Kansas City Man Blues,* he even used some horse whinnies (derived no doubt from New Orleans cornetist Freddy Keppard) and brought them off with dignity. And within a few

months, Bechet had recorded not only passionate slow blues
and faster stomps, but an exceptional ballad solo on *Old
Fashioned Love*. There is no question of Bechet's rhythmic
verve, confidence, and swing as a jazz player. He understood
the relaxed, legato New Orleans phrasing that Armstrong's
predecessors introduced so tentatively and that Armstrong
himself elaborated so brilliantly. And although there was an
occasional fleeting echo in Bechet of the clipped accents of
the previous decade, it diminished over the years.

The year of Bechet's earliest recordings is the year in
which New Orleans Negro jazz began to be recorded regularly, but Bechet's soprano saxophone style already represents an important step within that music. He based his work
on that instrument on a combination of the lead style of the
cornet or trumpet and on the clarinet's obbligato in the New
Orleans ensemble. Bechet therefore needed to take the lead
voice in the polyphonic ensemble, and he gave problems to
trumpeters throughout his career. There are two 1924–25
recordings of *Cake Walkin' Babies* which also feature the
young Louis Armstrong. On the first (labeled the "Red
Onion Jazz Babies") Bechet is uncannily responsive in polyphony and all poised excitement in his breaks. On the
second (by "Clarence Williams Blue Five") Bechet's breaks
again are statements in controlled excitement, but the climax
of the performance is awarded to Armstrong in solo.

A 1938 session involved Bechet's lead with Ernie Caceres's
baritone saxophone in obbligato, and it is particularly successful on *What a Dream*. Trumpeters were usually wise not
to compete with him (but, alas, some of them did), and this is
quite evident in some 1940 duets with cornetist Muggsy
Spanier. Spanier did not push the limits of his resources but
remained his simple self, and some of the resultant interplay
between the two horns is exceptionally effective.

A unique expression of sympathetic, integrated New Or-

leans polyphony can be heard on *Blues of Bechet*. By an early
example of over-dubbing (done before the days of tape and
therefore done on successive acetate discs by means of full
studio playbacks) Bechet himself plays variously clarinet,
soprano and tenor saxophones, piano, bass, and drums.

We owe *Blues of Bechet* to Bechet's 1940–41 association
with Victor records and his various pick-up groups which
were given the unpretentious collective name of the "New
Orleans Feetwarmers." There were some earlier 1932 Feetwarmers recordings, but I confess that they seem to me to
have more uninhibited energy than ensemble swing or musical success. However, Bechet evidently did find the atmosphere inspiring at least for the first half of *Maple Leaf Rag*.
And in the opening section of *Shag* he offered the first non-
thematic use on records of the *I Got Rhythm* chord progression.

The 1940–41 Feetwarmers series contributed the plaintive
re-make of *Nobody Knows the Way I Feel This Morning*.
And it offered *Blues in Thirds* with Bechet in the company
of Earl Hines, a pianist whose relative sophistication was, of
course, no deterrent. Between them, Hines and Bechet also
worked out a beautifully paced arrangement of Hines's fine
little piece.

The Feetwarmers series also offered at least one ensemble
which works because of a subdued trumpeter (*I Ain't Gonna
Give Nobody None of This Jelly Roll*, with Gus Aiken). The
Ellington pieces Bechet did for Victor (*The Mooche, Stompy
Jones, Old Man Blues, Mood Indigo*) may not all be among
the best of the series, but they do remind of one of the great
losses in the recorded repertory: it was Bechet's passionate
presence in Ellington's early Kentucky Club orchestra that
helped the pianist find his way as a bandleader and composer,
and no aural evidence of that historic association has survived.

Bechet's Victor *When It's Sleepy Time Down South* has a lovely non-thematic half-chorus on soprano saxophone. Such improvisation was of course not at all beyond his inventive powers; he is equally inventive on *Sweet Sue* in the Spanier duets, and there is a 1947 showpiece treatment of *Just One of Those Things*. Indeed, Bechet seems to have loved Cole Porter (he also left us a strong *Love for Sale* and an eloquently simple reading of *What Is This Thing Called Love?*), and that, in turn, reminds us of his—and Porter's—understanding of major-minor relationships. Bechet also loved Puccini, and that should not surprise us either.

Bechet recorded intermittently for Blue Note in 1939 and regularly in 1944–45. The results included his affecting showpiece *Summertime* and his slow blues clarinet masterpiece, *Blue Horizon*.

Sidney Bechet was not always the sublime soloist he was at his best, of course, and there was a banal, turn-of-the-century sentimental streak in him that occasionally showed in his choice of showcase material (*Song of Songs*), or in the trite, bravura endings he was so fond of. And if, on the whole, his ornaments and his inventions do not show the sustained originality and imagination of an Armstrong, nor of Armstrong's best successors, one should not expect that of him. He was true to the limits of his style and truly creative within them.

He was an eloquent musician, a musician whose range could encompass the fundamental passion of *Blue Horizon*, the elegant simplicity of *What Is This Thing Called Love?*, and the unpretentious invention on *Sleepy Time Down South*. And he was a pioneer jazzman who could collaborate, late in his career, with Martial Solal with singular success especially on *It Don't Mean a Thing, Rose Room,* and *The Man I Love*.

My praise of his eloquence, as well as my occasional reservations about his taste, is ultimately subjective of course. And I will conclude my comments even more personally. It has been said that Bechet's strong, constant wide vibrato is an acquired taste. For me, it was a taste I willingly acquired without thought as a teenager. And it was one night in 1949 or 1950 in Philadelphia when I saw Bechet play, and watched as the man, the instrument, the sounds, the emotion—all of these became by some magic process one thing, one aesthetic whole. I think it was then that I was first in touch with the essential miracle of music.

5

LOUIS ARMSTRONG

Style Beyond Style

The history of jazz conventionally begins with music from the western Congo and evolves as a style in New Orleans around the turn of the twentieth century. The contrast between the percussive music of Africa and New Orleans jazz is startling, not so much in that these musics seem similar as that, in some very basic ways, they do not seem similar. To be sure, jazz is played on European melody instruments and has borrowed from European melody and harmony. But the gross dissimilarity is in rhythm. Congolese music is so sure and so complex rhythmically as to make early jazz seem child's play, and for some of the players, rather awkward child's play.

There is a point of view which holds that Louis Armstrong brought rhythmic and melodic order to jazz out of crudeness or chaos. It may seem so, and because of his remarkable freshness it may even have seemed so in the 'twenties. But actually an honorable and often aesthetically successful tradition had preceded him and prepared his way.

It is only in quite recent developments that jazz has begun to approach the rhythmic complexity of African music. The history of jazz represents a gradual coming together of ideas of melody and ideas of rhythm. The sizable task that every major innovation has performed—in cakewalk music, in ragtime, in New Orleans jazz, in swing, in bebop—is basically rhythmic and shows itself in phrasing, in melodic rhythm, as well as in percussion. It is as if the music had to have a constantly renewed rhythmic vitality as it changed in melody and harmony. Each step finds jazz expanding its rhythmic and harmonic language while retaining its immediacy and its emotional concurrency with contemporary life.

A major step in this evolution was taken in New Orleans in the first two decades of this century. It was taken gradually and it happens that we have it documented on records in almost all its stages, from the rather clipped cornet phrasing of Freddy Keppard and Mutt Carey to the easier more legato melodies of Tommie Ladnier's trumpet and Sidney Bechet's soprano sax. It culminated in the durable genius of Louis Armstrong.

There are difficulties inherent in discussing Armstrong. For one thing, he has been called a genius. Call a man a genius often enough, no matter how justly, and his work gets to be beyond comment. On the other hand, Louis Armstrong has been treated by some as a sort of embarrassment. He has functioned as a vaudevillian and, partly because he uses the stage manner that many black *and* white performers employed during the 'twenties and 'thirties, he has been dismissed as an Uncle Tom. Also, with the constant demands placed on him in almost nightly performances, he has learned, as many jazzmen of all schools inevitably have learned, to coast and shuck his way genially through many nights. One cannot be truly creative and truly concerted emotionally six nights a week on demand, and one finds substitutes. Finally, jazz has had at least one major innovative soloist (Charlie Parker) since his first contribution was

made, and since the late 1950s and the "new thing," has offered further innovation. To some jazz listeners Armstrong
seems only a piece of history.

New Orleans contributed a durable ensemble style, of
course, popularized as Dixieland. I think that it was also the
New Orleans players who established improvisation as basic
to jazz. Most of the world's musics involve some kind of
improvisation, but before New Orleans it had not been so
important in any American style. Earlier players employed
embellishment and casual spontaneous change in performance, but many of the New Orleans players really worked
on improvisation and many of them thought of it as a crucial
part of their equipment. New Orleans musicians made a
basically emotional contribution. Even before Armstrong's
appearance, players from all over the country knew that New
Orleans musicians had impressively preserved the depth and
the immediacy of the idiom, both the sacred and secular,
in a comparatively sophisticated instrumental style.

It has been said that the New Orleans style evolved as the
musical sophistication of the downtown colored Creole
players came together with the earthier passion and rhythmic
vitality of the uptown black performers: to put it briefly,
European melody and harmony plus blues feeling. The
various traditions which came together in New Orleans were
more complex than that but the equation may stand for
what happened. Once that music had been established at
home, it was assimilated by others and began to spread. But
in New Orleans it continued to develop. I think what Armstrong did was to reintroduce at a later stage an even larger
measure of the blues emotionally, rhythmically, and melodically.

Certainly Armstrong's first elaboration of the elements
of his style was even more than a brilliant sum of its parts,
and it went quite beyond anything that had happened

before him. He also opened up even greater possibilities both for himself and for all jazzmen for twenty years and longer.

Despite the importance of such near contemporaries as Sidney Bechet, Armstrong's achievement was also more responsible than anything else for the fact that jazz irrevocably became not so much a collective ensemble style as a soloist's art. Armstrong's impact was startling and almost immediate. Through the crudeness of the recording techniques and the complexity of the collective improvising, his part in the 1923 King Oliver Creole Jazz Band recordings is clear largely because of his phrasing. He has acknowledged Oliver as his stylistic mentor, and the Oliver whose phrasing is closest to Armstrong's is probably the most familiar: Oliver, the poised and flowing soloist of *Dippermouth Blues.* Conversely, Armstrong is closest to Oliver on the Clarence Williams Blue Five recording *Everybody Loves My Baby* and in accompaniment to Ma Rainey's *Countin' the Blues.* However, some older players remembered the ideas Armstrong uses in his *Chimes Blues* solo as having come from Bunk Johnson, and they remembered Johnson as an inspiration for Armstrong's generation of New Orleans trumpeters. Johnson's first records were made in 1942, but if they reflect Johnson's earlier style, then he was a more legato and rhythmically relaxed player than his predecessors, and his work might well have been the basis for the later New Orleans trumpet style.

During 1924 with the Fletcher Henderson orchestra in New York, Armstrong made his message even more clear, and his solos with that group still shine through beautifully on the records.

On these earlier recordings by contrast some of Armstrong's fellow players seem to flounder rhythmically. His ideas of rhythm and phrasing were not established among

other instrumentalists, even among many New Orleans instrumentalists. Some men used an earlier rhythmic tradition.
Some tried to emulate him and wobbled between two traditions. Some few did grasp his message, and I suspect the
grasp was easier for those who knew and felt the blues idiom
and could play it well.

Armstrong's early work remains fascinating, but in the
light of what he later accomplished early Armstrong seems a
prelude. Perhaps to establish his idiom for himself as well
as others, he used a great many notes doubled and tripled—
repeated eights—which have a primarily rhythmic function.
This often makes it appear as if his early playing has an
excess of notes in comparison with his later solos. It is not
that these notes do not fit melodically, but that the early
solos do not have the sublime melodic ease of his later work.
Many players who learned from his early work continued to
use the predominantly rhythmic embellishments, notes
whose primary function was to make accents. Muggsy Spanier
was one who did, and there are comparable "rhythm notes"
in the phrasing of men like Coleman Hawkins, Don Byas,
even Roy Eldridge—indeed players in every style of jazz use
ornamentation with a primarily rhythmic function.

An instructive Armstrong record is *Twelfth Street Rag*
(1927, but unissued until 1940). As written, *Twelfth Street*
is a fair rag-style piece, but its manner was already dated by
the 'twenties and it is still used today as a vehicle for a
deliberately corny quasi-jazz. Armstrong's performance, a
brilliant revelation, opens up the jazz tradition. To recompose the tune so drastically, he slowed it down and removed
its jerkiness. In effect, he rephrased it into a passionate blues,
and there is hardly a note that is not directly consumed
with melody. In its way, *Twelfth Street* is more interesting,
or at least more indicative, than such justly celebrated Armstrong performances as the brilliant stop-time choruses of

Potato Head Blues, the series of sublime descents on *Gully Low* (*S.O.L.*) *Blues,* the recomposition of Morton's *Wild Man Blues,* the sustained exuberance of *Hotter Than That,* or the lovely and sober form of *Big Butter and Egg Man.* With *Twelfth Street Rag,* we are prepared for the beautifully free phrasing on the 1928 recordings with Earl Hines, *West End Blues* and *Muggles.* We are prepared for the later passionate melodies that swing freely without rhythmic reminders and for the double-time episodes that unfold with poise. We are prepared for a fuller revelation of Armstrong's genius.

By the late 'twenties, Armstrong in effect had reinterpreted the jazz tradition although he used all the familiar forms, all the melodic and harmonic patterns. Some of the records with Hines (*Skip the Gutter, Knee Drops, Two Deuces,* and the like) reinterpret episodes from his own earlier recordings with the Hot Five and Hot Seven, and the brilliant duet, *Weather Bird,* even reaches back to the Oliver repertory. It soon became obvious that so compelling a player was to become a popular musical figure with a large audience.

In *Early Jazz* Gunther Schuller remarks of Armstrong's subsequent work that, "Records like *West End Blues, Weather Bird, Potato Head Blues,* and *Beau Koo Jack* showed Louis Armstrong at the full extent of his mature powers. It would have been beyond even his genius to develop past this point, even if the temptations of commercial success had not been as strong as they now were." I cannot agree. I think that not only some of his best improvising, but also some of his most far-reaching work, were still ahead of him.

It was not simply for reasons of popular expediency that Armstrong undertook new materials, popular songs, and more sentimental Tin Pan Alley ballads. What other ma-

terial was there for him to try? And he had to in another
sense. To a player of Armstrong's abilities such pieces, although they might not be as good in one's final judgment
as Fats Waller's *Squeeze Me* or King Oliver's *West End
Blues,* were written with greater sophistication and offered
harmonic and structural challenges which did not exist in
the jazz tradition as Armstrong found it. One result of course
was that he created a new tradition: piece after piece that
Armstrong undertook after 1928 has remained in the
repertory.

I expect that if Louis Armstrong had one jot of taste con-
cerning the kinds of materials he has used, if he had the kind
of taste that would reject some of the trite, silly, and sentimental ditties he has played, and about the shallow, soggy,
and affected musical accompaniments with which he has
sometimes played them, then he would have been able to do
nothing at all. For a moment's critical reflection, were he
inclined to it, would have cut him off from all material and
all performance. And his genius is such that he can apparently take any piece, add a note here, leave out a note there,
condense or displace this melodic phrase a bit, rush this
cadence, delay that one, alter another one slightly, and transform it into sublime melody, into pure gold. He can turn
something merely pretty into something truly beautiful and
something deeply delightful. Conscious taste has little to do
with such transformations; they are products of an intuitive
genius, and of the kind choice where reason cannot intrude.

There are times when Armstrong has totally, or almost
totally, departed from melody into a free invention within
an harmonic framework, as with the celebrated 1938 version
of *I Can't Give You Anything But Love, I Double Dare
You* from the same year, the 1932 *When It's Sleepy Time
Down South, Swing You Cats* from 1933, and a few others.

However, Armstrong's most innovative work can be heard

in a select group of recordings which begins with *West End Blues* and includes, chiefly, *Sweethearts on Parade* (1930), *Between the Devil and the Deep Blue Sea* (particularly the faster, third take, 1931), and his second version of *Basin Street Blues* (1933). It is a commonplace that great figures outline and suggest many more possibilities than they are able to develop in their own work. But for any development, or even acknowledgment, of the brilliant ideas of phrasing and melodic rhythm in these Armstrong recordings we must wait for Lester Young in the late 'thirties and, even more decisively, for Charlie Parker and the jazz of the mid-'forties.

Armstrong's contributions to *West End Blues* represent a beautiful balance of brilliant virtuosity and eloquent simplicity. His arresting opening cadenza leads him to his opening theme statement, which begins simply and then rebuilds to the complexity of rising triplet arpeggios of its final measures. It ends on a high *b* flat. A passionate *b* flat held for almost four measures marks the simple beginning of Armstrong's reentry for his final chorus on *West End Blues*. Then follow the bursting, descending virtuoso phrases that lead him to his conclusion.

In the beginning and conclusion of this performance in Armstrong's fresh and unexpected accents and rhythmic patterns, it seems to me we are very far from the simple, double-time effects of *I'm Not Rough* and *Muggles,* and have entered into a quite different kind of rhythmic thinking.

Armstrong begins his opening chorus on *Sweethearts on Parade* so obliquely off the melody that one gets the effect of an introduction and opening statement all in one. Indeed, he seems almost to be tossing random asymmetrical phrases in the air until a particular phrase comes along that somehow ties the previous phrases together. And when he does allow us to glimpse the melody, he quickly veers away from it again into inventions of his own, usually complex ones that dance around the beat and offer hints of what is to come. After the vocal, a repeated, blues-inspired paraphrase of the song's opening idea leads to a deliberately earth-bound, drum-like phrase,[1] thence to his flying interpolation of the motive of the *High Society* obbligato (here is where Charlie Parker must have gotten that favorite lick). From this point to the end of the chorus, we are once again into a kind of rhythmic thinking that was innovative even for Armstrong.

Sweethearts on Parade, then, is built up in brief, intriguing but ultimately logical fragments. *Between the Devil and the Deep Blue Sea* takes a different approach. Armstrong's first contribution to the performance in both versions is a vocal chorus, a free invention that barely glances at the melody as written (did any other singer take up this idea until Sarah Vaughan?). On the faster, third take of the piece, Armstrong plays his first chorus (minus the bridge) with a straight mute—a rare event for him. Again, his thinking is quite bold rhythmically, but melodically his phrases link and flow together uniquely: his first covers only two bars, but his second is an unbroken six bars, and his third (granted a quick breath in the middle) consumes eight. The only flaw in this singular performance comes after Armstrong removes his straight mute during the song's final eight bars and for the reprise of eight more that finishes the record. On open horn he rather abruptly introduces an episode of Armstrong grandiloquence which, this time, he had not properly prepared for.

The 1933 *Basin Street Blues* is an improvement over the earlier, 1928 version, and a good arrangement of which the leader takes superb advantage. The first trumpet chorus

1. The *Nagasaki* lick, one might call it, later to become the *Salt Peanuts* octave jump and drum lick in a bebop jazz dialect.

ends on a hint of the virtuosity to come. The vocal chorus, "scat" sung without words, is an invention and it is virtually as bold rhythmically as the astonishing trumpet solo that follows, in which the episodes of eloquence are prepared for by the soaring grandiloquence of the more complex phrases.

At the same time, along with such bold, improvised invention and rhythmic innovations, the years 1931–33 saw some of Armstrong's most brilliant melodic paraphrases and transmutations.

The recordings Armstrong made for Victor during that period I think reflect such playing at its peak. There is that eloquently recomposed *I Gotta Right To Sing the Blues,* with Armstrong's melody suspended almost above the piece, certainly floating majestically over his accompaniment, yet in perfect time and perfect swing. One has to wait almost until the jazz of the 'sixties for such freedom of musical phrase. In an almost opposite approach, he juggles and rejuggles the phrases of *I've Got the World on a String.*[2] There is also the justly praised *That's My Home* from 1932, where Armstrong's lovely paraphrasing and compelling passion transform a silly and mawkish ditty into stark experience. And there is the version of *St. James Infirmary* that makes beautiful melody more beautiful.

Thus, it was in the years 1928 through 1933 that Armstrong found the highest expression of his genius.

Certainly there are failures from the great years, and a number of them are all of a piece. Armstrong's greatest work came at slow and medium tempos; the fast things—the *Shine, Ding Dong Daddy,* and *Tiger Rag* showpieces—sound oddly unfinished and rather like amiably raucous build-ups

2. In view of the excellence this recording of *I Gotta Right To Sing the Blues* and of *Between the Devil and the Deep Blue Sea,* it might be pointed out that the author of these pieces, Harold Arlen, was one of the first of our popular songwriters whose work shows the effect of Armstrong's ideas.

for events that never take place. It seems to me that a major contribution of both Roy Eldridge and Dizzy Gillespie was that they did something sustained and musical within such fast tempos, as Armstrong often did not.

I have said nothing so far about Armstrong's singing, and that is partly because I am of two minds about it. It is usually said that his vocal style is like his trumpet style. On his 1932 version of *When It's Sleepy Time Down South,* for example, the vocal and instrumental choruses are very similar in ideas and phrasing, particularly in the release. Yet the emotional import of Armstrong's voice seems to me different from that of his horn. Armstrong's trumpet has a melodic sweep and a sometimes staggering emotional comprehension and depth; his voice often seems to carry only a part of the power of the majesty of his horn. There is much of the stage manner, of the "genial Satchmo," in his voice, and his stage humor has sometimes seemed to me forced and embarrassingly unfunny. In contrast I find Fats Waller's spontaneous humor and presence still a delight on many of his recordings and in the few films he made. Armstrong's manner has a likeably engaging surface, to be sure, but I think it sometimes solicits our feelings in order to buttress a certain frank amateurishness. His horn instructs us; his comments and jokes might even invite our willing indulgence if he were not so honestly being himself and so likeable a man. But so likeable a man, if he is as complex as Louis Armstrong, must have an opposite side to his nature. Both sides and all of his complexity show in his horn.

Louis Armstrong functioned as a musical entertainer, as a vaudevillian, but to see this only in its narrowest terms is to miss his essence. When we see a celebrated American vaudevillian like Al Jolson or Judy Garland, I think we see the appealing dramatization of an ego and the dramatic projection of a kind of emotional self-indulgence which off-stage and in reality might be repulsive. At any rate, the musical "act," the vaudevillian, the torch or cabaret singer, is not necessarily musically interesting and is more often emotionally narrow. By contrast Louis Armstrong is nearly always musically interesting.

If we do not hear anything truly new from Armstrong after 1933, we often hear an ability to sustain the eloquence of his earlier discoveries from the 'thirties. I will cite *Jubilee, The Skeleton in the Closet, Ev'n Tide,* and *Lyin' to Myself.* There was inevitably a kind of solidification and simplification in much of his work. And I suppose it was this simplification which prepared the way for a greater popularity. But actually the popularity which has made him a kind of international figure did not begin for him until after 1947, when he reverted to a small quasi-Dixieland format. It is surely a confirmation of all theories about cultural lag that Louis Armstrong gained his largest audience only after his ideas had been imitated and popularized—sometimes grotesquely so—by scores of trumpeters and arrangers, and after his own playing had suffered from inevitable simplifications and the inevitable nights of emotional lassitude. At the same time, when the popularity did come, Armstrong rediscovered something of the sweep and the bravura which had often been subdued during the mid-'thirties.

It is a commonplace that Armstrong's groups have always been inferior to Armstrong. Inevitably so, but many of them have been grossly inferior to him as well as to the other jazz groups around him, even when their personnels might lead one to expect much more than one got. When he used Earl Hines in the late 'twenties, he also had Jimmy Strong, who despite his technical abilities could give no emotional competition to Armstrong's earlier clarinetist, Johnny Dodds. But in the 'forties, in the group which reunited him with Hines and which included Jack Teagarden and Sidney Cat-

lett, he had an exceptional jazz assemblage, individually if
not collectively. His art continued in the 'fifties; he recorded
new versions of *Struttin' with Some Barbecue, Basin Street
Blues, Lazy River,* and *Georgia On My Mind* which are a
credit to a major jazzman. And he redid *King of the Zulus*
in a version as emotionally powerful as any of his recorded
performances.

Well into his sixties, Armstrong would play on some evenings in an astonishing way—astonishing not so much because of what he played as that he played it with such power,
sureness, firmness, authority, such commanding presence as
to be beyond category, almost (as they say of Beethoven's
late quartets) to be beyond music. When he played this way,
matters of style, other jazzmen, and most other musicians
simply drop away as we hear his eloquence. The show biz
personality act, the coasting, the forced jokes and sometimes
forced geniality, the emotional tenor of much of Armstrong's music early and late (that of a marvelously exuberant
but complex child)—all these drop away and we hear a surpassing artist create for us, each of us, a surpassing art.

6

BIX BEIDERBECKE

The White Man's Burden

One commentator has called cornetist Bix Beiderbecke the baby-faced darling of the 1920s. If he was that, it was only in retrospect, and the Shelleyan, Keatsian, Billy-the-Kid-like jazz myth about him is decidedly a product of the 'thirties. Notes to a reissue LP reveal that he was mentioned in the public prints only twice during his life (there were no jazz journalists then) but he was a kind of demigod to musicians. Louis Armstrong has even said that he and Bix were working on the same thing, presumably on making jazz improvising primarily a soloist art.

I doubt if one should discuss Beiderbecke without offering at least some preliminary and general remarks about white jazzmen, at least the white jazzmen of the 'twenties and early 'thirties. Perhaps the best approach is by means of some remarks about players other than Beiderbecke. Bill Evans's harmonic language has affected that of all pianists, even some of his elders. But perhaps I should pick players closer to Beiderbecke's generation. A discussion of drumming might be incomplete without a mention of Dave Tough's name. Jack Teagarden was an exceptional and dedicated jazzman. And Pee Wee Russell seems to me one of the most interesting clarinetists in jazz history.

For one thing, Russell was a dedicated improviser; in his

own modest and shy way he dared, explored, and took chances. He may sometimes have failed, but he seldom played without a real effort at musical adventure and a genuine belief in improvisation. Perhaps too much so, for one even gets the feeling that he had to summon up the proper way to handle his horn each time he used it. His style was a thoroughly personal expression; if he had a major inspiration, it was Bix Beiderbecke.

I think that Beiderbecke's work has affected the whole of jazz. Such a thing has been said of Jimmy Dorsey, but Dorsey, whatever one's final evaluation of him as a jazzman, was a challenge, I expect, only because he was such a good saxophonist. Older recordings by, say, Rex Stewart, Benny Carter, "Hot Lips" Page, Jimmy Noone, and more recent recordings by Johnny Hodges and Roy Eldridge have made direct interpolations from Beiderbecke or obvious use of his ideas. In a sense the same might be said of phrases from Grieg or from a dozen second-rate "light classics." Eldridge has said that his youthful models included Red Nichols and Beiderbecke, and I am sure that the experience directly affected the way he later used the trumpet, although his style became much transformed. However, a comparable tribute might be paid to cornetist B. A. Rolfe whose playing inspired Louis Armstrong to seek the full range of his instrument. On such a basis one could argue that everyone from John Phillip Sousa to David Raksin has affected jazz, but I am arguing for an important contribution within the idiom that eventually affected not just a few obvious followers but nearly all jazz players.

One problem in any discussion of jazz and race involves a holdover liberal cliché from the 'thirties. Having heard so many racial generalizations that are destructive, demeaning, or absurd, we have become afraid of any kind of generalization. It might help clarify matters to return to the well-worn phrase, to the dictum that I have mentioned above, that "Negroes have natural rhythm," which has become horrendous. But what if blacks did have "natural rhythm"? Would it be a sign of inferiority to have "natural rhythm"? Is it insulting to say that they have dark skin? Why is it really enlightened or unprejudiced to assume that Negroes could *not* have something called "natural rhythm"?

Does it imply an inability to treat Orientals as individuals to say that they have black hair or brown eyes? We may know the subtle touchiness of the subject but, after all, is it not the truth, rather than a counterstatement, that shall make us free?

Our liberal clichés long ago put us in the position of assuming that differences imply an innate moral or intellectual superiority on the one hand and inferiority on the other. We cannot allow for differences or allow them to be differences. And we assume thereby, surely without realizing it, that all men are equal only if they are the same. (Or is it that all men are equal only if they are willing to accept American middle-class standards?)

I realize that I have discussed these questions before in the first chapter of this book, but perhaps they bear repetition and perhaps there are some things to add.

It would be perfectly easy to show that not all blacks have "natural" rhythm nor very good acquired rhythm necessarily. And one can think of black jazz musicians who have had rhythmic problems and have overcome them, and of some who have had them and have them still. There are Negro players who swing but keep poor time and there are some who keep time well but don't swing. There are Negroes who can't really improvise, and for whom jazz is merely a style with a set of devices that is not too difficult to acquire. Still, it seems to me perfectly valid to say (whether the basis is racial, ethnic, environmental, or whatever) that black jazzmen in general have had fewer rhythmic problems than white jazzmen.

On the other hand, one apparently cannot hold that white jazzmen, even the most derivative white jazzmen, generally do not sound like Negroes without somehow being insulting to someone (but insulting to whom?). Of course, one response to this proposition is that "those white men are not playing real jazz." If one chooses to call what white musician A is playing "not jazz," one invites a fruitless, semantic argument on the meaning of the word *jazz*. By an objective or technical definition, musician A plays jazz. By aesthetic judgment he may play good jazz and good music.

My proposition is that the white players of the 'twenties and early 'thirties brought a particular lyric sensibility to jazz and this sensibility has had an effect on its subsequent development. Bix Beiderbecke was the most gifted and important of those players, important not only because his work was the most influential, but also because he was intrinsically an exceptional, original soloist. Certainly Beiderbecke's effect was not as grandiose, not as pervasive, and nothing like as important as Louis Armstrong's. But it is there. And jazz would not be the same if it had not been there.

Bix Beiderbecke is the first white jazzman whose work one can take seriously, and that is at least partly because he took jazz seriously. The Original Dixieland Jazz Band of 1917 seems to me to have caught little more than the surface irreverence of the music. The New Orleans Rhythm Kings caught more, but they were sincerely and admittedly trying to sound like the Negro players. Beiderbecke heard something more than the spirited irreverence. In his best work he is not merely imitating the Negro idiom but, inspired by it, he is working out his own idiom. Beiderbecke took jazz seriously enough to be personal, and he was gifted enough to be more than simply personal. Certainly he did not sound like a Negro; it is to his everlasting credit that he did not and that he did not try to. It was his tribute to the music that he perceived that to do so would be to go against its deeper purport and meaning.

Bix Beiderbecke knew records of cornetist Nick La Rocca and the Original Dixieland Jazz Band, and those were almost the only jazz records that were made between 1917 and 1923.

It is remarkable how many white players worked out comparable styles, apparently independently, by knowing La Rocca and following through on what they heard. Next to Bix, Red Nichols is the best known. Whatever one may think of the music and intentions of the ODJB, they gave Beiderbecke an important impetus. (There is talk of the influence of a cornetist named Emmet Hardy, but he is only a name to us now.) Bix later heard others, of course, and was affected by them. A recently rediscovered solo of his in *I Didn't Know* might almost be the young Louis Armstrong, and several years earlier he had flashed through *Big Boy* in much the way Armstrong burst through the records by Erskine Tate's Chicago pit band.

In some ways Beiderbecke's earliest records outline his career. They were made with a midwestern group called the Wolverines. Their intentions were serious, but the Wolverines didn't make much more creditable jazz than the less dedicated big dance bands, or the almost equally dedicated small groups, that Bix later recorded with.

The Beiderbecke we hear with the Wolverines is both ahead of his times and behind them. His commitment and integrity show on *Tiger Rag*. It was a pretty corny showpiece as the ODJB played it, and it has led many a player to banality since. Beiderbecke avoids the corn and the banality, and he does not attempt to have it both ways with the

kind of bravura that Armstrong later developed. He simply
works on fairly legato, improvised melodies within the frame
of the piece.

Beiderbecke had rhythmic problems. He was basically
working with La Rocca's rhythmic ideas and smoothing
them out, if you will, but a lot had happened in jazz rhythm
meanwhile. We can take it that La Rocca was playing a
rather stiff version of the early rhythmic ideas of New Orleans jazz, the clipped accents we hear on Freddy Keppard's
few records and that Mutt Carey retained throughout his
life.

I do not believe that it is entirely useful to declare that
Louis Armstrong first arrived at that magic, illusive, but
empirical rhythmic phenomenon that came to be called
"swing." I believe that in an earlier rhythmic style Keppard
and Carey both "swing."[1] However, in his brief *Royal Garden Blues* solo with the Wolverines Beiderbecke is playing
a kind of parade horn that does not even seem intended to
swing, whatever the rhythmic style.

Beiderbecke could swing within the outlines of his style.
And he could also fall between two stools when he reached
for something like Armstrong's delayed, behind-the-beat, or
even his anticipatory phrasing. The dilemma sometimes

1. The term "swing," although it remains undefined and continues to be care-
lessly used, is a part of the technical vocabulary of jazz music. It came into
general use with Louis Armstrong, indeed may even have been introduced by
him, and was at first a musicians' term to describe Armstrong's early rhythmic
contribution to the music. Subsequently, the word was used as the name of
the style, largely built on his contribution and that of the early "big band"
arrangers, the kind of jazz that was popular during the 'thirties. But the term
has been retained in the jazz vocabulary and applied to subsequent styles and
players. Similarly, it has been applied to earlier, pre-Armstrong styles, and
fruitfully so, I think. That is to say, it is possible to play pre-Armstrong jazz,
and even ragtime, with or without the appropriate rhythmic character and
momentum, i.e., "swing," and swing is empirically present or not present in a
performance.

made his time seem shaky, but the same sort of thing was happening to many jazz players during the late 'twenties—on occasion even to so authoritative a man as King Oliver. However, in his best solos, Beiderbecke handles his ideas of rhythm with ease and they answer to his basic conception, answer to his ideas of melody and his exceptional harmonic ear.

Some of Bix's Wolverine solos—*Sensation, Riverboat Shuffle*—may almost seem patchworks of the jazzy mannerisms and clichés of the 'twenties. His problem, we realize, was to make something out of the musical materials available to him and he did not really have a background of folk sources on which to draw. But even in the *do-wacka-do* and *voe-dee-o-doe* figures one can hear a rare sense of melodic order trying to assert itself, and an emotional dedication to improvisation. Comparing this *Riverboat* to the one he made three years later, we hear an enormous improvement: he has discovered lyric melodies of his own. His ear and sense of melody are central. He was self-taught but could make even a fairly mechanical follow-through on the cornet valves an expressive part of a solo. Even with the Wolverines, his unique approach to improvising can already be heard in his memorably fluent and original solo and last chorus lead in *Jazz Me Blues.*

There soon began the association with C-melody and alto saxophonist Frankie Trumbauer which was to carry both of them through the big dance orchestras of Jean Goldkette and Paul Whiteman, and into recording studios with groups under their own names. Beiderbecke's small groups attempted jazz even if the men weren't up to it; Trumbauer's groups sometimes attempted it but at other times sounded like little brothers to the Whiteman band.

Trumbauer too was an influential man. Johnny Hodges has indicated that almost the only guides he had as a young

saxophonist were Sidney Bechet and Trumbauer. Trumbauer worked in many of the same musical areas as Bix (and
I expect he got most of his ideas directly from him) but,
although there is a kind of melodic purity in him at his best,
he never had any swing, and his playing projects far less
emotional expressiveness and conviction than Beiderbecke's.
Trumbauer's solo in *Way Down Yonder in New Orleans*,
for example, has good ideas, an interesting and provocative
handling of saxophone sound and phrasing, and steady time
(more dependably steady than Bix's?), but no swing. It is
almost a merely historical phenomenon. (One might also
note the shocking deterioration in Trumbauer's playing
after Beiderbecke's death.)

Beiderbecke on the same piece does not show the same
effort at invention but leans more heavily on a paraphrase
of the melody. And the paraphrase is not Bix at his best,
being less interesting than, say, the way he handled the
bridge of *Sweet Sue* with Whiteman. Still there is an urgent
emotional cohesion and melodic logic in Bix's *Way Down
Yonder* solo that makes Trumbauer's seem almost an
abstraction.

I don't think you could say that paraphrase or melodic
embellishment[2] was the rule for these men. More often they

2. The distinction which Gunther Schuller makes in *Early Jazz* between embellishment and improvisation does not seem entirely satisfactory to me as applied to jazz, however well it fits eighteenth-century European practice. One
may not wish to celebrate the improvisational aspects of certain simple and
obvious embellishments in jazz. However, by the early 'thirties jazz had produced so dazzling an embellishment and ornamental style as that of Art
Tatum, and one would surely want to celebrate the improvisational prowess
with which Tatum used such resources. It *is* useful, it seems to me, to make
a distinction between an improvisation that is thematic and one that is non-
thematic, i.e., an "invention" or "harmonic variation." Furthermore, André
Hodeir's borrowing of the grammarian's term "paraphase" seems to me most
useful in describing the particular kind of thematic variation at which Louis
Armstrong was so superb, one that moves away from embellishment and is
part thematic transformation and part invention.

seemed to be reaching for original variations made on chord structures. Frequently they succeeded, and this was before such inventions were really the rule in anything but blues playing or in a blues approach adapted to a few, simple chord progressions in music other than blues. *For No Reason at All in C,* improvised in the chords of *I'll Climb the Highest Mountain,* is an obvious example. There are also Bix's and Tram's solos on the justly celebrated *Singin' the Blues,* and several of the solos with Goldkette and White-man, like Bix's fine episode in *Lonely Melody.* There are also things like Bix's *Dardanella* solo which use the opening melody phrase almost as a recurring motif around which to build an original line.

Despite the inferior surroundings, the integrity and beauty of Beiderbecke's best work survives. In its own time, Bix's work came at the right moment. When jazz was irrevocably becoming a soloist's art, he made crucial steps away from simple embellishments and arpeggios toward melodic invention. He gave jazz harmonic and linear enrichments and showed how lyric it might become. He also affirmed from his own perspective, something that many jazz melodies affirm: that melodic completeness need not obey traditional ideas of form, that a melody can be a continuous linear invention, without the rather mechanical melodic repeats of popular songs, and still be a satisfying aesthetic entity. Bix's personal melodic intervals, his warm tone, his handling of sound, his plaintive bent notes, and his easy phrasing are a part of his contribution too. But they are all only manifestations of the real import of his playing, which was emotional. It suggested that there was a largely neglected kind of lyric feeling which might also find expression in jazz.

Many jazzmen got these things directly from Beiderbecke. Many more got them when his message was caught, absorbed, and elaborated so brilliantly by Lester Young, and through him they have affected almost the whole of jazz since the mid-'thirties. Young himself gave most of the credit to Trumbauer, which would mean it was a saxophonist's debt and at second hand, but I doubt if a man who carried *Singin' the Blues* around in his tenor case was unaffected by Bix's part in it.

There is more than coincidence in the echo of Beiderbecke that people hear in Miles Davis, for Davis owes a debt to Lester Young. Perhaps there is the same kind of link in the pairing of Davis with Lee Konitz; Young was a major influence on Konitz too. And for me *For No Reason at All in C* seems at least the indirect ancestor of the best of the Lennie Tristano–Lee Konitz–Warne Marsh recordings.

If Beiderbecke's short life was a tragedy, it was the tragedy of an artist for whom there was little or no tradition that was meaningful, and few guides available. It has been said that he was misguided about jazz, looked in the wrong places for his inspiration, was too preoccupied with impressionistic concert music, etc. I expect he looked wherever he could for whatever would help him. Growing up an American of German descent in Davenport, Iowa, he heard all the jazz he could hear. Ragtime was widespread but it had already been sifted of its meaning for jazz by the early 'twenties. Like many young men of his generation he virtually stood in awe of Bessie Smith and King Oliver, yet I doubt if the blues could have been essential to him as a guide for his own sensibilities. He could not rely on that rich interpolation of folk and blues phrases and devices that so many players were employing in improvising—even white players by this time—not because he did not know, did not love, or could not absorb these things, but because for him they did not really carry the unique story he had to tell and the lyric contribution he was to make. Beyond a point, the jazz tradition that existed then, remarkable as it was, could not help him. He had to work much of it out for himself.

7

COLEMAN HAWKINS

Some Comments on a Phoenix

Periodically jazz musicians and listeners rediscover tenor saxophonist Coleman Hawkins. Even during the time of major changes in the mid-'forties, the avid bebop partisan accepted Hawkins as a part of the jazz scene, as he accepted no others of Hawkins's contemporaries of the 'twenties and few of his companions of the 'thirties. One might call Hawkins a thorough professional, but he was also a major performer and he belonged to a generation in which these two things might go together as a matter of course.

Periodically Hawkins also seemed to rediscover himself. He listened to everyone, but however much his own playing reflected what he heard around him, Hawkins remained Hawkins.

Probably everyone who knows Hawkins's work has a favorite, relatively late recording on which he feels the saxophonist played particularly well. My own is the Shelly Manne–Hawkins LP called "2 3 4." Not only did Hawkins remain an exceptional player for decades he also recorded prolifically. An exhaustive survey of his records would be a lengthy and perhaps pointless task. But it might be useful to suggest the nature of his early style, indicate the course of his development, and point out what seems to me some of his more durable performances.

Coleman Hawkins's contribution has been so comprehen-

sive that it is impossible for any tenor saxophonist to avoid
some reflection of his influence unless that player were to
do a fairly direct imitation of Lester Young or perhaps Bud
Freeman. Yet, when one listens to Hawkins on his very
earliest records, one hears no promise of his stature as a
player. One hears a young man performing with calculated
and rather superficial raucousness, a slap-tongue tenor player
with little more than shallow irreverence to recommend
him.

However, one can note that this clowning soloist obviously knows his instrument, knows his chords, and has a sure
sense of time and tempo. Thus the Coleman Hawkins heard
on his 1923–24 solos with the Fletcher Henderson orchestra.
However, the Coleman Hawkins heard on Henderson's
T.N.T., recorded in October 1925, is a very different player.
The basis of the difference is quite apparent: rhythmically
and melodically, Hawkins's brief solo is early Armstrong.
The Stampede, made a few months after Armstrong's departure from the orchestra, is even more revealing. Cornet-
ists Rex Stewart and Joe Smith burst forth with brass hy-
perboles, reaching for Armstrong's excitement. Coleman
Hawkins follows Armstrong's lead too, but he treats his
style not as a series of effects but rather as a series of definite musical ideas in a cohesive structure.

A year or so later, on *Goose Pimples,* the young Hawkins
has become more himself, cutting through with the hard
staccato phrases that characterize his playing of this period.
However, on the 1928 version of *King Porter Stomp* we hear
Hawkins still echoing the young Armstrong fairly directly.

The disappointing Hawkins of this period is the Hawkins
of the twelve-bar blues. He is not a blues man, and he seems
to have known it. But unlike some of the early stride pianists, he was not content merely to play the blues form without the feeling. And unlike, say, Earl Hines or Benny

Carter, he was not prone to work out a personal and intro-spective style within the idiom. Hawkins set out to learn to play the blues with blues feeling. He did learn and he has played some very good blues, but to the end of his life he sounded as if the slow blues were, for him, something acquired.

Blazin', from early 1929, seems to me one of the best early revelations of a developing Coleman Hawkins style, and in it we hear the increasing reliance on the vertical, on Hawkins's exact and growing knowledge of chords, and on spreads of arpeggios. From a sound, youthful grounding in music, especially in piano instruction, Hawkins knew the notes in chords and learned to form passing chords between assigned ones. He also had the clear example of jazz reed players like Jimmy Noone and Buster Bailey who played arpeggio styles. But it is interesting to learn that an en-counter with the harmonic and embellishmental sophistica-tion of pianist Art Tatum was a turning point in Hawkins's development.

His solos on the Mound City Blue Blowers' *Hello Lola* from 1929, and Henderson's *Chinatown* from the following year, show some of the dangers of his new approach. It is as if in making all the chords, Hawkins also became deter-mined to make all the beats, and he made them in a more or less regular, heavy/light/heavy/light pattern. At faster tempos, once he was past his entrance, Hawkins's phrasing settled into a rhythmic regularity, and an almost brilliant articulation of proper notes sometimes trails off into a kind of rhythmic mutter. The risks involved became increasingly obvious in later performances: his knowledge of harmony, his regularity of rhythm, and his hardness of tone could lead him to mechanically formed solos delivered with a forced emotion.

On *New King Porter Stomp, Underneath the Harlem*

Moon, Honeysuckle Rose, and other pieces from 1932,
Hawkins found a temporary rhythm solution. He would
assume a momentary rhapsodic stance: triplets and more
complex phrases flutter and curve away from the beat, apparently without intending to swing. Although the ideas in
these solos are fine, the rhapsodic phrases are delivered with
an earnestness that is almost affected. He was using the same
approach as late as 1937 on the justly celebrated recordings
of *Honeysuckle Rose* and *Crazy Rhythm* done with Benny
Carter in Paris.

Hawkins's early celebrated ballads, *One Hour* with the
Blue Blowers (1929) and *Talk of the Town* with Henderson (1933), are both exceptional and both indicative of the
mood that would yield his later masterpieces. But both are
imperfect in revealing ways. *Talk of the Town* is a good
improvisation weakened by lush effusiveness. *One Hour* is
a better solo, a combination of lyric ideas and traditional
jazz phrases; it makes all the chord changes properly and it
is showy without being untidy. But Hawkins's tone is still
especially hard and brittle, as if his only protection against
sentimentality were to take on the mask of toughness.

A blues man might not have had problems with excess of
tone and emotion because he might not have had sentimental temptations. Not that the Hawkins of this period
had no emotional protections. On *Wherever There's a Will,
Baby,* with McKinney's Cotton Pickers, he combines a fine
sense of musical fun and hokum with firm musical ideas.[1]

One should also mention *Queer Notions* that Hawkins
made with Henderson, on which the increasingly sophisticated Hawkins provided himself with just the sort of challenging medium-tempo vehicle he wanted. As one would

1. On Henderson's *Sweet Music* (1931) and *I Wanna Count Sheep* (1932), however, Hawkins momentarily returned to Armstrong and, remarkably, the mature Armstrong of 1928–33.

expect, the challenge is largely harmonic. But I think that Hawkins's two choruses on *Hokus Pokus* from 1934 are probably the best of all his solos with Henderson. They are perhaps not typical, being more directly melodic and less arpeggiated, but they combine the robustness of his early work with a sophisticated melodic sense and a touching, almost nostalgic lyricism. The choruses seem also to have been highly influential: they outline the essentials of the style used by Herschel Evans and his associates and successors, Buddy Tate, Illinois Jacquet, and (most recently) Yusef Lateef. Of course it is possible that Hawkins, as a constant listener, may have picked up such phrases as these touring the Southwest with Henderson, but it is also possible that this so-called Southwest tenor style was first expounded by Coleman Hawkins in a New York recording studio.

When Coleman Hawkins returned from Europe in 1939, he entered his great period as a jazz soloist. He had continued to expand his basic harmonic techniques. He had come to terms with his own lush and sentimental temptations, which means that he had learned to sustain a true lyric mood and therefore no longer needed the sometimes forced and usually brittle edge to his tone that he had apparently found necessary before. The sharpness of vibrato heard on *One Hour* cannot be heard on *Body and Soul*.

Rhythmically, however, there sometimes seems to have been no solution, and Hawkins's double chorus on *The Sheik of Araby*, recorded in January 1940, fails almost as it succeeds. It is a *tour de force* of the sort which dazzled and delighted his fellow musicians, yet Hawkins's swift, knowing harmonic disentanglements are nearly lost in a predictably regular accentuation. In such moods Hawkins is in effect attempting to be not only his own soloist, but his own harmonist and his own rhythm section as well. However, he

does build these choruses gradually, both emotionally and
technically, without resorting to bathos or musical banality.
Other solos from the same period show Hawkins's final and
best rhythmic solution. His chorus on *Dinah,* recorded with
Lionel Hampton a month earlier, is another harmonic
delight. Rhythmically it frankly sets up the expectation of
more or less regular heavy/light/heavy/light accents and
varies them just briefly enough, often enough, and obviously
enough to relieve any encroaching monotony.

Body and Soul (1939) is the accepted Hawkins's masterpiece. The record reveals not only Hawkins's knowing use
of increasingly sophisticated techniques but his brilliant use
of pacing, structure, and rhythmic relief. He saves his
showiest arpeggios, opening melodiously and introducing
implied double-time along the way. His second recorded
improvisation on the *Body and Soul* chords, originally called
Rainbow Mist (1944), is not quite the equal of the original
but his absolute sureness and ease at what he is about, and
his ability to let the performance build, are the work of a
great musician.

They are also the work of a great improviser. I have heard
Hawkins's work deprecated as "just arpeggios," and the
complaint has been lodged that in his solos he leans heavily
for a sense of order on the fact that the modifying chords
in popular songs repeat in relatively short cycles. But arpeggios and cyclical patterns of harmony are Hawkins's means,
much as they were J. S. Bach's in certain moods, never his
end. Anyone who has heard him replay a standard Hawkins
piece, or heard him play the same piece successively, will
understand the committed creativity with which Hawkins
approaches his means.

I would say that the great period that began in 1939 for
Hawkins continued through 1944. That latter year was a
prolific one in records for an always prolific player, and it

found Hawkins present on several very good sessions and
two excellent ones. One of the finer sessions was with players
who had also been outstanding in the mid-'thirties, Teddy
Wilson and Roy Eldridge, and produced *I'm in the Mood
for Love.* The other excellent session produced *Sweet Lorraine, Crazy Rhythm,* and the superb *The Man I Love* by
Hawkins and a rhythm section.

Sweet Lorraine, the one slow ballad recorded on the date,
shows Hawkins forming his chord-spreads into meaningful
melodic phrases. Rhythmically he glides easily from one
heavy beat to the next, variously curving around the light
ones. His tone is firm but not harsh. Hawkins's decision to
play *The Man I Love* at medium tempo, but with the
soloists taking it in "long" meter, set up a dramatic basis
for exploring Gershwin's chord changes. Hawkins plays
with uncompromising involvement and a plentitude of ideas.
A variety of traditional-sounding riffs and blues phrases
interplay in surprising cohesiveness with showy arpeggios.
Brief phrases which break up Hawkins's regular accents are
placed with great effectiveness, and the performance is perhaps Hawkins's masterpiece of relieving rhythmic contrast.

The fact that the years 1939–44 found Hawkins at a peak
had a more than personal importance, for in these years
most young saxophonists were under Lester Young's influence, and Young often overrode harmony in the interests of
melody and his original rhythmic ideas. After 1944 Hawkins
fell in easily with the young modernists because his knowledge of chords, both theoretical and pragmatic, allowed him
to. Rhythmically, he continued to live in the early 'thirties—
but, again, with more regular accents than many players of
that period. Hawkins also did not seem out of place, I expect, because younger players like Dexter Gordon had arrived at a synthesis of Hawkins and Young.

Hawkins did begin to sound dated harmonically by the

mid-'fifties. On a Thelonious Monk date, made in 1957, he
was momentarily intimidated by some of the thick complexity Monk gives to his chords. However, Hawkins's quick
solution, to go ahead and play what he knows, is the solution
of a mature man, and his solos show it. Hawkins continued
to listen: later he used simple scalar embellishments in his
solos that echoed the more complex ones of John Coltrane.

Among Hawkins's more direct pupils, one thinks most
particularly of two men. The most brilliant is Don Byas,
but Byas was never as successful as Hawkins in varying his
phrasing; even the staggeringly sophisticated techniques of
finger and harmony on Byas's *I Got Rhythm* or *Indiana* are
phrased and accented with freight-train regularity. Perhaps
the greatest pupil Ben Webster, was almost Byas's opposite.
Long an exceptional soloist, Webster became a great one, I
think, after he accepted the limitations of his fingers and
embouchure and became a simple and eloquent melodist.

The standard term for Hawkins's sensibility is romantic.
Terry Martin has suggested, however, that, if Johnny Hodges
and Ben Webster were romantic saxophonists, then Hawkins's work was by comparison both too ornate and too detached to be called romantic, and that it would be better to
describe his talent as dramatic. I am inclined to agree, and I
further suggest that the best critical touchstones and analogies for Hawkins's kind of drama lie outside jazz. His sense
of drama was like that of the great aria and lieder singers,
the special declamatory drama of the concert singer and the
concert stage, a tradition which Hawkins himself deeply admired.

One might call Webster a player of great natural musical
instincts, and Hawkins a player of great natural musical
curiosity making use of the techniques that his innate
curiosity led him to acquire and assimilate. Thus Hawkins
survived more than four decades, a player whose commitment to improvisation was essential.

8

BILLIE HOLIDAY

Actress Without an Act

"All I ask of popular songs," a journalist once wrote, "is that they be beautiful"—which is to ask everything or nothing. Pretty they may sometimes be, but beautiful they often are not. And if they were beautiful, an artist like Billie Holiday might have nothing to do. Her repertory abounded in trivial melody, in ugly melody, in merely pretty melody. To be sure, a part of the meaning of jazz comes from its spontaneity—improvisation and variation have meanings of their own. But in another sense there would be no point in Miss Holiday's changing a melody if it were already beautiful. Her particular musical talent was that she could find emotional and melodic beauty in banality.

Her style evolved in the early 'thirties, when she began singing professionally, and although she picked up a couple of mannerisms from later players, she stayed with it all her life. She was respected by jazzmen of all eras. That respect had to do, in part, with her stage manner: she came out, sang, bowed, and left—no vaudeville showmanship. It had to do also with the special emotion of her performances, and with her superb musicianship.

Some of the qualities of her musicianship are dramatized on an LP done at one of her late public appearances, a 1956 Carnegie Hall concert. She was in good spirits and good voice that evening, and she varied her program in tempo and mood from song to song. She sang *Yesterdays*; in her first version of the piece she had found in its calculated nostalgia a real pathos, and here again she moved into an up-tempo section without interrupting her continuity or mood. She took *I Cried for You* very fast and with such poised rhythmic sureness that she seemed to be teasing her accompanists about the speed—or paying no attention to them at all—and she did not falter. More musicians gathered on stage for *What a Little Moonlight Can Do*. They were more enthusiastic than discreet or appropriate in accompanying her, but they did not faze Miss Holiday. She sang *Fine and Mellow* (one of the very few true blues in her repertory, by the way) patiently and beautifully, and it is a piece she must have done many hundreds of times. Swing, rhythmic poise, and emotional presence were crucial parts of her equipment, but she was a jazz singer and her real greatness rested on her ability to extemporize. Basically hers was a musicianship not of voice but of rhythm and melody. On occasion she sang a song straight, without much variation; then she might be an interesting and even moving singer, but she was not a great one.

Billie Holiday began recording regularly, first with Teddy Wilson's studio groups in 1935, then on her own the following year. If we know how these early records were made, we respect them even more. They were primarily intended for an urban black audience, and during those depression years they sold largely to jukebox operators. Like Henry "Red" Allen and Fats Waller before them, Teddy Wilson and Billie Holiday were asked to come to the studio with a group of the best musicians available (they would most often be drawn from the Fletcher Henderson, Count Basie, Duke Ellington, and Benny Goodman bands). There were no preparations or rehearsals. The performers would be given "lead sheets" to the latest popular songs, many of which they had not seen or heard before, with indications of melody, simple harmony, and words. They did some "standard" songs too, but the new material seems to have been selected with little care or taste, and it sometimes reached ludicrous proportions. The jazzmen proceeded to transmute the material into their own idiom—they worked up fairly innocent arrangements and they improvised solo variations. Certainly not all of what they did was good—inspiration falters and some songs can't be helped much—but they apparently felt much at ease in handling material they had never laid eyes on before. When they succeeded, they succeeded brilliantly—Miss Holiday perhaps most of all.

The quality and timbre of Billie Holiday's voice was entirely her own, and it can be rather a shock when one hears it for the first time. It is not like that of any blues singer one knows of or any earlier jazz singer. But the more one hears it the more one realizes how perfect it was to the import of her singing. Her very earliest records, 1933 ditties with the titles *Your Mother's Son-in-Law* and *Riffin' the Scotch,* are obviously the work of a younger Billie Holiday, but she was still using some of the mannerisms of the "hot" singer of the late 'twenties (of Ethel Waters, perhaps). By the 1936 *A Fine Romance,* it was entirely clear where her allegiance lay. As she said herself, she liked Bessie Smith's feeling and Louis Armstrong's style. And her taste led her to the greatest Louis Armstrong, the Armstrong of 1928–33. On *A Fine Romance,* she glides above her accompaniment with perfect poise and perfect rhythm, and without the rhythmic filigrees that even the younger Armstrong had found necessary to his development. This allegiance is confirmed by one performance after another, and particularly on pieces that Armstrong himself had done: *I Can't Give You Anything But Love, Georgia on My Mind, Pennies from Heaven.* One comparison is most revealing: her 1939

I Gotta Right To Sing the Blues directly echoes Armstrong's
version. But it is not Armstrong's voice alone that she respected. She also followed his trumpet; she went beyond
Armstrong the singer and grasped some of the technical and
emotional possibilities of his horn. Certainly her voice did
not have the commanding sound of Armstrong's horn or its
grandiose import of feeling, but it is perhaps in just that
subtle difference of the sound and the emotions it implies
that we might find the essence of her art. In her own way,
Billie Holiday probably developed the musical language of
Louis Armstrong as much as any other performer and carried jazz more directly along the path he implied.

Billie Holiday did absorb Armstrong's phrasing in its best
aspects early in her career. More important, she had a comparable talent for altering a few notes, a few accents, a few
rhythmic contours to make a popular ditty into real music
as in *Time on My Hands* (1940), *All of Me* (1941), *I Cover
the Waterfront* (1941), and many another. And, perhaps
most important, she took the crucial step of barely echoing
or virtually abandoning a melody if it did not suit her and
improvising a new one, as in the main strains of *The Man
I Love* (1939), *Body and Soul* (1940), *Love Me or Leave
Me* (1941). It might be argued that when Billie Holiday
raises the opening notes to a song like *Moanin' Low* she is
merely making the song more comfortably suited to her
own, admittedly small, range. Or it might be said that her
alterations in Gershwin's *Let's Call the Whole Thing Off*
actually avoid a rather tricky chord change. But the effects
of these changes are musically and melodically fascinating.
One's final judgment is that her point of departure (the
song at hand), her natural voice and emotional equipment,
her innate melodic taste and perception, have come together
to produce a work of *individual* art of a kind which only
jazz—in its dependence on both the individual's virtues and

shortcomings—can countenance. And further, if we decide that it was her natural sense of drama that enabled her to find substance in such ephemera as *Painting the Town Red* or *You Let Me Down,* we should also acknowledge that she never changed a song merely for a passing dramatic effect, and that, for her, dramatic effect and musical effect are the same thing. (Certainly there were precedents: when Bessie Smith approached a pop song she did so as an authoritative blues singer. For *I Ain't Got Nobody* or *After You've Gone* this meant that she bent its melody into a different shape.)

It must have been a revelation to Billie Holiday to work with members of the Count Basie rhythm section, for they actually played the kind of even, swinging, light accompaniment that Armstrong's lines had implied—the Basie rhythm section not only played them but played them so well that they could begin to take liberties with them. But I cannot agree that the meeting of Lester Young and Billie Holiday was the meeting of like styles. It may have been the meeting of similar approaches to musical sound or of compatible personalities. (But would Lester have been capable of her implied sarcasm and bitterness?) In style, however, it is the meeting of a brilliant and personal extension of Armstrong and a sublime departure from him. In Buck Clayton, she found the stylistic kinship of another jazzman who was indebted to Armstrong's ideas. In Lester Young she found rapport but emotional and stylistic contrast, and two eras of jazz met in a sometimes transporting musical discourse.

The younger Billie Holiday could not bring off everything, to be sure. The near monotone of *The Very Thought of You* (1938) does not inspire her, nor does she overcome the "pretty" steps in *The Mood That I'm In* (1937). In her 1936 version of *These Foolish Things,* the chord changes of the piece intimidated her a bit, and she relied heavily on simple blues devices and riding the tonic—almost the way

Bessie Smith might have done. But as André Hodeir has pointed out, in her 1952 version of the song she became its master, making its chord changes, providing new melodies for its inferior ones, giving the piece a superior recomposition. Other indications of her growing abilities came when two versions of a piece done at the same recording session happen to have been issued. The take of *I'll Never Be the Same* in "*Billie Holiday: The Golden Years, Vol. I,*" for example, was much better than a previously issued one, and was probably done after the performers had the material down a bit better.

On her January 1938 date, with Teddy Wilson and some of the Basie sidemen, she is not intimidated by a familiar piece like *Back in Your Own Backyard,* and she changes it boldly. But as is remarkably often the case, her bridge comes off close to the original. Yet on *On the Sentimental Side* and *When a Woman Loves a Man,* she is suddenly subdued and almost complacent, which might give pause to those who believe that her only successful subject was unrequited love. Similarly, she does *If Dreams Come True* as if she half-believed its absurdly rosy lyric. Perhaps the great paradoxical summary of this period is *Trav'lin' All Alone* in which medium tempo and perfect swing are in suspenseful tension with the bitterness of her emotion. At any rate, this sort of paradox seems more lastingly effective than the spiritedly sardonic way she treats *Getting Some Fun Out of Life* or *Laughin' at Life.*

Her response to the presence of the Basie men was, as I say, always special: *I'll Get By, You're A Lucky Guy, Mean to Me, I Must Have that Man,* and *I Can't Believe That You're in Love with Me* are excellent Holiday, particularly the last two.

Even if one's subject is Billie Holiday, one cannot leave

these early recordings without further praise for the musicians involved: for Teddy Wilson's improvisations on *The Way You Look Tonight, Pennies from Heaven, These Foolish Things, Laughin' at Life.* For the contrasting inventiveness both of Miss Holiday and of Teddy Wilson on *More Than You Know,* a brilliant record and possibly their joint masterpiece. For Lester Young's beautiful solo on either take of *When You're Smiling,* and on *The Man I Love* and *All of Me.* For the accompaniments of Wilson and Buck Clayton, especially, on many of the early performances. And for the simultaneous improvising of Holiday and Young on *Me, Myself and I,* particularly, along with *A Sailboat in the Moonlight* and *He's Funny That Way.* They are among the great and revealing pleasures of the recorded jazz of the 'thirties. *Body and Soul* clearly reveals Roy Eldridge's position in jazz history in his brief solo; it departs from the melody virtually into an invention, but in a style still indebted to Armstrong's.

Some performances with the Count Basie orchestra taken from broadcasts have been issued on records, and they find Billie Holiday singing with rare optimism. The rhythmic rapport between Billie and the Basie band on *Swing! Brother, Swing!* is even more revealing than the studio dates with only men from the rhythm section.

By the 1937 *Without Your Love,* bold melodic departures were the rule for Billie Holiday. But gradually her accompanists used more formal arrangements—the price of a growing fame, perhaps. Soon Miss Holiday was a success with much the same sort of supper club following that earlier heard the jaded, sometimes self-deluding emotions of a Helen Morgan, and that later attended an Edith Piaf. Her tempos got slower and slower, her material more and more that of a torch singer. But there could be no better comment on her art than the emotional directness and depth with which she transformed the affected and self-conscious decadence of *Gloomy Sunday*.

With a new record company and a new contract in 1944, her songs were still sometimes not well-selected. The stilted atmosphere—which often included arrangements for still larger orchestras, sometimes with strings—did not encourage quite her former emotional and melodic freedom. But at this time she did record at least one really beautiful song, *Lover Man*.

Probably she needed more emotional rapport, if not with her fellow musicians, then with an audience. Each time an "in person" performance has come to light it has been special, and there is a concert from April 1946 on records that is more distinguished than most of her recordings of the time. She did her *Strange Fruit* (moving propaganda perhaps, but not poetry and not art), *Body and Soul,* her beautifully transformed *Trav'lin' Light, He's Funny That Way, The Man I Love,* and *All of Me,* almost all but the last of them at slow tempos.

After 1952 her recordings were again less formal, with fewer musicians accompanying her, and a variety of tempos restored. Her sense of variation had become even surer, but her voice had not. We can account for this by saying that most untrained voices, and some trained ones, are very apt to deepen and deteriorate with the years. Possibly so with Billie Holiday. But for me the frayed edge of her sound in her later years seems to come from a deeply suppressed sob which, if she ever let go, would bring tears she might never be able to stop. Perhaps I mean that quite literally; perhaps I mean that she seemed so determined not to feel a deeper self-pity that she couldn't see the terrible sadness of her self-destruction. Oh, she may have indulged in sympathy-begging, feeling sorry for herself, but that is not the same thing. Her life was truly tragic in that no one could help her and she could not help herself.

Through it all she maintained artistic distance; she was not merely indulging her feelings in public. In a sense, she was an actress, a great natural actress who had learned to draw on her own feelings and convey them with honest directness to a listener. And like a great actress, she did not entirely become what she portrayed, but in some secret way she also stood aside from it, and gave us the double image of character and of an implied criticism.

She was an actress. And she was a great musician. But she never had an act.

9

ART TATUM

Not for the Left Hand Alone

When Louis Armstrong first arrived in the early 'twenties, the reaction of his fellow musicians was generally positive. His elders, most of them, and particularly if they were from New Orleans, heard him as a fulfillment of what they had been working on. And younger players seem to have felt that here was someone who could serve as an inspiration and guide, from whom they could take at least a part if not all, and go on to develop something of their own.

When Art Tatum arrived about a decade later, the first reaction of many musicians seems to have been one of delight and despair. If this is where it's going, they seemed to say, I can't follow. And some of them decided, perhaps temporarily, to hang up their horns.

What they heard in Tatum was, first of all, an exceptional musical ear, and beyond that, an unequalled capacity for speed and for musical embroidery. And those things remained for years a source of frustration to many a musician. But not so (one learns with gratification) to Coleman Hawkins, who heard something more, perhaps even something else, and found inspiration in it.

The speed and the embroidery were dazzling of course. Tatum played with an array of ascending and descending arpeggio runs, octave slides and leaps, sudden modulations,

double-third glissandos—a keyboard vocabulary in which
swift, interpolated triplets were a small matter. His left hand
could walk and it could stride; he also liked to use a kind of
"reverse" stride, the chord at the bottom, the note on top.
And he could execute all these at tempos that most players
could not reach, much less sustain. Indeed, his early *Tea for
Two* seemed to be a textbook summary of what one could
learn from Earl Hines; *Tiger Rag* all one could get from
Fats Waller; and by *Get Happy* in 1940, more than Waller
was ever likely to get to.

Was Art Tatum then only a kind of superior, jazz-oriented
cocktail pianist who borrowed the styles of certain leading
players and elaborated them with cool keyboard showmanship?

From the beginning, Tatum's rhythmic sense was absolutely sure, and over the years it seemed to grow even lighter
and more flexible. One might say that, by the late 'forties,
Art Tatum's command of musical time and tempo was rare
by any standard, rare for a player of any genre of music.
Beyond that, his swing was infallible. Yet it is so subtly and
perfectly assimilated to all aspects of his art that a listener
will often find himself responding to it, not with his feet or
his head, but inwardly, with his feelings. That subtlety was
also an aspect of a keyboard touch that seemed capable of
evoking endlessly varied sounds from the piano without ever
seeming to strike its keys—and this on a percussive instrument in a music which tends to treat all instruments percussively.

Tatum's repertory tended to remain stable, but it was
added to over the years, and the additions were mostly
medium-tempo ballads. That fact seems to me indicative.
Also, by the late 'forties, *Tiger Rag* and *I Know That You
Know* were less often heard; *Get Happy* had slowed down;
Tea for Two was slower and had become a succession of

chromatic modulations, some of them delivered a bar at a time. The newer pieces contained some unusual harmonic challenges (the stark simplicity of *Caravan,* for one example; the relative complexity of *Have You Met Miss Jones?* for another). The inflated "light classics" (*Humoresque, Elegie*) lay relatively neglected, and there were no additions of their kind.

Art Tatum's capacities for melodic invention were limited. Indeed, given a solo chorus on *Mop Mop,* with nothing but the chord progression of *I Got Rhythm* to work with, he could come up with a building succession of pianistic plati-tudes whose dexterity could not disguise their essential emptiness. But Art Tatum's harmonic imagination was so challenging that a performance could include fluid, altered voicings, unexpected passing chords and substitutions, left-hand counter-melodies—toward the end of his career he seemed capable almost of providing his ballads with whole substitute progressions every eight measures.

An Art Tatum bass line is a paradox of absolute depend-ability and rhythmic sureness, lightness and deftness of touch, and at the same time harmonic and rhythmic adven-ture and surprise. Has any other jazzman reached the level of integration of rhythm and harmony that was Art Tatum? In him they could become inseparable, an identity, inte-grated also with his touch, his momentum, and his swing. And there are those sublime moments when he moves from an ad lib section into a sustained tempo—or sometimes only apparently ad lib. If I cite *Tenderly* or *There'll Never Be Another You* or *Someone To Watch Over Me* or *I Gotta Right To Sing the Blues* or *What's New,* I necessarily neglect many such ravishing transitions.

By calling Tatum's melodic imagination limited, and denying him the ability to sustain spontaneous, invented melodies, I risk denying him one of the most gratifying aspects of his work. He was basically an artist of the arabesque, true, but he also functioned in that middle ground which André Hodeir has called paraphrase, where fragments of the original theme take their place beside invented phrases, to form allusive structures in variation. And there, Tatum's choice and placement of terse transitional phrases can be all verve and elegance. Art Tatum's best harmonic and melodic adornments help us discover what is potentially beautiful in a popular song; his invented, passing phrases subdue what is not.

Tatum's maturity came in the late 1940s, and it is worth remarking that it came after the modernists of Charlie Parker's generation had established themselves, and after Tatum had largely abandoned the trio format with bass and guitar which brought him the only public popularity he ever had—and which, like any role but that of solo pianist, inhibited Tatum's inventive powers. That maturity was announced in a series of recordings he made for the Capitol label in 1949.

The Capitol performances display a heightened harmonic imagination and a firm confirmation of Tatum's always evocative touch on the keyboard—*My Heart Stood Still* or *Dancing in the Dark,* or, for simpler structures, *Blue Skies, Willow, Weep for Me* or *Aunt Hagar's Blues.* And, again, there is firm command of tempo, of musical time, and a growing use of rhythmic suspense and surprise evident everywhere, but particularly on *I Gotta Right To Sing the Blues* or *Someone To Watch Over Me.*

If there is a masterpiece of the series it would have to be either *Willow Weep for Me* or *Aunt Hagar's Blues.* Both offer in abundance the Tatum paradox that all surprises quickly assume an inevitability as one absorbs them. Indeed this Capitol *Aunt Hagar's* seems so perfect in its overall pattern and pacing, with every short run and every ornament appropriate and in place, that it may be the masterpiece of all his recorded work.

Pianist Dick Katz has written that Tatum approached each piece in his repertory through a kind of loose arrangement, and the general patterns of opening ad lib (if there was one), of movement into and out of tempo, of certain ornaments and frills tended to be there consistently—or, rather, versions of them did. (Even Tatum's interpolated "quotes" tended to be consistent: *In a Sentimental Mood* usually contained a fragment of *Swanee River* and ended on *My Old Kentucky Home; Somebody Loves Me* glanced at *Pretty Baby; Indiana* ended wryly with the traditional *Funky Butt; Blue Skies* with *In and Out the Window;* and over the years *Sweet Lorraine*'s Sousa allusion was joined by a fragment of Paderewski's minuet and a quote from "Narcissus.") But the patterns were all loosely held, and, like the pieces themselves, always a basis for spontaneous rephrasing and paraphrase, reharmonization, re-accentuation, and elaboration. If the Capitol recordings are the best introduction to Tatum, the second best might be a successive listening to all versions of one of his often-recorded standards, *Sweet Lorraine,* say, or *I Cover the Waterfront* or *Tenderly,* or such widely separated, early-and-late pieces as *Sophisticated Lady, Moon Glow,* or *Ill Wind.*

The series of 1953–56 extended solo recordings which Tatum did under Norman Granz's auspices (issued on Clef, Verve, and more recently collected on Pablo) are a singular documentation of a remarkable musician. To expect each performance of each piece to be definitive is perhaps to misunderstand the nature of the improviser's art and the pleasures and rewards of attending him. And to pick, let us say, thirty excellent titles from that series (as one easily could) is perhaps to provide the listener with the kind of guide he might prefer to arrive at for himself.

I will single out *Jitterbug Waltz* for its overall design, for its control of tempo and movement, and for its particular grace in the counter-movements in Tatum's bass line. I will cite *Have You Met Miss Jones?* for its high adventure in modulatory risk and daring, and for its mastery of musical time both in its "free" and its in-tempo sections. And there is the ease and daring of *Tenderly*, a kind of triumphant climax to his several versions of that piece—indeed, Tatum's art might almost be defined through his surviving versions of *Tenderly*.

The series does have its failures, of course: it has further examples of Tatum's wasting his time on puzzling material (*Taboo, Happy Feet, Blue Lou*), and of Tatum's finding relatively little where one might have expected more (*Stardust*). And I cannot say that for me Tatum's taste in free tempos, or his choice of ornaments always avoids the pompous and vulgar (*All the Things You Are*).

To be sure, to raise the question of vulgarity is to raise the question of taste, and the question of opposing Tatum's taste to one's own. But it is also to raise the important question of Tatum's sly, redeeming, pianistic humor. Time and again, when we fear he is reaching the limits of romantic bombast, a quirky phrase, an exaggerated ornament will remind us that Tatum may be having us on. He is also inviting us to share the joke, and heartily kidding himself as well as the concert hall traditions to which he alludes.

Opposing one's own taste to Tatum's is ultimately the critic's business, of course. But raising the issue here can also serve to remind us of the aesthetic miracle that was Art Tatum. For somewhere among the melodies he chose, the ornaments with which he enhanced them, the lines he altered, the phrases he added, the sense of musical time and momentum he evoked in us, the unique harmonic adventure he brought us each time, and each time differently, somewhere among all these, the alchemy of a great jazzman brought his performances to the highest levels of compositional solidity, integrity, and strength.

As with many other major jazz artists, the revelation of broadcast and privately recorded material enlarges our image of Art Tatum. The so-called "discoveries" recordings, taped at an informal evening in the home of a prominent Hollywood musician, offer a generally heightened Tatum, and in *Too Marvelous for Words* we have probably the supreme example of Tatum's wending his adventurous way into an absolutely "impossible" harmonic corner, and then dancing free on his bass line, while executing a fluid treble line to ornament the feat.

Was Tatum, as a master of ornament and paraphrase, out of the mainstream in a music whose emphasis fell increasingly to harmonically oriented invention? I think that Tatum's influence, although it may have been somewhat indirect, has been crucial. I have mentioned Coleman Hawkins, and Tatum was Hawkins's second great influence after Armstrong. What Hawkins heard in Tatum was the core concern, the harmonic impetus, and Hawkins, probably helped by his own early training on piano, understood. Hawkins's arpeggio-based style and his growing vocabulary of chords, of passing chords and the relationships of chords, was confirmed and encouraged by his response to Art Tatum.

Similarly, Charlie Parker. We learn with delight that Parker once took a kitchen-help job in a club where Tatum was working in order to absorb him live. And Parker proved to be the pianist's equal in the imaginative use of harmony. The saxophonist proved to be a superb, inventive melodist as well, but we should also acknowledge the clear effect that Tatum's rhythmic language, his patterns of accents, his speed with short notes—his melodic rhythm—had on Parker.

The final effect of Art Tatum has to be between his key-

board and his listener, of course. One can return to a familiar
Tatum recording and discover something new, or delight in
something previously unnoticed, or discover that what we
already thought we knew still seems surprising. Or one can
come upon an unfamiliar version of any Tatum standard
and discover that, as anticipated, it truly does offer something
new.

For the listener, the Tatum adventure seems unending.

10

DUKE ELLINGTON

Form Beyond Form

Main Stem was recorded in 1942 and therefore comes from
a great period for Duke Ellington as a composer, orchestrator,
and leader of a large jazz ensemble. I am not sure that it is
one of the masterpieces of that period, but it is at least excellent. On the face of it, *Main Stem* may seem casual enough:
a blues in a relatively fast tempo. It opens with a theme
played by the orchestra, followed by a succession of one-
chorus solos by sidemen, and a final return to the theme. It
is a big band blues, then, apparently like many another
casually conceived and executed big band blues of the time.

The opening chorus of *Main Stem* is its twelve-bar theme.
But the theme involves some interesting accents and phrases;
it is not the usual repeated two-bar riff moved around to fit
blues chords. Then there is its orchestration: a casual listening would probably not reveal which instruments and which
combinations of instruments are playing what. Also, there is
an interplay of accents from the brass: the phrasing and the
manipulation of plunger mutes by the trumpets set up one
kind of rhythm, while a more conventional accentuation of
notes sets up a different pattern.

The second chorus offers Rex Stewart's cornet, apparently
taking over for the band's recently departed plunger-mute
soloist, Cootie Williams. However, the chorus is not a solo
but an antiphonal episode in which the saxophones deliver

simple statements—simple, but taking off from one of the phrases in the opening theme—to which Stewart gives imitative, puzzled, plaintive, or humorous responses. Next is an alto saxophone solo by Johnny Hodges, and Hodges the melodist is left to himself with no background but the rhythm section. Then Stewart returns in his own style. He gets a background, with saxes predominating, obviously in contrast to his own brass instrument. But the background is also an imaginatively simplified version of the opening theme. Then trumpeter Ray Nance solos, and behind him the theme returns more strongly, almost exactly. The next soloist is clarinetist Barney Bigard; he juxtaposes a melodic fragment, suggested by the theme, over still another simplification of the theme, this time appropriately scored with the brass predominating. And behind Joe Nanton's plunger-muted trombone solo there is another sketch of the main melody, this one with saxes predominating.

Perhaps *Main Stem* approaches monotony at this point. What we hear next begins with a six-measure modulatory transition, almost lyric in contrast to what has preceded it. Then there are four measures by the ensemble and a fourteen-measure solo by Ben Webster, the hint of lyricism continuing in his accompaniment. We are into a second section of *Main Stem*. Webster's earnestness is followed by another four measures from the ensemble and a fourteen-measure virtuoso trombone solo by Lawrence Brown, but with a brass accompaniment that is increasingly rhythmic, preparing for what follows. And what comes next is a recapitulation of the opening theme, but not an exact one. As if to balance both sections of the piece, Ellington extends the twelve-bar theme with an eight-measure coda.

Main Stem, then, with such organization and unity, is a far from casual performance. Yet it is relatively casual for Duke Ellington.

I suppose it is the greatest tribute to Ellington's music that, from *The Duke Steps Out* and *Ring Dem Bells* on, some of his most effective pieces have basically been strings of solos by his musicians. Yet those pieces are truly Ellington works, and not just because his soloists are men whose styles we associate with Ellington. It is a high achievement to have been able to parade Rex Stewart, Johnny Hodges, Stewart again, Ray Nance, Barney Bigard, Joe Nanton, Ben Webster, and Lawrence Brown in rapid succession on *Main Stem* without overloading, and with no loss of the effect of a single, purposeful piece of music. And when one notes the details of theme-orchestration, background, and transitional scoring that contribute variety and yet help make such unity of effect possible, one also notes that these group effects are essentially simple—and very nearly perfect. And how perceptively Ellington could use, for example, the very special qualities and limitations of Nanton's trombone, Stewart's cornet, and Bigard's clarinet.

Duke Ellington lived long enough to hear himself called our greatest composer, or at least to have it acknowledged that the decision would be between his accomplishments and those of Charles Ives. Ellington left an enormous body of music: simple songwriting; theater songs; background music for dramatic films and television melodrama; solo piano works; duets for piano and bass; music for small jazz ensembles from sextet through octet; hundreds of short instrumental compositions for jazz orchestra; extended works, usually suites, for large jazz ensemble, sometimes with singers and (for the later "sacred" concerts) also with tap dancers; works for jazz ensemble and symphony orchestra combined. But Ellington's core reputation depends on his skill and art as a composer-orchestrator of instrumental miniatures for his orchestra.

Ellington is probably the largest and most challenging

subject in American music for our scholars, our critics, our musicologists, our music historians. And I do not intend here to undertake a survey of his career or an evaluation of his output. But perhaps I can suggest some ways in which he moved from his rather curious beginnings on records to the masterpieces of 1939–42; that is, give an account of some aspects of his development from, say, *I'm Gonna Hang Around My Sugar* in late 1925 to *Ko-Ko* and *Dusk* in 1940— or perhaps from *Choo Choo* in 1926 all the way to that wonderful 1947 alliance of atonality and Harlem strut, *The Clothed Woman.*

Ellington's very earliest recordings may seem to preserve an inauspicious beginning for a major talent; they may make him seem a jazz musician on the wrong track, even in danger of derailment; or in some ways they may make him seem no jazz musician at all. They are stiff rhythmically and they abound in the superficial jazziness of the period. But I think we can now see that, for him, Ellington was on the right track.

If You Can't Hold the Man You Love imitates King Oliver's Creole Jazz Band, and does not do it very well. But in *Rainy Nights,* Ellington showed that he had gone to the right source to learn what would be most useful to him about orchestrated jazz. It is apparently impossible to be sure about which came first, but *Rainy Nights,* credited to "Trent, Donaldson, and Lopez" as composers, is the same piece, and has a similar arrangement, as Fletcher Henderson's *Naughty Man,* credited to "Dixon and Redman" and arranged by Don Redman.

Ellington also had several strong instrumentalists, including trumpeter Bubber Miley. And as we shall see, it was Miley particularly as the dramatic soloist and the carrier of strong, sometimes indigenous themes who affirmed for Ellington the nature of his destiny as a leader of a jazz orchestra.

Although there are some few questionable moments in his playing on the early records, Miley was obviously an authentic and developed jazz musician. And through Miley we can gain insight into how much feeling and expressive depth might be retained in a developing and increasingly sophisticated instrumental music.

The earliest recorded Ellington is basically in the dance band style of the day, but a fairly sophisticated version of that style. From just such music, and from Fletcher Henderson's particularly, Ellington first absorbed the basis on which to build his own. He needed ideas of harmony, melody, orchestral color, and form, and, like all jazzmen in all periods, he readily absorbed many ideas from the music he heard around him, then sifted them, and soon learned to transmute and expand them into a musical language that became distinctly his own.

I do not mean to dismiss the Ellington of 1924 through early 1926—Ellington before *East St. Louis Toodle-oo* and *Birmingham Breakdown*. Besides Miley's work on several of them, there is *L'il Farina*, with its succession of solos, which compares favorably with the orchestral jazz being recorded in New York at the time. In *Choo Choo* we meet Ellington the composer and, especially in its chord pattern, meet him interestingly.

Then there is the fact that Ellington's piano (what one can hear of it on these records) reflects his upbringing in the Eastern "stride" school. The traditions of that school may possibly go back even earlier than the ragtime style of the late 1890s, but its players did learn from the great rag men, and by the middle 1920s stride piano was at a peak in New York. All of the stride men were interested in technical expansion and were busily absorbing everything they could from musical comedy scores and "light classics"—even some heavier ones. There are times when the stride men seem bent on developing a kind of Afro-American version of "proper" parlor piano. Admittedly, few of them could play with real blues feeling, and most of them were a bit stiff rhythmically compared to the New Orleans men. But each of them felt required to evolve his own style, settle on his own harmonic devices, and I think such standards tellingly influenced Ellington's ideas of music. Also, the stride style is largely orchestral; it imitates a band.

In retrospect, we can say that Ellington faced three basic problems in his first fifteen years as a band leader and composer with a potentially unique orchestral language to offer. He needed to bring his own inquisitive urbanity and relative sophistication into some kind of balance with the sometimes earthier and more robust talents of his sidemen. Ellington also needed to come to terms with the innovations of the New Orleans players, and with the brilliant elaborations of those innovations that Louis Armstrong was making. Symbolically at least, Louis Armstrong would have to be brought into the orchestra.

Also, the stride piano style held limitations for Ellington as an orchestrator by its very nature. As it imitated a band, so Ellington's early orchestrations imitated the piano keyboard virtually finger by finger. Gunther Schuller points out that Ellington's early approach to orchestration is succinctly revealed if we compare the piano and orchestra versions of *Black Beauty* from 1928. Ellington's third problem, then, was to learn to write directly for his horns without taking the route through his keyboard.

In late 1926 Ellington began recording Bubber Miley's pieces—*East St. Louis Toodle-oo* was the first. He was also still acquiring other outstanding instrumentalists: Nanton was present, as were baritone saxophonist Harry Carney, and Johnny Hodges, and Barney Bigard.

Late 1927 saw a crucial event in Ellington's career. King

Oliver turned down an offer from a new New York night
club, the Cotton Club, and Ellington took the job. It meant
steady work and keeping the orchestra together. It also meant
national fame through nightly broadcasts. Most important,
it meant playing the Club's shows, its miniature reviews. In
working on these shows; in preparing overtures, chorus
dances, accompaniments to specialty dances, "production"
numbers; in working with featured singers and contributing
some of their songs; in preparing musical transitions and
"fill," Ellington began to discover what kind of music he
was to make, and he began his singular expansion of the
orchestral language. Ellington took the idiom that Miley
represented, took what he had learned from Redman and
Henderson, took his own innate urbanity, and in effect
started all over again with a new approach to the large ensemble. King Oliver had tried a big band style that basically
substituted a reed section (saxophones frequently doubling
on clarinets), with written parts, for the single improvising
clarinet of his earlier New Orleans group. And Redman and
Henderson had converted the American dance band, with
its compartmentalized reed, brass, and rhythm sections, into
a jazz band. Ellington now made his big band over by making it also a show band, a theater orchestra.

Some of the sketches and production numbers in the Cotton Club shows were lurid affairs, with "jungle" nonsense,
or sheiks kidnapping fair maidens, etc., and the music occasionally had to be bizarre and always immediate in its
effect. Ellington approached his tasks with his own kind of
urbane but optimistic irony, and he could use preposterous
titles like *Jungle Nights in Harlem* for the benefit of the
"slumming" white crowds at the club at the same time that
he was expanding the sonorities, the color, the orchestra-
tional resources of his ensemble and creating a memorable
and durable music. The superficially sensational and quasi-

primitive effects actually had a deeper role: they were kept quite musical and compositionally intrinsic, and they were a means of exploration and growth for the orchestrator and the orchestra.

Stanley Dance reminded us in his eulogy at the composer's death that Edward Kennedy Ellington retained his youthful nickname because he was a natural aristocrat. He was also a democratic aristocrat. Much as the great dramatists have worked with the talents of their lead actors and the resources of their companies, and the great dance directors have learned to work with the accomplishments and potential of their dancers, the great European composers with specific instrumentalists and singers, each learning from the other, so Ellington worked with his sidemen.

Ellington not only learned to cut across the compartmentalized trumpet, trombone, and reed sections of other jazz orchestras but he came to know he was scoring for the individuals in his ensemble and their sounds. He thereby became the jazz composer *par excellence*. He knew that Harry Carney's baritone sound was crucial to the sound of his saxophones and to the sound of his orchestra. But what genius was it that told Ellington not to score Carney's sound always as the *bottom* of his harmonies, where it might seem to belong, but move it from one position to another for its strongest effect? Indeed Ellington was so attuned to the sounds of his men that the very originality of his textures and the daring of his harmonic language were determined not in the abstract but in his inquisitiveness about, let us say, how this reed player's low A-flat might sound when juxtaposed with that brassman's cup-muted G.

Ellington's works were produced in an atmosphere of improvisation and experiment. The solos usually came from the soloists, and, as alternate "takes" and the surviving broadcast versions confirm, the players were free to stick to them from

one performance to the next. They were also free to reinterpret and ornament them, and—depending on the context
and if so moved—to reject them and come up with new
solos.

All the great Ellington works depend on a relationship
between soloist and group, between what is written (or perhaps merely memorized) and what may be extemporized,
between the individual part and the total effect, and a relationship among beginning, middle, and end. A great Ellington performance is not a series of brilliant episodes but a
whole greater than the sum of its parts. He learned how to
discipline improvisation and extend orchestration—to the
enhancement of both.

Ellington was coaxing a temperamental and brilliant
group of soloists and players into discovering and developing their own best resources, into contributing constantly to
the act of mutual composition, orchestration, and performance, and paradoxically into integrating their own talents
into a total effect.

There is a moment in *Shout 'Em Aunt Tillie* that I think
is a small but succinct revelation of Ellington's role. It is his
striking and original piano accompaniment to Cootie
Williams's solo. His left hand is not striding, and in rhythm,
sound, melody, and harmonic relationship to the soloist, the
piano becomes an effective piece of contrasting orchestration. The maturing Ellington learned to think directly as
an orchestrator—a jazz orchestrator—even when playing
piano.

As Gunther Schuller has pointed out, there was an im-
balance in the earlier works with Miley, as exciting and
important as they are. The first important Ellington-Miley
collaboration, *East St. Louis Toodle-oo,* is impressive, but
Miley's anguished *wa-wa* horn dominates it, as it does the
second important joint work, *Black and Tan Fantasy.* Elling-

ton's orchestral effects and secondary themes seem weak, out
of place, and perhaps affected by comparison. *Creole Love
Call,* another early collaboration, is better balanced perhaps
because Ellington did not contribute any thematic material.

In their later versions, both *East St. Louis Toodle-oo* and
Black and Tan Fantasy are improved works, less dominated
by the themes and the interpretations of a single musician,
more balanced and appropriate in the contributions of their
orchestrator-leader.

Miley's contribution to *East St. Louis Toodle-oo* is a
dramatic combination of themes in AABA song form. Ellington surely added the piece's third theme, a melody intended
for contrast. But it seems a rather inappropriate melody, and
it employs almost archaic ragtime-like accents—indeed, it
suggests one of the themes in Scott Joplin's *Heliotrope Bou-
quet.* In the 1937 "new" *East St. Louis Toodle-oo,* featur-
ing Cootie Williams, that theme is gone, the whole is much
better orchestrated, the juxtaposition of the featured soloist
against the orchestration and against the other soloists is balanced and proportioned. And to cite one detail, the plunger
response executed by the full trumpet section on the first
entrance of the bridge is startlingly effective.

Similarly with the new *Black and Tan Fantasy* of 1938.
Ellington's secondary theme does not appear in the main section but is now the basis of an effective *Prologue to Black and
Tan Fantasy.* The piece is played more slowly, which gives
an introspection to Miley's broader proclamations. And the
Fantasy itself becomes a beautifully played and scored exploration of Miley's blues theme climaxed by Cootie Williams's solo. *En route,* it is enhanced by a middle chorus
which juxtaposes Nanton's plaintive trombone, Ellington's
piano, and Barney Bigard's superb glissando, which moves
from an upper register D-flat through D and into F, and from
a whisper to *forte.*

Thus Ellington's sophistication, sometimes inappropriate in its early manifestations, held the greatest promise.

I do not suppose that one could overestimate Cootie Williams's importance to Ellington, much as one could not overestimate Miley's. Not a great improviser, Williams was nevertheless a great player, and it was he who brought the Armstrong style and spirit into the Ellington orchestra. He also brought a sound brass technique and the ability not only to take over the plunger trumpet role that Miley had created but to expand it, in flexibility, in varieties of sonority, and in emotional range. It is fitting that one of the durable successes of early Ellington should be Williams's contribution *Echoes of the Jungle* (1931). It is also fitting that his work on that piece is in a sense a pastiche of the work of his predecessors, the plunger-muted trumpeters, Miley and Arthur Whetsol. And it is most fitting of all that one of Ellington's later masterpieces should have been his *Concerto for Cootie.*

The years 1930–32 were important for Ellington, a first flowering of his genius. With only twelve musicians in 1930 he produced the astonishing *Old Man Blues,* a masterpiece of orchestration and dense sonorities in AABA song form. And in the same year there was *Mood Indigo.* The first version is exceptionally well composed and orchestrated, but not very well played, and it is prophetic in its singular juxtaposition of muted trumpet, trombone, and lower-register clarinet.

The haunting opening chorus of *The Mystery Song* from the following year is one of the unique moments in Ellington, and is probably undecipherable for even the keenest ear in its instrumentation and its voicings. It is an early confirmation of André Previn's famous tribute that Duke Ellington could lower one finger, some musicians would play something, and every composer and orchestrator in the house would respond with "What was *that*?"

By 1932 a rhythmic turning point had been reached in *It*

Don't Mean a Thing, with its prophetic subtitle, *If It Ain't Got That Swing.* The piece was obviously conceived as an instrumental, although it was first recorded with a vocal by Ivie Anderson, taking over (it seems clear) passages first designed for Cootie Williams's plunger and Johnny Hodges's alto. *It Don't Mean a Thing* is an orchestral and not a pianistic piece, and it is composed and performed with an Armstrong-inspired, swing phrasing throughout.

I should also mention the astonishing *Daybreak Express* from 1933, a part of a series of virtuoso pieces for the orchestra which would include *Hot and Bothered* (1928), *Braggin' in Brass* (1938), *The Flaming Sword* (1940), and the *Giddybug Gallop* (1941)—all except the last, by the way, *Tiger Rag* derivatives.

The accomplishments of 1937–39 provided a prologue to the sustained accomplishments of 1940. From 1937 there is *Azure,* a small masterpiece, and a part of the by-then-established tradition of outstanding Ellington instrumental ballads—or "mood" pieces, as they were called. Otherwise, it became clear in these years (if it had not been clear already) that Ellington was capable of seeming to do one thing while doing quite another, and on occasion of injecting something quite unexpected by anyone. In 1938, while offering what could pass for more medium and fast "swing band" instrumentals like *Hip Chic* or *Slap Happy,* he could also offer *Blue Light* and *A Gypsy Without a Song.*

Blue Light is a beautifully self-contained slow blues for only seven instruments. Again, it may seem largely a succession of solos but *Blue Light* is structured in contrasts. Ellington himself sets the mood with a piano introduction, provides mobile but unifying comments throughout, and a kind of summary in his own final solo. Barney Bigard's opening clarinet solo provides a series of thoughtful, liquid ascending-descending phrases. The twelve-measure passage which fol-

lows uses a version of the *Mood Indigo* alliance of trumpet,
trombone, and lower register clarinet; it is a simple succession of half and whole notes, beautifully voiced for the three
horns, compellingly effective, but without strong melodic
content. Lawrence Brown's trombone chorus which follows
is a robust, climactic melody. (It was Brown's own, and an
improvisation, by the way, and so strong that Ellington later
used it as the basis of *Transblucency* in 1946.)

A Gypsy Without a Song is in no way typical of the big
band music of the times, nor is it typical of its composer except in its excellence. *A Gypsy Without a Song* in AABA
song form has its compositional elements so perfectly in balance that one is brought up short by the realization that
Juan Tizol's and Lawrence Brown's trombones are both
heard in solo, as are Cootie Williams and Johnny Hodges—
Tizol twice and Williams thrice.

In 1939, Ellington had the daring to transform the obvious, sure-fire effectiveness of the *Bugle Call Rag* into *The
Sergeant Was Shy,* an array of subtle—even elusive—effects.
He offered what passed for big band riff tunes (*A Portrait of
the Lion*) and big band boogie woogie (*Bouncing Buoyancy*),
but, as we have come to expect, each was more than what it
seemed to be. And Ellington recorded another slow blues,
Subtle Lament, with five choruses, again virtually theme-less
in the orchestrated sections. The opening ensemble is a series
of descending half and whole notes in fascinating voicings for
the saxophones, but with one of the tenors doubled by Joe
Nanton's plunger-muted horn. And in the second chorus
Ellington uses the typical touch of introducing new thematic
material on his piano while having the brass respond with
allusive, carry-over phrases in a faint echo of the opening
ensemble.

Both *Blue Light* and *Subtle Lament* are experiments in
blues composition with ensemble portions that are almost

theme-less, and with a bare burden of melody falling to some of the soloists. It is an idea Ellington would return to.

There is nothing extrinsic, nothing out of place, in either *Blue Light* or *Subtle Lament,* but until he wrote them, there was, I think, a still-lingering tendency in Ellington to introduce inappropriate secondary themes in otherwise successful works. *Bundle of Blues* from 1933 brilliantly juxtaposes Cootie Williams's resilient growls against keenly timed responses from the orchestra. But then Ellington has Lawrence Brown state a second theme whose chic lyricism interrupts *Bundle of Blues.* Similarly, *Echoes of Harlem* from 1936 begins robustly and memorably but has a secondary theme for the saxophones (borrowed from the earlier *Blue Mood*) that seems jarringly out of place—but which does take on life when Williams interprets it later in the performance.

In *Blue Light* and *Subtle Lament* and *Gypsy Without a Song,* Ellington prepared for the consistency of 1940–42, for *Ko-Ko, Conga Brava, Concerto for Cootie, Dusk, Sepia Panorama, Blue Serge, Moon Mist.* And for the shining satellites that gather around their brilliance, *Cotton Tail, Never No Lament, Harlem Air Shaft, Warm Valley, Across the Track Blues, Sherman Shuffle,* and the rest.

The *Concerto for Cootie* is in a sense the ultimate refinement of the influence of ragtime structures on later jazz composition. It opens, after its eight-bar introduction, with an AABA in song form, but the A theme is ten bars rather than eight, and each use of that A theme in the *Concerto* is a variation on its first appearance for both the soloist and the ensemble. The second section of the *Concerto* is its sixteen-measure C theme. And the performance ends with a brief variation of A, limited to six bars, followed by a beautifully sustained ten-measure coda.

Such comments may of course make the piece sound like a technical exercise in breaking down the standard four- and

eight-bar phrases—something which Ellington had worked
on in *Creole Rhapsody* in 1929, for example. In the *Concerto,* in any case, the extensions are successful and flow
naturally. Williams and the orchestra share ten-bar segments,
not eight-bar phrases with an extra two bars tacked on. The
piece is for Cootie Williams, balanced against the orchestra
but not dominating it, and once again he plays beautifully.
He uses all his sonorous resources, from a tightly cup-muted
sound, through the *wa-wa* of a plunger mute in motion, the
plunger held close, the hard "growl" with the plunger held
partly open over a straight mute, open horn on the C theme,
etc. The scoring is simple harmonically but constantly
varied, and the settings and transitions, dominated by the
saxophones, are beautifully conceived and beautifully
played.

Portions of the *Concerto* had been previously tested. The
forceful B melody is an adaptation of one of Cootie's blues
phrases, one which introduces the 1938 *Mobile Blues.* The
coda is an adaptation of one Ellington used on *Moonglow*
in 1935.[1] The new portions are the lyric themes, A and C,
and they are the work of Ellington the composer in 1940.

Ko-Ko could be called the *Concerto's* opposite. Its point
of departure is simple, a succession of twelve-bar blues
choruses in minor, using two main themes or sections; however, its orchestration is far from simple, particularly in its
harmonic voicings. The *Concerto* undertakes a variety of
material in a brief performance; *Ko-Ko* undertakes a simplicity of material without letting the results seem monotonous.

Ko-Ko begins with a brooding, eight-measure introduc-

---

1. What of the Will Hudson–Eddie Delange *Moonglow,* incidentally? Its
structure obviously owes a great deal to the 1932 Ellington piece *Lazy Rhapsody* and its melody to *Lazy Rhapsody* and an interlude in *It Don't Mean a
Thing.*

tion. The main twelve-measure section or theme is then given antiphonally by the ensemble and Juan Tizol's valve trombone. The piece moves immediately to its second section, and in contrast to Tizol's fluid instrumental sound, offers Joe Nanton's slide trombone in a continuous twenty-four-measure exposition. And Nanton's accompaniment includes saxophone figures which derive from *Ko-Ko*'s main section, thus linking the two sections and the performance's first three choruses.

The main section then returns as Ellington provides an increasingly bold obbligato to relatively basic antiphonal ensemble figures. A simple ensemble variation on the main section follows, but with carry-over brass figures from the previous chorus.

We then return to the second section for a call-and-response chorus between the ensemble and breaks for Jimmy Blanton's solo bass statements. A full, richly orchestrated almost optimistic variation on *Ko-Ko*'s opening theme follows. The piece then ends with an approximate recapitulation of the introduction completed by a four-measure coda.

In *Ko-Ko,* Ellington's talent reaches a full expression. The piece provides evocative primary and secondary material, all of it derived from elementary, even primitive, blues phrases. He handles these with appropriate robustness, continuity, and contrast, with the composer's sophistication used to enhance the themes and enhance the work of his soloists. And the final variation, before *Ko-Ko*'s ending, is one of the most richly orchestrated moments in all of Ellington and all of jazz.

Ko-Ko might be sketched as follows:

Introduction (eight measures)
A   Ensemble and Tizol (twelve measures)
B AND B1   Nanton and the ensemble (twenty-four measures)
A1   Ensemble and Ellington (twelve measures)

A2   Ensemble (twelve measures)
B2   Ensemble and Blanton (twelve measures)
A   Ensemble variation (twelve measures)
ENDING   Recap of the introduction plus a coda
         (eight plus four measures)

Ko-Ko again returns to the idea, heard in *Blue Light* and
Subtle Lament, of an instrumental blues without a strong
written melody in the conventional sense, without even a
conventional riff theme. *Ko-Ko* has, in basic terms, nothing
we would come away whistling or humming, even in its
solos. But *Ko-Ko* has a singular and memorable character as
an instrumental entity, and it succeeds in an area of "pure"
music as perhaps no other previous Ellington work.

The stature of the Ellington orchestra at this period reveals itself in details as well as in full performances. There
is the original, contrasting saxophone line behind the simple
trumpet riffing that opens *Harlem Air Shaft*; the band's playing on *Never No Lament,* especially behind Cootie Williams's solo; the beautiful saxophone ensembles on *Rumpus
in Richmond,* especially as they move upward through the
piece's chordal steps behind Cootie Williams's second solo;
or the polyphonic opening choruses of *I Don't Know What
Kind of Blues I Got,* a small marvel in the Ellington repertory.

For *Blue Serge,* Ellington turned to the most challengingly
simple and potentially monotonous of forms, the eight-bar
blues. He and the orchestra meet the challenge with an ingenious variety of techniques, including unobtrusive modulations, always with a probing sustained emotion.

The introduction to *Blue Serge* is six measures, but for
good reason it is broken into four measures plus two. The
opening four give the main theme, by clarinet and brass, but
only for its basic melodic figure. This exposition is interrupted for a brooding, two-bar transition, a sort of vamp

by the trombones, that sets the mood for the performance. It also sets up the idea of a "floating" two bars which ingeniously reappears several times, extending one chorus to ten measures, or breaking another into six plus two.

In the first chorus of *Blue Serge* Ray Nance's trumpet restates the theme in a full exposition, and in a full realization of its introspective character. The second chorus is a thematic variation scored for reeds and muted brass, a thing of marvelous color and one of the hundreds of examples in Ellington where only the closest listening will reveal what combinations of what instruments with what mutes are playing what, to produce this shifting sonority. This chorus also offers the first extension of the eight-bar chorus; it is unobtrusively and quite effectively eight plus two.

The next two choruses are tied. The first is a non-thematic plunger solo by Joe Nanton. As is usual with Ellington's settings for Nanton's dramatic simplicity, the chorus is excellently accompanied. By a slight harmonic manipulation, this chorus is joined to the next, which is a written (but non-thematic) variation, with plunger trumpets predominating. This episode, however, ends after six bars, leaving two bars for the piano. This "premature" introduction of the piano ties the fourth chorus to the fifth, which is a thematic piano variation for a full eight bars. The next chorus is a secondary theme, a twelve-bar solo by Ben Webster played over the trombones. (But is it actually four bars plus eight bars?) The record concludes with a return to a beautifully orchestrated variation, just barely thematic but strong enough to leave the performance with a feeling of resolution and with no lingering need for a recapitulation.

The successes of 1938 to 1942 obviously have to do with a coming together of specific talents: the leader in maturity, and the sidemen with whom he had worked for years, like Williams, Stewart, Brown, Nanton, Tizol, Hodges, Bigard,

Carney, and so on. Tempering the more sophisticated talents in the orchestra in 1940 were those of the musically robust midwesterners who joined at about the same time, Jimmy Blanton and Ben Webster. Then there is the presence of the orchestra's second composer-arranger, Billy Strayhorn, who joined in early 1939. Strayhorn's was a talent compatible with Ellington's in several ways, and perhaps we shall never know in detail who has contributed what to the Ellington book from the day Strayhorn joined him. Strayhorn had his moments of chic sophistication as his early songs *Lush Life* and *Something To Live For* will reveal. But he could alter the chords of *Exactly Like You* perceptively for *Take the "A" Train*, and he was soon producing *Johnny Come Lately, Day Dream, Chelsea Bridge,* and *Rain Check.*

Inevitably the less imaginative arrangers of the 'thirties and 'forties borrowed from Ellington's themes, effects, and backgrounds, two and four bars at a time, sometimes to turn them into simple, repeated riffs. Pieces like *Slap Happy* and *The Jeep Is Jumping,* for example, are ahead of their time in that they use a variety of riffs to form continuous melodies. The more perceptive students of Ellington did not undertake to grasp the subtler aspects of his orchestral language until the late 'thirties, and at first such efforts were likely to go on in orchestras, like those of Charlie Barnet and Erskine Hawkins, that were frankly engaged in tributes to his talent.

Some commentators have seen Ellington as an impressionist. Surely we are invited to do so by his own descriptive and programmatic titles—*Daybreak Express, Misty Morning, Harlem Air Shaft*—and also by the manner in which he has coached his soloists, almost as though they were a group of actors, into evoking specific emotions appropriate to specific situations. Perhaps impressionism is his means on occasion, but his highest ends include *Concerto for Cootie, Ko-Ko,* and *Blue Serge,* which are pure instrumental music.

I have neglected here the question of Ellington the distinguished composer of instrumental ballads (*Sophisticated Lady, In a Sentimental Mood, Lost in Meditation, Prelude to a Kiss, I Let a Song Go Out of My Heart, Warm Valley*) and the subject of Ellington the songwriter (*I Got It Bad, I'm Beginning To See the Light*). But since those two subjects are often (too often?) the same subject, the question is obviously not a simple one.

As I say, by 1940 he had dealt with the nature of his talent and brought it to a fulfillment. During the early 'thirties, he learned to orchestrate less as a pianist and more as the leader of a group of instrumentalists, individually and collectively. He had also absorbed the challenging rhythmic and melodic idiom of Louis Armstrong. And by 1938 he was using the possibilities of his own sophistication in orchestration in balance with the statements of his sidemen. Ellington refined jazz beyond the achievements of anyone else. He orchestrated and enriched its message without taking away its spontaneity, its essential passion and life.

One problem in Ellington's later career was that he sometimes ceased to work quite as closely with the specific talents of his players. Often he could not because of the departures of some of his key musicians. Choosing to maintain a continuity of his basic style, he was required to get new players to take over what Cootie Williams had done earlier, what Joe Nanton had done, etc. Carney remained, however. And fortunately, Ellington lost Johnny Hodges only briefly, and the combination of communal earthiness, rhythmic drive, and sophisticated lyricism which Hodges possessed made him perhaps the perfect Ellington sideman.

However, there is the related example of Ellington's willingness to return to his own standards and try to discover something new or something still challenging in them. He could succeed superbly. His 1950 "concert" version of *Mood*

Indigo, with one section a waltz, is (its vocal aside) his best version, and one of his best recordings.

Particularly since his death, the question of Ellington's longer works has been raised anew. It seems to me that it might best center first on *Reminiscin' in Tempo* (1935); *Diminuendo and Crescendo in Blue* (1937); *Suite Thursday* (a pun after John Steinbeck and an integrated blues suite in which all parts are ingenious variants of the simple riff which opens the first section); and perhaps *The Queen's Suite* (1968, for Elizabeth II). Ellington's most ambitious long work, and perhaps his most challenging, remains *Black, Brown, and Beige* from 1943, and it may be the best. In view of the often subtle relationships of some of its themes and motives (the third section's "Emancipation Celebration" is, appropriately, a variant of the sacred "Come Sunday" theme of the opening section, for example) and the fine ingenuity of the blues section, Ellington's own evident dissatisfaction with the work—and particularly the last two movements, which he changed several times and finally dropped—seems puzzling.

Ellington remained the major leader of a large jazz ensemble, and there are excellencies from every period of his career. True, he sometimes misjudged his audiences in his later years. He sometimes offered a medley of Ellington "hits," or a facile and banal use of saxophonist Paul Gonsalves's fine talent, or of trumpeter Cat Anderson's phenomenally high "screamers" to audiences who would rather have heard his *Such Sweet Thunder* suite, or a full version of his exceptional score for the film, *Anatomy of a Murder,* or for the *Asphalt Jungle* television series.

Nevertheless, Ellington remained on the surface the supreme popular artist. His audience still had at its core couples who danced to his *Sophisticated Lady* on their honeymoons, and he knew it. And if it interested him to provide a program of popular dance band ballads, he would provide one, and very possibly do so with brilliance.

Throughout his career, Ellington met audience after audience on its own level and transported it up to his own. He made his music, guided his sidemen, and reached his listeners with a perceptive sense of the realities of his situation. He made his music out of a positive optimism, a capacity for seeking the best and making the best of any situation and any individual. But he also made a music that denied nothing in the American experience. He embraced it all.

11

COUNT BASIE AND LESTER YOUNG

Style Beyond Swing

Since the mid-'fifties, the Count Basie orchestra has been a superb precision ensemble, and perhaps the greatest brass ensemble of the century. And that fact adds an irony to a distinguished career, for it was not always such.

The Basie orchestra of the late 'thirties was praised for its wonderful spirit, and certainly the relaxed power of the ensemble was compelling enough to make one overlook—virtually forget—many things including a manifest lack of polish, of unity, even of good intonation. It had perfected ensemble swing, some said. There is no question that the ensemble did swing. But it seems to me that the Basie orchestra had discovered that it could do more than swing, that there were more things to be done in jazz than had been done before, and that its collective joy came from such discoveries.

The year 1932 was probably the key year for big band swing. By then the Fletcher Henderson orchestra had learned how a large jazz ensemble could perform with something of the supple rhythmic momentum of Louis Armstrong. Also by 1932 there were enough Ellington performances that manifest an Armstrong-inspired ensemble swing to underline the point. But in that same year, the midwestern orchestra of Benny Moten made some recordings which not only showed a developed ensemble swing but a basically simple style on which something else might be built.

The Moten orchestra was an unlikely one to make such a discovery. Some of its earlier scores owed an obvious debt to Jelly Roll Morton, but it took the Moten band until 1929 and a performance like *Jones Law Blues* for it to be able to play a Morton-derived style with sureness and accomplishment. Otherwise its arrangements were overstuffed affairs, full of effects that were at once simple and pretentious, and some of its soloists were apt to be embarrassingly indebted to the likes of Red Nichols or Frankie Trumbauer—when they were not simply faking.

Yet in December 1932 this orchestra, after the merest hints in its early records, had a marathon recording date on which it revealed a four-square swing so nearly perfect that some of its passages are classic—the final riffing on *Blue Room* for example.

The transformation came about less abruptly than the recordings make it seem, and it came about because the Moten band gradually borrowed the members of another band, the Blue Devils of bass player Walter Page. No matter how much credit one gives where it is due—to trumpeter "Hot Lips" Page, to trombonist Dan Miner, to trombonist-guitarist-arranger Eddie Durham, to clarinetist-saxophonist-arranger Eddie Barefield, to tenor saxophonist Ben Webster, to singer Jimmy Rushing, to pianist William (later Count) Basie—the crux of the matter on the 1932 Moten recordings is Walter Page and the firm, strong, and sometimes joyous four beats to a bar that his bass provided. Around its virtues all other things seem to have gathered.

Even the style had developed in Page's Blue Devils orchestra, and at its best it was simplicity itself. The most effective ensembles on the 1932 Moten records are simple riff figures, shouted out by the brass or saxes or tossed back and forth from one section to another in antiphonal call-and-response figures. Thus the finale of *Blue Room*. Thus the finale of *Moten's Swing*. Thus older-style pieces like *Milenburg Joys* and *Prince of Wails* could be reinterpreted in a new rhythmic manner. And thus the group could play a more elaborate piece like *Toby* and play it well. But the Moten band was to drop the style that *Toby* represents, leaving it to powerhouse orchestras like Jimmie Lunceford's.

Therefore the best Moten ensembles were simple and direct, and the more complex passages in the music were up to the soloists. And so it was not that the Basie band could swing in 1937; the Moten band had had such things in hand five years before.

The story is fairly well known that Basie's orchestra did not begin as a big band but as a smaller one of nine pieces which the pianist led after Moten's commercial potential had collapsed. But many of the stylistic virtues of that small ensemble were evidently borrowed from those of the Blue Devils and the later Moten band. So it is perhaps not quite miraculous that Basie was able to expand his small group to a large one, while retaining its informality, spontaneity, and verve.

The early Basie book was casual and frequently borrowed, either in bits and pieces or, sometimes, whole. The ultimate source was often Fletcher Henderson's orchestra. Basie's arrangement of *Honeysuckle Rose* is a slight simplification of Henderson's. Basie's *Swinging the Blues* comes from Henderson's *Hot and Anxious* and *Comin' and Goin'*.[1] *Jumpin'*

---

1. A more complete history of this piece is interesting and revealing. The 1929 Ellington-Miley *Doin' the Voom Voom*, in AABA song form (an obvious Cotton Club specialty), became the 1931 Horace Henderson-Fletcher Henderson pair of pieces called *Hot and Anxious* (a blues) and *Comin' and Goin'* (partly a blues). Those pieces also added the riff later called *In the Mood*.

at the Woodside (as Dan Morgenstern points out) comes from the Mills' Blue Rhythm Band's *Jammin' For the Jackpot,* with perhaps a glance at the arrangement of *Honeysuckle Rose* that Benny Carter did for Coleman Hawkins and Django Reinhardt. *Jive at Five* from the same ensemble's *Barrelhouse.* The Mills' Blue Rhythm Band was a Henderson-style orchestra.

On *One O'Clock Jump,* one hears a riff lifted from one piece, and then another riff lifted from another piece. Or, one hears a simple ensemble figure that reflects the style of one Basie soloist, and then another figure that comes from the vocabulary of another Basie soloist. The understructures are also simple, often borrowed from *Tea for Two, Digga Digga Do, I Got Rhythm, Lady Be Good, Shoe Shine Boy,* and the like. And everywhere and always one hears the blues, often in medium tempo and with a kind of joy unheard in the blues before.

A history of the jazz rhythm section is virtually a history of the music. In the early 'twenties one might find a pianist's left hand, a string bass or tuba, a guitar or banjo, a drummer's two hands, and perhaps his two feet, all clomping away, keeping 4/4 time, or two beats out of the four. It was partly a matter of necessity; keeping time was difficult for some of the players individually, swinging more difficult, and consequently both keeping steady time and making it swing were difficult for many of the groups as well. When such elementary time-keeping became less needed by the hornmen, it began to drop away, to be sure, but not only

---

These, in turn, became Count Basie's *Swinging the Blues.* Meanwhile, *Doin' the Voom Voom* had also obviously inspired the Lunceford-Will Hudson specialties *White Heat* and *Jazznocracy,* and these in turn prompted the Harry James-Benny Goodman *Life Goes to a Party.* In the last piece, the background figure (an up-and-down scalar motive) to one of the trumpet solos on *Voom Voom* had been slightly changed and elevated into a main theme.

because the musicians didn't need it any more. It dropped
away also because the rhythm section men found something
to put in its place.

It is another of the Basie miracles that the pianist, Count
Basie, the bassist, Walter Page, and the drummer, Jo Jones,
came together. Jones not only played lightly and differently,
he gave jazz drumming a different role in the music. He
pedalled his bass drum more quietly and he moved his hands
away from his snare drum to keep his basic rhythm on his
double, high-hat cymbal. Unlike some of his imitators, he
achieved a momentum, a kind of discreet urgency in his
cymbal sound by barely opening the high-hat as he struck it.
All of which is to say that Jo Jones discovered he could play
the *flow* of the rhythm and not its demarcation. And he
perceived that the rhythmic lead was passing to the bass,
which he could complement with his cymbals.

From one point of view, the styles of the members of the
Basie rhythm section were built on simplifications of previous styles. Walter Page had heard Wellman Braud, but
(right notes or wrong) counted off four even beats, and in-
frequently used the syncopations that were sometimes so
charming in Braud's playing. Guitarist Freddie Green struck
chords on the beats evenly, quietly. Jones played his *ching-
de-ching* differently, in a sense much more simply, than, say,
Baby Dodds played his drums. And Basie, more often than
not, neither strides nor walks with his left hand. But the
simplifications, the cutting back to essentials, also involved
rebuildings.

Basie's melodic vocabulary came from Fats Waller, with
flashes of Earl Hines, and some soon-to-be-acquired bits from
Teddy Wilson. He could stride skillfully and joyously, as he
did on *Prince of Wails* with Moten. But when he dropped
the *oom-pa* of stride bass, Basie's right hand accents were no
longer heavy or light, but all equal, and, with Page taking

care of the basic beats, the pianist's rather limited melodic
vocabulary was suddenly released. Basie could form solo
after solo out of a handful of phrases that quickly became
familiar but were always somehow fresh because they were
always struck, shaded, enunciated and pronounced differently; he discovered the superbly individual piano touch
which defies imitation, and which can cause subtle percussive and accentual nuances in the most apparently repetitive ideas.

Similarly he shifted the very function of jazz ensemble
piano. He no longer accompanied in the old way: he commented, encouraged, propelled, and interplayed. And in
his own solos, his left hand commented, encouraged, propelled, and interplayed with his right. One need only listen
to those moments when Basie did revert to a heavy stride
bass (as when he did behind Lester Young on *You Can
Depend on Me*) to hear what a sluggish effect it could have
in the new context, or listen even to those moments when
Basie's left-hand stride was so light and discontinuous as to
be almost an abstraction of the style (as on *Time Out* or
Twelfth Street Rag) to realize how brilliant were his discoveries about jazz piano.

Basie's playing on *Lester Leaps In* seems perfect, perhaps
(one is tempted to believe) because he is in the company
of a select group from his own orchestra, men whom he
understood and who understood him. But when he sits in
with the Goodman sextet on *Till Tom Special* and *Gone
with 'What' Wind*, every piano animation and comment is
precisely right in timing, in touch, in sound, in rhythm. If
there is anything left in Basie of the oldest tradition of jazz
piano, that of imitating an orchestra, it is an imitation of an
orchestra somehow made spontaneous and flexible and never
redundant. Probably the greatest moment for Basie the accompanist comes during the two vocal choruses on *Sent for*

You Yesterday, in a delicate balance involving Rushing's voice, Harry Edison's trumpet obbligato, the saxophone figures, and Basie's discreet feeds, interjections, punctuations, and encouragements.

Perhaps the best introduction to Basie both as soloist and accompanist is the alert exchange of two-bar phrases between him and the horns on *Shoe Shine Boy* and of four-bar phrases on its variant, *Roseland Shuffle,* on *You Can Depend on Me,* and *Lester Leaps In.* In those moments, his piano is discreet enough to dramatize the phrases of the hornmen, yet too personal and firm to be self-effacing.

Basie's solo on *One O'Clock Jump* shows how rhythmically self-assured he had become, for it is clearly he who leads the rest of the rhythm section. And *John's Idea,* the second piano solo, shows what personal humor he had discovered within the broader genialities of Fats Waller's style.

Basie's opening solo on *Texas Shuffle* is a good example of spontaneous logic of phrase and sound. His solo on *Doggin' Around* is a classic of linking and occasionally contrasting melodic ideas, and is probably his masterpiece.

Basie does not wail the blues, to be sure, but he has an obviously respectful concern for the blues tradition, and on a slow piece like *'Way Back Blues* he shows what concentrated introspection he achieved in the style. Here is stride piano (and touches of Hines piano) cut back to its essentials, and almost ready to "play the blues," as stride piano can with latter-day stride men like Monk and Bud Powell.

Many of the best early Basie arrangements were casually worked out by the band's members in the act of playing, and many others were revised by them in the act of replaying. But when scores were written for the band, Basie himself would frequently cut and simplify them, and one can well imagine that this happened to Eddie Durham's *Time Out.* Durham seems to have profited from, and improved on,

Edgar Sampson's *Blue Lou,* and his structure encouraged a fine effect of suspense during Lester Young's solo. The resultant *Time Out* is an exemplary Basie arrangement: its ideas are sturdy and it is flexible; it might be expanded almost indefinitely—by more solos, longer solos, and by repeats of its written portions—without losing its casual, high effectiveness. (And incidentally, the performance of that piece shows how much technical polish the band could achieve by 1937.)

The great moments from drummer Jo Jones are the moments when he rises to the music most subtly. One is apt to sense his splashing cymbal in its response to Lester Young's arrival on *One O'Clock Jump* without really noticing it. That response or the way he shifts and varies his cymbal sound behind Young on *Shorty George* or on *Exactly Like You.* His cymbal and bass drum accents propel Young during his fine, rolling solo on *Broadway,* particularly at the end of the bridge. (Was Jo Jones the first drummer to use a bass drum for such accents?)

My examples all come from accompaniments to Lester Young, and that is as it should be. On Basie's records we listen to the group spirit and to the soloists. We hear what a highly personal style Basie made of Waller. We may note that Buck Clayton formed a personal approach within outlines suggested by Armstrong. That Harry Edison built a more complex trumpet style with less obvious use of Armstrong. That Herschel Evans knew the Hawkins of the early 'thirties. But when we discuss Lester Young we enter his own musical world.

An account of Lester Young's historical importance has often been given, but it is an account always worth giving again. He created a new aesthetic, not only for the tenor saxophone but for all jazz. One compares him usually with Coleman Hawkins, and the comparison is handy and instruc-

tive, but one might compare him with everyone who had
preceded him.

Like any original talent, Lester Young reinterpreted tradition, and we may hear in him touches of King Oliver, of
Armstrong (even of the most advanced Armstrong), of
Trumbauer, and Beiderbecke. But in pointing them out,
we only acknowledge a part of the foundation on which he
built his own airy structures.

There seems to me no question that Lester Young was
the most gifted and original improviser between Louis Armstrong and Charlie Parker. He simply defied the rules and
made new ones by example. His sound was light, almost
vibratoless. He showed that such a sound could carry the
most compelling ideas, that one could swing quietly and
with a minimum of notes, and that one could command a
whole orchestra by understatement. His style depended on
an original and flexible use of the even, four beats which
Armstrong's work made the norm. The beats were not in-
flexibly heavy or light in Young—indeed an occasional accent might even fall a shade ahead of the beat or behind it.
And he did not phrase four measures at a time. (If he had
any important precursor in the matter of flexible phrasing
besides Armstrong, by the way, it was trumpeter Henry
"Red" Allen, Jr.)

Lester Young's solo on Count Basie's *Doggin' Around* is
a handy example, and one of the best. He begins, actually,
by phrasing under the final two bars of Basie's piano chorus
(thus does "Lester leap in"). His own chorus starts with a
single note in a full bar of music—many a reed player and
many a horn player at the time would have used at least four
notes. His second musical phrase begins at the second bar
and dances gracefully through the seventh, unbroken. His
eighth bar is silent—balancing the opening perhaps. In nine
he begins his third phrase, which links logically with his

second. But the basic impulse here is not breaking through the four and eight-bar phrases, nor in the daring symmetry of balancing one casual note at the beginning against a silence eight bars later. It is in his accents, in a sort of freely dancing rhythmic impulse, which seem almost to dictate how his melodies shall move. Then in his bridge, he consumes the first half with a series of one-measure spurts and the second with a single phrase spun out of them.

With a marvelous ear, and a refusal to allow a literal reading of chords to detain him, he might freely, casually, and tantalizingly phrase several beats ahead of a coming chord change. Similarly, he might phrase behind an already departed chord. His opening chorus on *Taxi War Dance* contains a bold enough use of such horizontal, linear phrases to have captivated a whole generation of players, and to seem bold still.

Thus one might say that his originality was not harmonic, but a-harmonic. He announced it on his very first recording date in the dense and ultimately self-justifying dissonances of *Shoe Shine Boy,* rather different from the simple harmonic ignorance of some of his predecessors. And he affirmed it with a fine harmonic high-handedness in solos like *I Never Knew.* In general what he did was hit the tonic chords, and read through the others as his ear and sense of melody dictated.[2]

He was an exceptional sketch artist and a master of a kind of melodic ellipsis. As Louis Gottlieb has said, he could make one hear a scale by playing only a couple of notes, as on his introduction to *Every Tub.*

Sometimes one even suspects a perverseness perhaps born

2. A recorded rehearsal from 1940 (released on an unauthorized LP in the 'seventies) with Benny Goodman and guitarist Charlie Christian, finds Lester Young being more careful about his chord changes, and a challenging soloist results.

of a defensive introversion. He leaves out beats other players would accent. He offers an ascending phrase where one expects a descent. He turns a cliché inside out. He uses melodic intervals no one else would use, in places where one would not expect to hear them, even from him.

But he was no mere phrase-monger. However original his phrases might be, his sense of order was sometimes exceptional. We are apt to think that the best of his solos delight us because they are so eventful that they maintain themselves only out of a kind of sustained unexpectedness and energetic surprise that somehow satisfies us. But on *One O'Clock Jump,* he begins with a light parody of the brass riff which accompanies him, and develops that parody into a melody. His first recording of *Lady Be Good* has a motific logic that is announced by his opening phrase. And a classic performance like *Lester Leaps In* is full of ideas that link melodically, one to the next. Perhaps the great example of this is his playing on *Jive at Five.* Every phrase of that beautiful solo has been imitated and fed back to us a hundred times in other contexts by Lester's followers, but that knowledge only helps us to affirm the commendable decorum and the originality of the master's work, whenever we return to it.

Lester Young could directly reinterpret a simple, traditional idea, as he does in his clarinet solos on *Pagin' the Devil* and *Blues for Helen.* And he could play jazz counterpoint—as with Buck Clayton on *Way Down Yonder in New Orleans* and *Them There Eyes,* or with Billie Holiday on *Me, Myself and I* and *He's Funny That Way*—in such a way as to make one reassess all New Orleans and Dixieland jazz one has ever heard. He is—or he should be—the despair of his imitators as much as Basie the pianist should be.

We have few examples of Lester Young's slow blues playing from the years with Basie, and almost every one of them makes us wish we had more. Besides *Pagin' the Devil* and *Blues for Helen* there is a beautifully simple chorus on a never re-released Sammy Price pick-up date, *Things About Coming My Way*; and the accompaniments to Jimmy Rushing on both *Blues in the Dark* (before Ed Lewis takes over to reproduce Armstrong's *Gully Low Blues* solo) and on *I Left My Baby*. The last is especially remarkable because Lester Young imitates a man in tears almost literally, yet aesthetically.

In 1939 Lester Young contributed a beautiful saxophone theme on the slow blues *Nobody Knows,* and under his guidance the sax section plays it, curving and bending its notes with the plaintive depth of Lester himself. And in 1940 he provided the Basie orchestra with an original theme called, with typical innocence, *Tickle Toe,* on which he had the group play a melodic line in eighth-notes. On this basis, one might have hoped for even further changes in style within the large jazz ensemble itself, with Lester Young showing the way.

His temperament was not universal. Indeed one sometimes feels he was gaily gentle to the point of deliberate innocence and innocent to the point of self-delusion. Yet his musical personality is so strong that, while one is in its presence, little else exists. He did create a world in which one can believe fully, but when his personal world came in touch with the real one, we know that the results might be tragic. The Lester Young of 1943, after he left Basie briefly and returned, was a somewhat different player, for some of the leaping energy was gone. And the Lester Young who returned from Army service in late 1945 was a very different player and man.

Young once indicated that he spent his early days with

Basie exploring the upper range of his horn, "alto tenor,"
as he put it. His middle days on "tenor tenor." And his last
years, on the low notes of "baritone tenor." Beyond question, his creative energy descended as he descended the
range of his horn, and his rhythmic sense gradually became
that of a tired and finally exhausted man. But there are
compensations, as perhaps there were bound to be from a
soloist of his brilliance. Slow balladry was seldom allowed
him in the years with the Basie orchestra, but his post-Basie
years produced the superb musings of *These Foolish Things*.[3]
And, perhaps inevitably, they also produced a further extension of his blues language with the profoundly ironic,
melancholy joy of *Jumpin' with Symphony Sid,* with its
touches of bebop phrasing, and the resignation of *No Eyes
Blues.*

I suppose that any man who loves Lester's music will have
favorite recordings from his later years in which something
of his youthful energy was recaptured. Mine are from a
1949 session which produced *Ding Dong* and *Blues 'n' Bells.*
Incidentally, the "cool" tenor players seem to have liked
the latter piece too, for it contains almost the only phrases
from Young's later career which they borrowed.

Lester Young created a new aesthetic for jazz but, whatever one says about his rhythmic originality, about his expansion of the very sound of jazz music, about his elusive
sense of solo structure, he was a great original melodist, like
all great jazzmen. Great Lester Young solos—*When You're
Smiling* with Teddy Wilson, or *You Can Depend on Me,* or
Way Down Yonder in New Orleans—are self-contained.
They seem to make their own rules of order and be their
own excuse for being.

3. A 1946 broadcast version of this piece survives with Young accompanied
by Nat Cole's trio. It is a fine complement to the studio recorded version, and
perhaps equally superb.

12

CHARLIE PARKER

The Burden of Innovation

It is now possible to discuss Bix Beiderbecke as a musician, but Beiderbecke has been dead since 1931. When Charlie Parker had been dead less than a year they still spoke of him often, but it became more and more unusual for anyone to discuss his music. They were beginning to speak of him as a god, perhaps because it saved them the trouble of reflecting either on his playing or on his life. Some prayed to him as a saint, but surely a saint must have a clear self-knowledge and acceptance of his destiny. Some said, in *non sequiturs* that passed for insight, that he was destroyed by big business and advertising. An uptown barkeep muttered, "I got no use for a man who abuses his talent." They proclaimed, "He never practiced." (But he *did* practice, of course, and in his youth he practiced day and night.) They said of the more careless performances and the reed squeaks, "He was a man in a hurry." Perhaps he once said it better: "I was always in a panic." His friends said, "You had to pay your dues just to know him." In a sense you have to pay them even to listen to him. Perhaps that is as it should be.

A Negro celebrity has said that Charlie Parker represented freedom. It is hard to be sure exactly what he meant, for surely there was little true individuality in the life of the man, so constantly was he, it seems, the victim of his own passions.

For Parker's music, perhaps *freedom* would not be the best word, but there should be no question that his music represented high individuality and an independent, inner determination. Charlie Parker the saxophonist was a conquering Tamerlane interpreting and revising the whole world on his own terms. He was, if you will, the bird that seemed to soar with grace and ease along its own flightlines. But a bird, it might be appropriate to add, does not always have its feet on the ground.

Parker the musician had made the first decision of maturity, knowing what he wanted and knowing how he could best obtain it. Those who knew him, those who tell you that you had to pay your dues to know him, will usually tell you also that he did exactly what he wanted to do, when he wanted to, regardless. And the negative side of knowing only what one wants and how to get it is a kind of heedlessness, a self-indulgent unawareness of the consequences or effects of one's actions.

This is not the place for an evaluation of Parker's personality and personal life, but perhaps in that life he did live the negative side of his self-determined musical persona.

What saves one from the ultimate, implicit *self*-destruction of heedlessness is of course the second step of maturity, knowing the consequences and effects of one's actions, and taking the responsibility for them. In any case, heedlessness was not a part of Charlie Parker's music. His music said that, although the choices are greater and more exciting, more promising, than one had thought, so are they more challenging and demanding, and they do have musical consequences.

Parker was indeed a complex being, yet his personal life seems to have been a chaos in which moments of perceptive kindness vied with moments of anger and panic, moments of gentleness contrasted with moments of suspicion. The opposites in him were indeed far apart, tragically far apart. But his music, for all its freshness, its expanded emotion and its liberated feeling, its originality, its seemingly unending invention, at its best presented an image of unexpectedly subtle and complex order and wholeness.

In his one-chorus improvisation on *Embraceable You,* Parker barely glances at Gershwin's melody. He begins with an interesting six-note phrase which he then uses five times in a row, pronouncing it variously and moving it around to fit the harmonic contours of Gershwin's piece. On its fifth appearance the six-note motive forms the beginning of a delicate thrust of melody which dances along, pauses momentarily, resumes, and finally comes to rest balanced at the end with a variant of that same six-note phrase. From this point on, Parker's solo interweaves that opening musical motive in remarkable permutations and in unexpected places. Sometimes he subtracts notes from it, changes notes within it, adds notes to it. But it is the core of his improvisation, and, speaking personally, I have seldom listened to this chorus without realizing how ingeniously that phrase is echoed in Parker's remarkable melody.

I think we sense such subtle musical order even though we may not hear it directly. Of course that order has nothing to do with repetitiousness. It represents a kind of organization and development quite beyond popular song writing. It fulfills the sort of compositional premise which a composer might take hours to work out on his own. But Parker simply stood up and improvised the chorus. And a few moments later, at the same recording session, he stood up and played another chorus in the same piece, quite differently organized and, if not quite a masterpiece like the first, an exceptional improvisation nevertheless.

Improvisation has a meaning of its own; if we know that a piece of music is being at least partly made up for us on the spot, that we are attending the act of creation, we hear that music with special receptivity. But in the final analysis, an improvised music needs to be improvised well, and the final defense of improvisation in jazz is that the best jazzmen can improvise superbly; they can compete with less spontaneous melodists and even surpass them.

Of course, I am not contending that creating melodic order by a recurring motive, by "sequencing," is new in jazz. And I am not contending that it is new with jazz, but I do believe jazzmen rediscovered it for themselves. Some of King Oliver's best solos (let us say *Dippermouth Blues*) use recurring motives and develop sequential phrases exceptionally well. Nor am I contending that the approach always works. There is a first take of *Hallelujah,* with Charlie Parker as a sideman in a Red Norvo group, on which he seems repetitiously and monotonously hung up on a single idea. But hear the second take of *Hallelujah*.

The six-note phrase is not the only principle of organization on Parker's first *Embraceable You*. The chorus begins simply and lyrically, gradually becomes more intricate, with longer chains of melody involving shorter notes, to balance itself at the end with a return to simple lyricism—a kind of curve upward and then downward. The second take of *Embraceable* has quite different contours, as Parker alternates the simple lyric phrases with more complex, virtuoso lines, and variations in light and shade, tension and release.

A great deal of misinformation has been put into print about music in which Parker was a major figure. It was at first called, onomatopoetically, bebop, then modern jazz. It has been said that the boppers often made their compositions by adopting the chord sequences of standard popular songs and writing new melody lines to them. So they did, and so had at least two generations of jazzmen before them. It has been said that they undertook the similar practice of improvising with only a chord sequence as their guide, with no reference to a theme melody itself—in classicist terms "harmonic variations," in the terms of jazz critic André Hodeir "chorus phrase." But the practice had become a norm and commonplace by the late 'thirties to men like Teddy Wilson, Henry "Red" Allen, Roy Eldridge, Johnny Hodges, Ben Webster, Lester Young, Coleman Hawkins, Charlie Christian, and hundreds of others; indeed one might say that in their work it had reached a kind of deadlock of perfection. For that matter, one can find choruses of non-thematic improvising in the recordings of players who were leaders in the 'twenties and earlier—Louis Armstrong, Earl Hines, Bix Beiderbecke, Jack Teagarden, Sidney Bechet, even Bunk Johnson.

The practices are, basically, as old as the blues. Certainly King Oliver's three classic 1923 choruses on *Dippermouth Blues* have no thematic reference to the melody of that piece. One might say that jazz musicians spent the late 'twenties and the 'thirties discovering that they could "play the blues" on chords of *Sweet Sue, I Ain't Got Nobody, Sweet Georgia Brown, You're Driving Me Crazy, I Got Rhythm, Tea for Two,* and the rest.

What Parker and bebop provided was a renewed musical language (or at least a renewed dialect) with which the old practices could be replenished and continued. The renewed language came, in part, as have all innovations in jazz, from an assimilation of devices from European music. But a deliberate effort to import "classical" harmony or melodic devices might have led jazzmen to all sorts of affectation and spuriousness.

Like Louis Armstrong before him, Charlie Parker was called on to change the language of jazz, to reinterpret its fundamentals and give it a way to continue. He did that with a musical brilliance that was irrevocable. But he did it simply by following his own artistic impulses, and Parker's innovations represent a truly organic growth for jazz and have little to do with the spurious impositions of a self-consciously "progressive" jazzman.

The music of Charlie Parker and Dizzy Gillespie represented a way for jazz to continue, but that way was not just a matter of new devices; it also had to do with a change in even the function of the music. Parker's work implied that jazz could no longer be thought of only as an energetic background for the barroom, as a kind of vaudeville, as a vehicle for dancers. From now on it was somehow a music to be listened to, as many of its partisans had said it should have been all along. We will make it that, Parker seemed to say, or it will perish. The knowledge that he was sending it along that road must have been at times a difficult burden to carry.

Today we are apt to see Parker as the most important of the pioneer modernists, chiefly because his influence has proved more general, widespread, and lasting; and because, for most of his brief and falling-star career, his talent grew and his invention seemed constant. Rightly or wrongly, we are apt to think of Dizzy Gillespie's influence as chiefly on brassmen, Parker's on everyone. And we know that Thelonious Monk's ideas were rather different from either Parker's or Gillespie's, and that their real importance would emerge only later.

It is perhaps hard for some of us to realize now, so long after the fact, what a bitter controversy modern jazz brought about, but it is instructive to look briefly at that controversy. Among other things, its opponents declared that the modernists had introduced harmonic values that were alien to jazz. Well, once jazz has embraced European harmony in any aspect, as it did far longer ago than 1900, it has by implication embraced it all, as long as the right players came along to show just how it could be unpretentiously included and assimilated into the jazz idiom. But the curiousness of this argument is clearly dramatized in the fact that bop's opponents are apt to approve of pianist Art Tatum and tenor saxophonist Don Byas, both of whom were harmonically as sophisticated and knowledgeable as Parker and Gillespie. But Byas does not really *sound* like a modernist, because rhythmically he is not a modernist. And rhythm is the crux of the matter.

The crucial thing about the bebop style is that its basis came from the resources of jazz itself, and it came about in much the same way that innovation had come about in the past. That basis is rhythmic, and it involves rhythmic subdivision. Any other way would surely have been disastrous. We should not talk about harmonic exactness or substitute chords and the rest before we have talked about rhythm.

Like Louis Armstrong, Charlie Parker expanded jazz rhythmically and, although his rhythmic changes are intricately and subtly bound up with his ideas of harmony and melody, the rhythmic change is fundamental. "Bebop," however unfortunate a name for the music, does represent it rhythmically and hence rather accurately, much as "swing" accurately represents the rhythmic momentum that Armstrong introduced.

We may say that Armstrong's rhythms are based on a quarter-note. Parker's idea of rhythm is based on an eighth-note. Of course I am speaking of melodic rhythm, the rhythm that the players' accents make as they offer their melodies, not of the basic time or the basic percussion.

For that matter, to speak of rhythm, melodic line, and harmony as if they were entities is a critic's necessary delusion. But such separations can clarify much. To many ears attuned to the music of Coleman Hawkins or Roy Eldridge and the rhythmic conceptions they use, Parker's music seemed at first pointlessly fussy and decorative—a flurry of technique.

Players at first found Parker's sophisticated blue lines like *Relaxin' at Camarillo* and *Billie's Bounce* almost impossible to play, not because of their notes but because their strong melodic lines demanded such a fresh way of accenting and phrasing. But once one is in touch with Parker rhythmically, every note, every phrase, becomes direct, functional musical expression. And of course I am giving only a rough rule of thumb; each style is more complex than such a description makes it seem. Parker, who showed that his notes and accents might land on heavy beats, weak beats, and the various places in between beats, was the most imaginative player rhythmically in jazz history, as his one dazzlingly intricate chorus on *Ornithology* might easily attest.

I do not think that one can hear the impeccable swing of a player like Lionel Hampton without sensing that some sort of future crisis was at hand in the music, that—to exaggerate only slightly—a kind of jazz as melodically dull as a set of tone drums might well be in the offing. In guitarist Charlie Christian, it seems to me, one hears both the problem and the basis for its solution, a basis which Lester Young had helped provide him with. Christian's swing was perfect. He was an outstanding melodist. And at times his rhythmic imagination carried him to the verge of some new discoveries.

To say that fresh rhythmic invention is basic to Parker's music is not to ignore the fact that he also possessed one of the most fertile harmonic imaginations that jazz has ever known. In this respect one can mention only Art Tatum in the same paragraph with him. Tatum must have been an enormous influence, one feels sure, harmonically and even in note values. But Tatum's imagination was harmonic and ornamental, and Parker—although he had a melodic vocabulary in which (as with most musicians) certain phrases recur—was perhaps the greatest *inventor* of melodies jazz has seen.

Still, one is brought up short by the realization that a "typical" Parker phrase turns out to be much the same phrase one had heard years before from, say, Ben Webster. The secret is of course that Parker inflects, accents, and pronounces that phrase so differently that one simply may not recognize it.

What was Parker's heritage? Such questions are always vexing for so original a talent. Someone has suggested that he combined on alto the two tenor saxophone traditions: the sophisticated and precise harmonic sense of Coleman Hawkins and his follower, Don Byas; and the rhythmic originality, variety, and looseness of phrase and penchant for horizontal, linear melody of Lester Young and his follower, guitarist Charlie Christian. But the closest thing on previous jazz records to Parker's mature phrasing that I know of are a handful of Louis Armstrong's most brilliant trumpet solos—*West End Blues* from 1928, *Sweethearts On Parade* from 1930, *Between the Devil and the Deep Blue Sea* from 1931, *Basin Street Blues* from 1933. In them we clearly hear Parker's melodic rhythm in embryo. No one jazzman, not even Roy Eldridge, undertook to develop that aspect of Armstrong until Charlie Parker.

However, it is fitting that Parker's first recorded solo, on *Swingmatism* with Jay McShann, does owe so much to Lester Young. Whatever his debt to others (and to himself) for the genesis of his style, Parker had obviously absorbed Young's language soundly and thoroughly. Charlie Parker's second recorded solo is also indicative—brilliant but perhaps exasperating. On McShann's *Hootie Blues* he played what might have been a beautifully developed and rhythmically striking chorus, one which introduces almost every-

thing Parker was to spend the rest of his life refining. But
the solo is not finally satisfactory; he interrupts it in the
seventh bar to interpolate a trite riff figure. Granted that he
showed the sound intuition of knowing that a contrastingly
simple idea was precisely right at that moment in his
melody, a simply commonplace one was not.

The best introduction to Parker's music is probably his
remarkable pair of choruses on *Lady Be Good*. Stylistically
he begins rather conservatively, in a late swing period manner rather like Lester Young's, and he gradually transforms
this into the style that Parker himself offered jazz.

These choruses are melodically fascinating in another aspect. Just as *Embraceable You* is organized around the interweaving and permutation of one melodic fragment, *Lady
Be Good* uses several which emerge as the choruses unfold.
Parker's first few notes are Gershwin's, but he uses these
notes as the opening to quite a different melodic phrase. His
second phrase is a simple riff. His third phrase echoes his
opening Gershwin-esque line, but in a kind of reverse-echo
reassortment of its notes, and it also has something of the
character of his second riff phrase—in a sense it combines
and continues both. And so on.

At the same time this brilliance was delivered in the most
adverse circumstances, at a "Jazz at the Philharmonic" concert in the spring of 1946 in Los Angeles. The solo thereby
refutes what is patently true, that Parker's playing really
belonged only in the small improvising quintets he established as the norm. The circumstances were made even more
trying by the fact that, as Parker begins to move further
away from the conventions of an earlier style, moving in his
own direction, he is rewarded with a wholly unnecessary
background riff from the other musicians on the stage at the
time. It is apt to distract a listener, but it apparently did
not distract Parker. Still, the solo is delivered with a kind

of personal and technical strain and pressure in his alto sound that was foreign to Parker at his best.

Almost opposite to the "classic" development of a *Lady Be Good* is another public recording made with a far more appropriate group, the Carnegie Hall concert of 1947 with Dizzy Gillespie. Here is Parker the daring romantic, using passing and altered harmonies, complex movements and countermovements of rhythm, unexpected turns of melody. Much of it is delivered with an emotional directness that makes the complexity functional and necessary. The celebrated stop-time break on *A Night in Tunisia* played on the same occasion shows Parker's intuitive sense of balance at its best: an alternation of tensions and releases so rapid, terse, and complete that it may seem to condense all of his best work into one melodic leap of four bars. One knows that on this occasion Parker was out to "get" his friend and rival Gillespie, and Gillespie was playing as if he were not to be gotten. This personal element influences the aesthetics of the music, sometimes for the worse. There was at times a sharper than usual edge, an apparent strain, to Parker's sound.

No one who has listened with receptive ears to Charlie Parker play the blues could doubt that aspect of his authenticity as a jazzman. Nor should one fail to understand after hearing his music that the emotional basis of his work is the urban, Southwestern blues idiom that we also hear running through every performance by the Basie orchestra of the late 'thirties. *Parker's Mood* (especially take 1) is as indigenously the blues as a Bessie Smith record, more so than several James P. Johnson records. But one also senses immediately the increase in the emotional range of the idiom that Parker's technical innovations make possible.

Charlie Parker was a bluesman, a great *natural* bluesman without calculated funkiness or rustic posturing. It has been

said that all the great jazzmen can play the blues, but that
is obviously not so. Earl Hines has played wonderful solos
in the blues form, but with little blues feeling. Neither did
James P. Johnson, Fats Waller, nor any of the classic "stride"
men. Johnny Hodges can play the blues; Benny Carter not.
But without counting, one would guess that perhaps 40 per
cent of Parker's recordings were blues. The best of them are
reassessments and lyric expansions of traditional blues
phrases and ideas, ideas reevaluated by Parker's particular
sensibility. The classic example is probably *Parker's Mood,*
but there are dozens of others. And his "written" (more
properly, memorized) blues melodies are also a valid introduction to his work. On the first record date under his own
name he produced two blues. *Now's the Time* is an obviously
traditional piece (so traditional that its riff became a rhythm-
and-blues hit as *The Hucklebuck*) which is given an original
twist or two by Parker, particularly in its last couple of bars.
But *Billie's Bounce* is a strikingly original, continuous
twelve-bar melody, in which phrases and fragments of phrases
repeat and echo and organize the line, and in which traditional riffs and ideas leap in and out rephrased, reaccented,
and formed into something striking, fresh, and unequalled.

Writing was an aspect of playing to Parker. He contributed durable pieces and durable melody lines to the jazz
repertory. But likely as not, he contributed them simply by
standing up and playing them out of his head when it came
time to contribute them. A traditional or borrowed chord
structure would take care of the basic outline; his own sense
of order as an improviser would take care of melodic order;
his own melodic and rhythmic imagination would take care
of originality. *Scrapple from the Apple,* one of his best and
most influential melodies, began with the chords of *Honeysuckle Rose,* but borrowed the bridge of *I Got Rhythm.*
His basic repertory included the relatively complex chal-

lenges of sophisticated structures like *How High the Moon*
and *What Is This Thing Called Love*. But it also included
the simpler challenges of the blues and *I Got Rhythm*. He
met both kinds of challenges successfully, both as a player
and composer, and therein showed the range of an artist.

Parker's best piece of writing is *Confirmation,* an ingenious and delightful melody. For one thing, it is a continuous linear invention. Pieces which use AABA song form
have two parts, of course, a main strain and a bridge or release or middle. The main strain is repeated twice before
the bridge and once after it, exactly or almost exactly. *Confirmation* skips along beautifully with no repeats, but with
one highly effective echo phrase, until the last eight bars
and these are a kind of repeat-in-summary to finish the line.
And Parker uses the bridge of the piece not as an interrup-
tion or interlude that breaks up or contrasts with its flow, but
as part of its continuously developing melody. Finally, *Confirmation* was in no way predetermined by a chord sequence;
its melody dictates one of its own. But note that the song
form dictates a cyclical harmonic understructure, whereas
Parker's melody is relatively continuous.

One frustration with Parker's recorded work is that, although a lot of it is kept in print, the brilliant records he
made for the Dial label in 1946 and 1947 had been spo-
radically available and in a rather scattered manner. In the
'seventies, they reappeared, edited well, and we heard *Bird
of Paradise* evolving from three takes of *All the Things You
Are,* and we heard the different variations on alternate takes
of *Embraceable You, Scrapple from the Apple, Klactoveedsedsteen, Dexterity, Moose the Mooche,* and the rest.

Also from the Dial catalogue there was a far better take
of *Quasimodo* than the one that was long generally available
on reissues. But the leaping solo on *Crazeology* tells as much
as any single performance about the ease with which Parker

handled harmony, rhythm, and line. *Klactoveedsedsteen* would be a wonder if only for Max Roach's drumming. It also has a breath-stopping Parker solo that at first seems built in brief spurts, placed ambiguously and vaguely around a bass line until he slides into the bridge. From that point he builds form simply by increasing complexity, and what previously seemed careless disparate fragments of melody now take their place in a firm, logically developed line.

The collected Dial issues present the final takes of four pieces from a highly productive recording date. There is *Moose the Mooche,* memorable not only for its writing but for Parker's bridge in the first chorus which seems to dangle us bitonally between two keys at once. There is the more tender Parker of *Yardbird Suite,* lyric in both the theme and the improvisation, understandably the favorite Parker of Lee Konitz. There is the famous fourth take of *Ornithology,* not only superb in its rhythmic ingenuity but in its alternation of long/short/long/short phrases, with some rests in between. There is *A Night in Tunisia,* with its famous unaccompanied break, and, again, the spontaneity with which Parker juggles tension and release, complexity and simplicity. There is a very different Parker on each of these pieces. He develops each in a manner he considered appropriate to the piece at hand, and those who will not allow that Parker had that kind of artistic discipline should listen carefully.

The personnel of the quintet that made Parker's 1947 records offered a fine collection of foils and counterfoils to Parker. The talent of a then still-developing and sometimes faltering Miles Davis was, in its detached lyricism, sonority, and lack of obvious virtuosity, an excellent contrast. What is perhaps more important is that, in a growing capacity for asymmetry and displacement, Davis was able to carry and refine a part of Parker's rhythmic message in a unique man-

ner, quite opposite from Dizzy Gillespie's virtuoso approach
to the idiom of "modern" jazz. Pianist Duke Jordan was a
balanced melodic player. Bud Powell or John Lewis replace
him on some of the Savoy records from the same period, and
with the former at least, the whole group quality changes;
Powell's ideas, his touch, and his strong emotion are perhaps
too much like Parker's. Max Roach was at the apex of his
early career in the mid 'forties. The simplest way to put it
is to say that he could *play* the rhythms that Parker used
and implied, and he knew exactly when and how to break
up his basic pulse to complement what the soloists were
doing with it. To call what he does interfering or decorative
is perhaps to misunderstand not only the whole basis of this
music but the function of all jazz drumming from Baby
Dodds forward. Hear Roach on *Crazeology* behind the
"guest" soloist on that date, trombonist J. J. Johnson, then
behind Miles Davis and throughout the piece. *Klactoveedsedsteen* represents Roach's work at a peak development.

Surely one of the most interesting documents in jazz is
the Savoy LP which preserves all the recorded material from
the record date that produced *Koko* and two blues we have
already mentioned, *Now's the Time* and *Billie's Bounce.*
It might be enough just to hear the various final performances gradually shape and reshape themselves as the various
takes are programmed in order, but the session was also one
of Parker's best, and its climax was *Koko. Koko* may seem
only a fast-tempo showpiece at first, but it is not. It is a precise linear improvisation of exceptional melodic content. It
is also an almost perfect example of virtuosity *and* economy.
Following a pause, notes fall over and between this beat and
that beat: breaking them asunder, robbing them of any
vestige of monotony; rests fall where heavy beats once came,
now "heavy" beats come between beats and on weak beats.
Koko has been a source book of ideas and no wonder; now

that its basic innovations are familiar, it seems even more a
great performance in itself. I know of no other Parker solo
which shows how basic and brilliant were Parker's rhythmic
innovations, not only how much complexity they had, but
how much economy they could involve. *Koko,* at the same
time, shows how intrinsically Parker's rhythms were bound
to his sense of melody.

Parker's career on records after 1948 is a wondrous, a
frustrating, and finally a pathetic thing. It was perhaps in
some search for form beyond soloist's form, and for refuge
from the awful dependency on the inspiration and intuition
of the moment (as well as a half-willing search for popular
success) that he took on the mere *format* of strings, the *doo-
wah* vocal groups, the Latin percussive gimmicks. A major
artist can find inspiration in odd places, but Parker with
strings still includes the strings and banal writing for them.
It seems a perversion of success to place a major jazzman in
such a setting, whatever he thought about it or would admit
to feel about it. (Yet hasn't Louis Armstrong had worse, and
more often?)

There is an arrangement of *What Is This Thing Called
Love?* whose triteness is gross indeed, yet Charlie Parker
plays brilliantly in it (as he usually did in that piece and
in its jazz variant, *Hot House*)—in effect he was a great,
creative musician battling pseudo-musical pleasantries. Then
there is *Just Friends*—Parker's part of it beautifully developed—which is the only one of his records he would admit
to like, and *In the Still of the Night* where he shimmers and
slithers around tritely conceived choral singing like a great
dancer in front of a chorus doing time-steps. The Latin
gimmickry is not as bad, and on *Mongo Monque* Parker
adjusts his own phrasing admirably. But to what end? One
cannot hear Dizzy Gillespie improvise without realizing that
his phrasing was influenced by his experience in rhumba

bands, but Parker's is always a development of jazz and jazz rhythms. It was perfectly natural for Gillespie to use Chano Pozo, the brilliant Cuban bongo player, as a second drummer; for Parker such things remain extrinsic effects, however well he adapts himself.

What remains otherwise from those years is often an expansive soloist. One cannot hear the fluent sureness of *Chi Chi*, the easy conservatism of *Swedish Schnapps*, the developed virtuosity of *She Rote* without knowing that a major talent is enlarging and perfecting his language. And there is the celebrated excitement of *Bloomdido* and *Mohawk* on the "reunion" recordings with Gillespie. But on several of these personal successes Parker is involved with Buddy Rich, a virtuoso drummer who simply did not feel the pulse in Parker's way.

By this time, Parker created a finely developed and natural means of expression out of a high virtuosity of short notes and intricate rhythms. It is from this Parker that Cannonball Adderley learned, much as it was from the earlier Parker that Sonny Stitt learned.

Even in the midst of the orderliness of Parker's best solos we sometimes return to the proposition that a lot of Parker's work is oddly incomplete. Sometimes a solo will leave us with a feeling of suspense rather than one of order restored or even of passion spent. Parker fulfilled a mission, surely, to salvage a music and set it on its course. Perhaps he was also the victim of that mission. In any case, one wonders if he really fulfilled his talent, even as one hears recordings on which he is so brilliant.

Perhaps to Charlie Parker invention sometimes came too easily, or perhaps he was tortured by its constancy. Perhaps, on the other hand, he did rely too completely on the intuitive impulse of the moment; it was his strong point, and he may therefore have come to believe it was his only point.

Perhaps it was. When he could blow everyone else away just by standing up and playing, he admitted hearing no call to any other kind of challenge, and thereby he may have been persuaded to take on the spurious challenge of flirting with popularity by standing in front of those strings. In his utter dependency, night after night, on the inspiration he drew from the act of playing itself, in his frequent refusals to coast and determination always to invent, he may have given himself the kind of challenge that no man of sensitivity could respond to without inviting disaster. Or perhaps Parker the man might have learned from the liberation *with* order and proportion that we can hear in Parker the musician.

I have said that Parker and his associates not only evolved a replenishment of the jazz language, but that they proposed a change in the function of the music. Players undertook the former simply because they could, because they heard the music that way and therefore had to play it that way. There can be no question that they succeeded in permanently replenishing the jazzman's vocabulary and usage. But they undertook to bring about the change in the function of jazz a little more deliberately and a lot more self-consciously, and there remains a question of whether or not they succeeded. There was and is relatively little ballroom or social dancing done to modern jazz, but for a large segment of its audience it is not quite an art music or a concert music. It remains by and large still something of a barroom atmosphere music. And perhaps a failure to establish a new function and milieu for jazz was, more than anything else, the personal tragedy of the members of the bebop generation.

New Orleans jazz began as a communal activity, played by men who were not professionals. The transition from such a communal music to a musical vaudeville was not too difficult. The early modernists wanted to take still another step, but as performers they had little or no tradition on which to draw in making that step: they had few traditions of presentation, of personal conduct before an audience, of stage manner, even of programming, to guide them. They did not favor the hoopla presentations of the vaudeville stage, and, I suspect, they did not want to borrow outright the stuffiness of the contemporary concert hall. On the one hand, they repudiated what they thought of as the grinning and eye-rolling of earlier generations of jazzmen; on the other, they sometimes refused to make even a polite bow to acknowledge the applause of their listeners. At the same time, some of them, Parker included, apparently courted a public success and a wide following that were defined in much the same terms as the popular success of some of their predecessors.

But if they had little tradition on which to draw in presentation, they had a rich one on which to draw musically. I think they treated that musical tradition honorably, and obviously they left it richer still.

13

THELONIOUS MONK

Modern Jazz in Search of Maturity

The rediscovery of Thelonious Monk in the late 'fifties is surely a curious event in the admittedly short history of jazz. The fan and trade press, which once dismissed his recordings with a puzzled or scornful two or three "stars," began to wax enthusiastic at the slightest provocation and listed his name in popularity polls where it had seldom appeared before. Musicians who once dismissed him as having long since made his small contribution to jazz listened attentively for ways out of the post-bop dilemmas. They found that his music had continued to develop through the years of his neglect, that it provided a highly personal summary and synthesis of fifteen years of modern jazz, and that it suggested sound future paths as well. And a public which had once barely heard of this man with the intriguing name soon began to buy his records and attend his public appearances.

It is fitting that so unusual a thing in jazz as belated discovery should have come to so unusual a man as Monk. Monk's is one of the most original, self-made talents. Unlike almost every other jazzman, Monk was not only a productive musician after more than fifteen years of musical activity, but seemed still to be a growing artist exploring his talent and extending his range. Such a thing just does not happen in this music, one is apt to say; if a jazzman can simply maintain the level of his first maturity, he is exceptional.

Monk's first recordings were not released until 1947 and are ours by accident. Jerry Newman was "on location" in the back room at Minton's Playhouse in 1941 to record guitarist Charlie Christian, and, above the din and through the low fidelity, he happened to take down some accompaniments and solos by Thelonious Monk. As it turned out, the two solos he subsequently issued indicate the basis for much of what was to come. On *Topsy* (called *Swing to Bop* on the LP recording) Monk plays a solo based on the melody itself; on *Stompin' at the Savoy* he improvises on the chords of the tune but with an original, harmonic, and rhythmic looseness. The pianist's "comping" accompaniments and those of drummer Kenny Clarke sometimes involve unusual displacements of the regular four-beat pulse of the performance and of the period.

The style of the *Savoy* solo is curious: it stems more or less from Teddy Wilson's fluent, many-noted approach. That solo, the ones he recorded with Coleman Hawkins in 1944, and such later variations as those on *Straight No Chaser* and *Who Knows,* should answer the question of Monk's "technique." Obviously Monk sacrificed techniques of manual dexterity for techniques of expressiveness—for the techniques of music, specifically of his own music.

Not that Monk's whole-tone runs are easy to play, with the unorthodox fingering that gives him the sound he wants. Not that his fast successions of ringing note clusters built on fourths are easy either. But Monk's virtuosity, and he has real virtuosity, has developed in the specific techniques of jazz. As when Monk offers a simultaneous, "inside" trill with the first fingers of his right hand, while playing melody notes with his outer fingers. Or when Monk actually *bends* a piano note: offers, by a special manipulation of fingers,

piano keys, and foot pedal, a true blue note, a curving piano
sound, not two tied-notes or a momentary resort to minor.
Or most important, in the virtuosity of Monk's jazz rhythm.

When the records with Hawkins were released in 1944,
Monk's introduction and solos on *Flying Hawk* and *On the
Bean* (based on *Whispering*) showed that an original talent
was emerging. But the records were obscure, had limited
distribution, and were pressed on fragile wartime material
with extremely poor surfaces.

Thus Monk was known about long before he had really
been heard by anyone but a handful of musicians and in-
siders. He was always named as one of those who had contributed to the evolution of the bebop style of the mid-
'forties during those jam sessions at Minton's, but it was fate
that he happened to be there—Monk had been hired as the
"house pianist."

Monk did not record again until 1947 when the series for
Blue Note records began. Meanwhile, whatever the truth of
the matter, it seemed that bebop was a kind of virtuoso
style full of fast tempos, cascading and jerky melodies, rapid
runs of short notes, and was based on a certain few linear
and chordal devices. In this setting, Monk's records were
received with puzzlement and confusion; he did not seem
to compose or play the way it had been decided he should.
There is hardly a bop cliché in the whole early Monk series,
and the ones that do appear are either deliberate parodies
(like *Humph*) or they are in two pieces Monk himself did
not write. Whatever his contributions to bop had been,
Monk was not a bopper. He had been working on something else all along. And those Monk recordings from 1947–
52 seem among the most significant and original in modern
jazz.

In the first place, they establish for jazz a major composer—the first that jazz had had since Ellington—and one

whose best work extends the concept of composition in the idiom. In speaking of his writing, the usual procedure is to point out that *'Round Midnight* is a beautiful piece and has long been a jazz standard, and to say that *Straight No Chaser, I Mean You, Ruby, My Dear, Off Minor, Well You Needn't, Epistrophy,* etc. have been used by other jazzmen and groups. Popularity often determines value for the bookkeepers of jazz. But not all of these seem the most significant works in the series. It is in pieces like *Four in One, Eronel, Evidence, Misterioso,* and *Criss Cross* that the real import of Monk's composing emerges.

The ragtime pieces of Scott Joplin and James Scott are instrumentally conceived in comparatively simple ways. So are the best jazz works of Morton and Ellington instrumental *compositions,* not "tunes" and certainly not "songs." In modern jazz, most of Charlie Parker's best pieces are instrumental lines whose purpose is to set up a chord structure for improvising (most frequently a borrowed chord structure).

Joplin leaned heavily on the tradition of European and American dance melodies, polkas and marches; Morton leaned on the same tradition. Ellington often works within the idiom of American (or more properly, Viennese-derived) show tunes. Even when Monk writes within the framework of a thirty-two-bar, AABA song form, his conception is not only instrumental but compositional; he writes for instruments in the jazz idiom. Even when Monk borrows a popular song's chord structure, he transmutes it compositionally. Perhaps the best approach to this aspect of his music are his blues pieces. While they are as fundamental as Jimmy Yancey's, they have absorbed and transmuted the vocal background of the blues, and have gone beyond the facile excitement of the riff-style blues, restoring and extending the instrumental conception of such pieces as Morton's *Dead Man Blues* and Ellington's *Ko-Ko.*

Try to hum *Misterioso*. The instrumental quality of
Monk's writing is easy to grasp, the best rule of thumb being
that we come away, not wanting to hum such pieces so much
as wanting to hear them played again.

The compositional aspect is most succinctly revealed in
the fact that the melody and the harmony of a good Monk
piece do not, almost cannot, exist separately. In order to
play Monk's pieces well, one must know the melody and
Monk's harmony, know how they fit together and understand why. Most of Monk's melodies are so strong and important and his bass lines (even those bass lines that are
fairly simple, straightforward or traditional) so integrated
with their structures that it is almost impossible for a soloist
to improvise effectively on their chord sequences alone: he
will do better also to understand their themes well and, one
way or another, make use of them. When Monk uses AABA
song form in things like *In Walked Bud* or *I Mean You*, he
is often careful to integrate the B, release, or "bridge"
melody by basing it on an elaboration or development of
bits of the final phrases of the A part.

It is even more striking that a close look at Monk's pieces
shows that they are often unexpected elaborations, extensions, recastings of simple musical phrases, traditional jazz
phrases, sometimes even clichés. This is obviously true of
pieces like *Epistrophy, Shuffle Boil, Straight No Chaser,* but
it is also less obviously true of pieces like *Misterioso* and
Criss Cross.

Monk's sense of form is innate and natural, and therefore
extends beyond composition to performance. Monk had
perhaps no less a sense of group form than had Jelly Roll
Morton or Duke Ellington, but in his smaller groups the
form is looser and more spontaneous—the "orchestration,"
one might say, is extemporaneous. Two of Monk's best compositions are, in their early recorded versions, two of the best

overall performances of Monk's music. They are *Misterioso* and *Evidence,* both, one should note, done in 1948.

Misterioso opens with Monk's blues theme, a succession of "walking" sixths, and a striking reassessment of a traditional blues bass figure. It is offered by Milt Jackson and Monk, the bass and drums phrasing with them. As the theme ends, Jackson begins to improvise on the blues, as the bass and drums begin to walk behind him, more or less conventionally now. But Monk is determined that this is not merely the blues, however beautifully Jackson can play the blues, but Monk's blues *Misterioso.* Monk accompanies the vibraphone, not with the comping, but in a stark, orderly pattern built on the next implied note, if you will, the "missing" note of his theme—the seventh. The sense of continuity continues in Monk's own improvisation, which is built around a commanding ascending figure, echoing the upward movement of the main theme. When that theme returns at the end of the performance, Jackson carries it, with the rhythm once more phrasing with him, as Monk spreads out the sevenths of his previous accompaniment across the theme, in melodic and rhythmic counterpoint.[1] Monk thus ties together all elements of the performance in a strikingly original, compositional, yet improvisational conclusion.

With *Evidence,* a little hindsight is an advantage; that is, the recording is even better if we know Monk's melody, at least in its later manifestations. Here it appears in Monk's introduction, darts in and out of Monk's fascinating accompaniment to Jackson's solo, is held in abeyance during Monk's relatively conventional solo. Then at the end of the performance, in the interplay between Monk and Jackson, this apparently jagged, disparate, intriguing tissue of related sounds has at last emerged, but not quite—a theme of great

1. This fine ending to one of the two takes of *Misterioso* may have been based on a sublimely handled mistake.

strength and almost classic beauty for all its asymmetry and surprise.

On *Criss Cross,* done in 1951, Monk allows the firmness of his harmonies and the percussive accents of Art Blakey to carry the performance once the opening theme is stated and the solos take over. But as the last soloist, Monk himself (entering at a quite unexpected point, by the way) realized it was time to reassert the claims of continuity and form, time to begin rebuilding his theme. He suggests it and then improvises on it more directly, preparing for its restatement. *Criss Cross* is perhaps Monk's classic piece, the one which above all others extends the idea of jazz as an instrumental music.

The early records also place Monk's piano style historically and establish his heritage in jazz. His earlier Wilsonesque solos don't fit that picture too well. Even if it were not for the stride bass line sections in *April in Paris* and the near-parody *Thelonious,* it should be clear that Monk's style (like Ellington's, an influence whose later development has been strikingly parallel to Monk's) is a development of the style of Harlem stride men like James P. Johnson, Willie "the Lion" Smith, Fats Waller, and the rest.

The link between pianists like James P. and Monk is Count Basie. Basie's earliest work is either Earl Hines piano or Fats Waller stride piano, but in the 'thirties he modified or dropped the stated beat of his bass line and developed a rhythmic variety which modified the regular (not to say monotonous) accents of the Harlem school.

We are always brought up a bit short when a phrase or a quality in Monk's playing reminds us of these earlier stride players, because their work depends so much on the regular fulfillment of the expected. Monk's (somewhat like Lester Young's) depends on the surprise twist, the sardonically witty phrase, and the unexpected rhythmic movement seem

fitting and inevitable once one has heard them. Monk was
authentically a blues man, as none of the older stride men
were.

Monk, like the other great jazz composers, is a unique and
largely unorthodox accompanist. He forms a frequently
"simple," polyrhythmic and nearly polyphonic, horn-like
line *between* the percussion (bass and drums) and the soloist
or front line horns. Even when Monk does "comp" chordally, he is a subliminal melodist. The best introduction to
his very personal approach is probably his accompaniments
to Milt Jackson, with whom he works excellently. And as
we have seen, such accompaniments involve something that
was noticed in his work only later: Monk can hold both
performances and inspiration together by the continuity he
gives to his accompaniments. He is a kind of improvising
orchestrator.

The only American critic who understood Monk in the
'forties was Paul Bacon, who wrote:

> His kind of playing isn't something that occurred to him
> whole . . . beyond its undoubted originality, it has the
> most expressive and personal feeling I can find in any musi-
> cian playing now. It has cost Monk something to play as he
> does—not recognition so much . . . I believe his style has
> cost him 50 per cent of his technique. He relies so much on
> absolute musical reflex that Horowitz's style might be un-
> equal to the job. . . . What he has done, in part, is quite
> simple. He hasn't invented a new scheme of things, but he
> has, for years too, looked with an unjaundiced eye at music
> and seen a little something else. . . . At any rate, Monk is
> making use of all the unused space around jazz and he makes
> you feel there are plenty of unopened doors.

As a matter of fact, to make his playing as personally
expressive as he wished, Monk had even altered his way of
striking the keys, his finger positions, and had largely con-

verted his piano into a kind of horn which was also capable
of stating harmonic understructures. And he did not fake,
doodle, decorate, or play notes only to fill out bars or fill
time.

The core of Monk's style is a rhythmic virtuosity. He is a
master of displaced accents, shifting meters, shaded delays,
and anticipations. Therefore he is a master of effective pause
and of meaningfully employed space, rest, and silence.
Fundamentally his practices in harmony and line are organized around his insights into rhythm. And as rhythm is
fundamental to jazz, so one who develops its rhythms also
develops jazz along just the lines that its own nature implies
it should go. The work of Lennie Tristano and his pupils
and of the "cool" post-Lester Young tenormen shows, I think,
that if attempts to impose innovations in harmony and
melodic line are not intrinsically bound to innovations in
rhythm they risk distorting some secret but innate balance
in the nature of jazz.

Actually, I am not sure that the term "harmony" is accurate when applied to Monk; he seems much more interested
in sound and in original and arresting combinations of
sounds percussively delivered, than in harmony per se. And
this aspect has also saved him from the neo-Debussyan senti-
mentalities of many of his fellow modern jazz pianists. When
he undertakes an unlikely popular ditty like *You Took the
Words Right Out of My Heart,* he keeps the performance
fairly straightforward melodically, except for Monkish nuances of accent and dynamics, but he pivots almost every
sound around a single tonic note. Monkian alchemy somehow distills granite from sugar water.

In the early 'fifties, Monk's music and his recordings were
even more misunderstood and ignored than before—after
all, hadn't the question been settled that Monk had little to

offer? But the records show that Monk was still productive and still growing.

He had not before recorded so obviously earthy a blues as *Blue Monk*. *Think of One* is, like the earlier *Thelonious*, ingeniously built on the metrical-accentual variations and harmonizations of one note. Pieces like *Nutty, Reflections, We See,* and *Gallop's Gallop* have melodies that maintain the good standards of *Introspection, Ask Me Now,* etc. *Trinkle Tinkle,* like *Four in One,* is built on the ingenious twisting of a fast run of short notes. *Let's Call This,* one of his most satisfying lyric melodies (on the chords of *Sweet Sue,* by the way), is continuous throughout, technically unresolved until its thirty-second bar.

Perhaps the greatest achievement of the time is Monk's exceptional 1954 recomposition of Jerome Kern's song *Smoke Gets in Your Eyes* into a piece for instruments. One might call the performance a miniature concerto, with Monk's improvising piano leading the horns in their written parts, but with both sharing in the total effect. The notes Monk adds do not have the effect of embellishments but integral parts of a recomposition, a new piece based on *Smoke Gets in Your Eyes.* Monk's splitting of the theme, his altered chords, his deeply forceful playing, his implicit humor, his commitment only to the best aspects of the original, rid it of its prettiness and its sentimentality and leave it with only its implicit beauty.

When Monk's solo on take 1 of *Bags' Groove* (1954) and his recital *"The Unique Monk"* appeared (1956), the re-evaluation of his work had begun. These recordings made more obvious what had been true all along: in Monk's work the changes in the melody, harmony, and rhythm of modern jazz were being ordered and organized. Monk was apparently the first modernist in whose work elements of the style were assimilated enough so that they could begin to be used in a compositional continuity, beyond the requisite continuity and order of a good soloist. Far from being "difficult" and "obscure" or "eccentric," Monk's performances were logical and structured. And so was the music of his groups.

His work had obviously long had a sense of *emotional* completeness. Perhaps the highest tribute I have ever heard paid to Monk's music was offered by a novice who said, after first hearing recordings by Bud Powell, Parker, and Monk: "Monk seems to finish things, to get them all said. I feel satisfied and sort of full when one of his things is over."

Monk's long improvisation *Bags' Groove* is based on the sustained exploration of a single musical idea and on an ingenious use of rhythm and silence. It is a strikingly spare, suspended, hardly self-accompanied line, full of musical space and air, but it soon appears that Monk has brilliantly elaborated his opening phrase into a continuum of variations, turning it this way, that way, rephrasing it to fewer notes, elaborating it with more notes, hinting at contrasting phrases, but returning to the original, and all the while suggesting rhythmic patterns perhaps yet unheard.

A similar but less subtle *tour de force* is Monk's first version of *Functional,* a sustained nine minutes of original variations on a traditional six-note blues phrase.

The improvisations on the LP *"The Unique Monk"* are rhythmic and thematic variations in interrelated, developing sets, based directly on the melodies of standard popular tunes. *Just You, Just Me* is exemplary for its continuity. The version of *Tea for Two* also brings Monk's otherwise subtly penetrating but pervasive humor to the fore. Monk approaches the piece in parody, beginning as if he were doing a wildly witty version of an old-style jazz pianist. But soon one realizes that the joke is not so much on jazz as it is on the kind of listener who thinks that the jazz pianist is someone who plays a ditty like *Tea for Two* in a corny, ricky-tick style. However, everything Monk is playing is entirely and unfrivolously musical. And by the end, Monk has converted the respectful joke into a performance of Pirandello-like dramatic seriousness and penetrating melancholy, in a brilliant stroke.

Monk's penchant for making his variations directly on a theme itself in a sense echoes earlier practice: the embellishment styles of the 'twenties, as continued by Art Tatum, and the probing melodic paraphrases of Louis Armstrong. But Monk has his own perceptive ability in getting inside a melody to seek out its implications; he can elaborate, expand, reduce, or abstract a theme to an intriguing sketch and tissue of notes. At the same time he approaches a standard piece, as we have seen, not as a melody plus harmony, but as a point of departure for a two-handed, semi-improvised composition for piano, a logical, self-contained succession of unique, pianistic, musical sounds.

We have spoken of Monk's sense of form as a composer, as leader of a group performing a semi-improvised music, and as an extended soloist. But orderliness is innate with him, and we ought to make at least a brief mention of Monk's more inventive, nonthematic variations. There is a two-chorus solo by Monk on *I Mean You,* as a "guest" with the Art Blakey Jazz Messengers, that has a striking inner logic. Monk bases his first chorus on a descending motive which he handles variously. The second chorus he bases on a brief, contrasting riff figure, which is turned several ways, is subjected to a counter-riff or two, and finally is complemented by a descending fragment which alludes to the first chorus and ties the two together. Once again Monk's music benefits from Blakey's presence and rapport, as it had on *Four in One, Criss Cross, Eronel, Blue Monk, Just You, Just Me, Tea for Two,* and the rest.

In the immediate foreground of Monk's rediscovery and
subsequent popularity was an engagement with a quartet—
Monk; John Coltrane, tenor saxophone; Wilbur Ware, bass;
and Shadow Wilson, drums—at a New York club called the
Five Spot during the summer of 1957. It was surely one of
the most important and exhilarating events in jazz history.
The group did record three selections, strong experiences
and exceptional jazz, even if they are not as good as the performances one heard those summer nights at the Five Spot,
when each man played with great enthusiasm, at the peak of
his abilities, and through Monk's music each discovered and
expanded his potential.

The leader and his saxophonist had exceptional emotional
rapport. Technically they were something of a contrast. John
Coltrane's techniques are obvious; Monk's piano techniques
more subtle. And at the same time that Coltrane, with
showers of notes and scalar "sheets of sound," seemed to
want to break up jazz rhythms into an evenly spaced and
fairly constant succession of short notes, Monk seemed to
want more complexity, subtlety, and freedom. Monk is a
melodist; his harmonies are intrinsic but his playing is ultimately linear and horizontal in its effect. Coltrane played
vertically; he found harmonic stimulation in Monk's music,
and he seemed to know where Monk was headed, as well as
where he *was,* as very few players did then. But he also knew,
as the recording of *Ruby, My Dear* shows, that Monk's
melodies are strong and that it isn't enough merely to run
their chords. Monk's pieces often disciplined Coltrane and
ordered his explorations as weaker material did not. *Ruby*
is a knowingly embellished performance, and Coltrane's
opening solo finishes with a beautiful, Monkish effect of
suspension. Monk's decision to begin his own solo with a
lightly implied double-time was a beautiful stroke of musical

contrast: Coltrane's many notes at a slow tempo, then Monk's fewer notes at a faster tempo.

Wilbur Ware was, like Monk, a melodist also able to find surprise twists in a use of traditional materials. Wilson, whose work once had the even smoothness of a Jo Jones, responded to Monk's music with some appropriate polyrhythmic comments.

Monk got a variety of textures from his four pieces, by playing with the saxophonist, by playing contrapuntally against him, by "laying out" and leaving him to the bassist and drummer: sometimes to one of them predominantly, other times equally to both.

On their version of *Nutty,* Coltrane having strayed further and more elaborately into the harmonic implications of the piece, the composer typically enters for his own solo with an eloquent reestablishment of the theme in paraphrase.

He does the same on *Trinkle Tinkle,* with an even more intriguing recasting of that intricate melody. *Trinkle* is the best of the recorded performances by the group. Its melody, unlike most of Monk's melodies, is conceived perhaps a bit too pianistically to be fully effective on saxophone. But at the same time, its somewhat scalar quality suits Coltrane's style. The spontaneous interplay between Monk and Coltrane in the performance is exceptional, but Monk's intuitive logic in knowing just when to stop it and let the saxophonist stroll alone against bass and drums is intuitive perfection.

From this point on, Monk was heard and reheard carefully and widely. What could be so "difficult" about a man who often based his variations on melodies themselves? And what is so difficult about an improvisation based not on melody but on a chord sequence, if it worked out the single phrase or idea that it announced when it opened? In the face of this kind of basic continuity, what trouble could his unusual revoicings of chords and his rhythmic displacements cause? A listener who can follow a melody, and who is not put off by Monk's uncompromising emotion, need not know immediately how intrinsic are Monk's dissonances, harmonies, and rhythms. Form will guide him eventually to sense those things.

Brilliance Corners showed the innovative Monk still at work. Its basis is the alteration of the tempos; *Brilliance Corners'* theme is effective played slowly and then exactly twice as fast, and the abrupt shift in pace does not interrupt the flow of the performance. It succeeds, partly because its melody notes dart about at unaccustomed intervals so that the changes of tempo are almost anticipated by the nature of the melodic line. In turn each player—Sonny Rollins, Monk, Ernie Henry, and Max Roach—is required to improvise at the alternate speed but has to keep the performance continuous.

Monk's first version of *I Should Care* is his piano solo masterpiece and a uniquely pianistic performance. Again Monk transmutes a popular song into a composition for piano. And he conceives this composition as a striking, resourceful tissue of unique piano sounds, in a kind of free tempo in which each phrase seems to have its own momentum. Among its several virtues *I Should Care* is evidence that Monk has carried the jazzman's concept of individuality of sound further than any other player on his instrument; indeed, he has carried it almost as far as the hornmen.

Thelonious Monk learned to explore and develop an original and unorthodox musical talent. And he endured years when his music suffered neglect and even disparagement. Neither of those things is easy, and especially not for an American. Then Monk was signed by a major record company, and his appearances began to draw crowds, and he was faced with perhaps the severest test of all—success, personal popularity, the problems of facing an audience night after night, the problems of sidemen and of keeping the right group together. Many a popular artist (and many a fine one), faced with the recognition he has awaited, is tempted to relax, admire his laurels, and pause now and then to count the house. And during the years of success there were indications that Monk was all too willing to coast a bit too.

His second version of *Bolivar Blues* does not have the anguish of the original, but Monk's solo is something of a minor wonder, moving from tripling dissonances (quasi-amateurish and quite humorous), through sustained splashes of sound which spread out in rings from a center (and echo his earlier accompaniment to tenor saxophonist Charlie Rouse on the piece), ending in quick spurts of sound that abruptly disappear beneath the surface, leaving no trace.

A new version of *Just a Gigolo*[2] condenses a range of sound into a quite brief solo performance by Monk, and again reveals, through Monk's left hand, that he belongs with the earlier Harlem stride players. Then, when his bass figures get a bit melodramatic, Monk kids them beautifully with a rattling tremolo in his right hand. *Sweet and Lovely,* another of the out-of-the-way standards in Monk's repertory, is perhaps better than his first version. He develops it to the point where his left hand boldly sings out an abstract of the melody line, while his right hand offers glittering pianistic embellishments above. On a solo version of *Body and Soul,* Monk has the daring to simplify a stride bass to the point of apparent amateurishness, yet its effect is of a powerful,

2. A scholarly (and thoroughly unimportant) essay might be written on Monk's affinity for Bing Crosby's repertory. Or Sonny Rollins's for Al Jolson's.

incantive, yet humorous series of sound clusters, as accompaniment to a shimmeringly original paraphrase of the theme.

Then there is a new version of *Five Spot Blues,* on which an archaic triplet figure is elaborated within the traditional blues framework. It is perhaps a measure of Monk's talent that he is willing to undertake something so totally unpretentious. And yet in his solos, he stretches out that little triplet motif, then abruptly condenses it into half the space it is supposed to occupy, embellishes it until it is almost lost, then rediscovers it and restores its unapologetic simplicity. I think that anyone with an ear for melody and rhythm could follow him exactly yet in its small way *Five Spot Blues* is perhaps a measure of his sense of order, of his rhythmic virtuosity, his originality, and his greatness.

On a 1964 "in concert" recording, containing the best realization of Monk's music for a large ensemble, there is a grand moment that shows the pianist's commitment to improvisation in his sudden, wildly witty interjections on Hall Overton's scoring of his theme, *Epistrophy,* a piece which Monk has obviously played many hundreds of times. And in the same recital, there is once again his innate sense of form, in his punctuations, his solo, and his accompaniment (particularly with Phil Woods) on *Evidence.*

It would not take too much psychological subtlety to see what Monk's achievement means. It means that some of the sensibilities that Parker, Gillespie, Powell, and Monk himself came upon and expressed with such masterful intuition could be made more ordered and rational, and could be handled with greater choice. Obviously a sense of form does not mean conventionality or depreciation of the idiom. Imagination, improvisation, spontaneity, and feeling—the fact that form for the smaller groups of modern jazz is more improvisational—these things alone might counter stylistic rigidity. At the same time, Monk's unresting harmonic, rhythmic, and melodic explorations have already led to further reorganizations of jazz. And within his own idiom Monk long continued to maintain the precarious, spiritually dangerous status of an innovator.

But, most important, and the thing that shows that it is all not a matter of mere "techniques," Monk at his best is a deeply, uncompromisingly expressive player. He is not an "entertainer"; he does not "show" us anything. Everything he says, he says musically, directly, unadorned; he is all music and his technique is jazz technique. His greatest importance lies in the fact that Monk is an artist with an artist's deeply felt sense of life and an artist's drive to communicate the surprising and enlightening truth of it in his own way. And he has the artist's special capacity for involving us with him so that we seem to be working it all out together.

Jazz has had precious few of his kind.

14

JOHN LEWIS
AND THE MODERN JAZZ QUARTET

Modern Conservative

One could say that the Modern Jazz Quartet actually began in 1946 as the rhythm section of Dizzy Gillespie's orchestra: two years later, in fact, four titles were rather obscurely recorded by Milt Jackson, John Lewis, Kenny Clarke, Al Jackson on bass, plus Chano Pozo on Conga drum. However, in August 1951 the "Milt Jackson Quartet" assembled for a recording date, and its members decided they liked playing together. Percy Heath came in on bass for Ray Brown, Milt Jackson on vibraphone, John Lewis on piano, Kenny Clarke on drums. Lewis soon became musical director, and the group was called the Modern Jazz Quartet. Success was gradual, and the Quartet's career was interrupted several times as its members briefly took other jobs. Then in 1955, Clarke left and Connie Kay became the group's drummer.

On the early recordings the music was built primarily around Jackson's exceptional gifts as an improviser and his delight in medium and fast blues, medium and slow ballads. The later recordings show the effects of John Lewis's leadership.

Lewis apparently felt that if the Quartet were to have an identity and stability, it needed to offer something more than

a quasi-jam session of four men improvising on fairly standard material, no matter how good those men might be as improvisers. Their music (like Jelly Roll Morton's music and
Duke Ellington's music) might become more than the sum
of the abilities of its players. He saw that the Quartet in some
sense needed to create its own audience beyond the core of
modern jazz fans that existed in the early 'fifties. He also
saw, clearly I am sure, that if the Quartet were to break out
of the regular round of jazz clubs and all-star touring "pack-
ages," it needed a music which could legitimately ask an
audience to sit attentively in a concert hall, a music which
needed to offer more than a succession of half-hour night
club "sets." One of the singular facts in John Lewis's leadership is that he has a realistic sense of the facts of the milieu
in which he functions, and that he usually knows what things
can be changed and what things cannot be changed.

Lewis knew—his work shows he knew—that modern jazz
itself needed more than the theme/string-of-solos/theme
conception. That approach had served well as a vehicle for
its best early players to work out its basic language. But the
idiom needed some sort of synthesis of its elements, some
sort of compositional order and form.

Inevitably, one cannot be entirely sympathetic with everything that Lewis has done as a composer, nor with all of the
ways he has searched for form outside the jazz tradition,
nor with all of the results his leadership has produced. Long
and frequently ponderous compositions like *The Comedy*,
with neoclassic "effects," during which Milt Jackson is asked
to employ his talent in executing some fairly mechanical
ideas, are puzzling, to say the least. Indeed, I do not think
one is wrong to hear in John Lewis's career at least an echo
of the sort of misguided but understandable efforts at prestige which led certain ragtime and Harlem stride pianists
and composers to undertake "symphonic" works and

"operas," or which has led some younger jazzmen to record "with strings."

But to turn to first principles, one cannot question the marvelous group swing and drive which the Quartet is able to achieve in an exceptional variety of moods and tempos and at so many levels of dynamics. Nor can one question the fact that the group is truly dedicated to improvisation: its various recordings of the same repertory would be proof enough of that without consulting its public appearances.

Lewis's failures, furthermore, are not typical of his talents as either a composer or an improviser, nor of his leadership of the group. Even in *The Comedy*, there are individual sections with eloquently simple John Lewis melodies, and a performance of the piece will feature improvisation that shows the group's capacity to be at once both controlled and marvelously spontaneous.

Lewis's achievements are real, and they have been important not only to the Quartet but to the course of modern jazz. His credentials as a jazzman are authentic. Milt Jackson is supposed to be the earthy, passionate, and spontaneous member of the group, but anyone who has heard John Lewis's solo on, say, *Bags' Groove* knows that John Lewis can play the blues unashamedly—indeed with pride. Lewis's own half-humorously protested ambitions to record with people like blues singer Joe Turner make perfect sense. And the expressiveness of his piano and his fine sense of musical phrase deepened during his years with the Quartet.

Lewis's virtues as a pianist do not include obvious finger dexterity, and his virtues as an improviser find greater expression in relatively simple frameworks than in complex ones. Early performances in which he undertook a Bud Powell-like virtuosity of notes or a rapidly shifting pattern of chords sometimes fail rather badly, and very fast tempos sometimes do still.

Lewis understands Count Basie. Contemporaneously, both Thelonious Monk and Miles Davis sensed that modern jazz rhythms needed a kind of relaxation and "opening up," that subtleties of space and rest in phrasing were called for. Lewis has achieved something of the same thing partly by recalling his knowledge of Basie, and of a time when Basie had done the same sort of opening up of jazz rhythms of the 'thirties. Lewis also knows the styles of swing period players like Earl Hines and Teddy Wilson; his *I Remember Clifford* is succinct evidence of that.

It is as if Lewis set about to reinterpret the modern idiom by directly using his knowledge of earlier jazz. Monk and Davis employed such knowledge, but less directly, I think. Lewis's approach to a use of the past is then comparable to Horace Silver's, but he has, both as a composer and as a musical director, a more developed sense of group form than Silver.

John Lewis's love and understanding of the music of the swing period, and his admittedly orchestral conception of the piano, allow him one spontaneous contribution to the music of the Modern Jazz Quartet. His accompaniments are seldom the percussively delivered chord patterns of the typical modern jazz pianist; he will automatically offer complementary countermelodies behind a soloist. These usually begin as riffs, the kind of repeated, rhythmic phrases that are as old as jazz and which big swing band reed and brass sections delivered all the time. Lewis often elaborates these brief phrases into a more complex but discreet jazz counterpoint. The results in the texture and the complexity of the Quartet's music are excellent, and it is as if Lewis had learned again, and independently, the lessons which King Oliver and Jelly Roll Morton had taught well—that contrapuntal effects can give the jazz ensemble a wonderfully heightened excitement. Also, Lewis's spontaneous accompaniments often give cohesion and orderly pattern to a performance, as he elaborates a theme-proper behind a soloist's variations or as he develops a single motif for several choruses. For example, there are the first few choruses of *Ralph's New Blues.*

Mention of counterpoint brings up one of the most critically delicate aspects of the Modern Jazz Quartet's work: John Lewis's obvious delight in European, baroque contrapuntal music. *Softly, as in a Morning's Sunrise* was one of the earliest pieces in the group's repertory. As Milt Jackson rephrased its melody and as the group spontaneously delivered it, this bit of operetta fluff became a real musical experience. But the Quartet later played the piece with a brief, Bach-derived introduction and conclusion that seems extrinsic and pointless, if not pretentious and arty.

The several fugal pieces in the group's repertory are more indicative. British critic Max Harrison has said that although the Quartet's first fugue, *Vendome,* sounds stilted and derivative, the later fugue, *Concorde,* decidedly moves in the right direction, and that *Versailles* and *Three Windows* are real jazz fugues, their materials assimilated and transmuted, and reminding us more of Oliver and Morton than of a conservatory exercise. I think this more successful quality also comes because the melodies of these later pieces sound less derivative and more like jazz melodies. They are truly improvisational—the written portion of *Concorde,* for example, is a mere eight bars; the rest was made up in each performance.

The jazz-fugue has been around at least since the 'thirties as a musical stunt, and pieces with the Bach-like steps of, say, *All the Things You Are* have tempted many a borderline jazzman to trot out what he learned in student exercises. The Quartet's accomplishments in *Concorde* and *Versailles* and *Three Windows* are a different and altogether

more authentic matter. But, one should note, they are still
only the Quartet's accomplishments—isolated phenomena
which no other jazzmen took up except in a few pointless
imitations.

On the other hand, one repeatedly finds this kind of paradox in Lewis's work: lines in his quasi-baroque scoring of
God Rest Ye Merry, Gentlemen sound quite straightfor-
wardly musical when played by the Quartet, but the same
effects sound stilted when a string orchestra executes them
under Lewis's direction. One is tempted to blame this on
the inexperience of string players with jazz phrasing, but
surely the writing must take part of the blame.

Because of this aspect of his work, there is a strong temp-
tation to think of Lewis as the kind of prodigy who would
get straight A's in any music school, and never do anything
really good thereafter. There were a number of musicians
who functioned on both coasts during the 1950s' popularity
of "cool jazz" about whom such things might be said with
accuracy; their rather academic and transparent efforts to
"do something artistic" were patently derivative and naïve.
John Lewis is a different sort of musician. And with the
Quartet's later fugues at hand, it is obvious that John Lewis
can find something really creative—and not merely derivative—in the idiom of the eighteenth century.

John Lewis is the kind of man who can rename *Two Bass
Hit* as *La Ronde, Moving Nicely* as *Baden Baden,* can name
his pieces after French châteaux, can say "create" when it
might be more discreet to say "write" or "compose." He is
also a man with knowledge of his own shortcomings, with
a sense of the realities of the milieu in which he functions,
and a universal taste in music—and in jazz music. He is as
much in touch with his own basic feelings as he is with anything he has learned. I say this, not in a personal defense
of John Lewis, but because these things show quite directly

in his work. They show in his own best playing and writing, and they are the best basis on which to hear him.

The directness of Lewis's phrasing as an improviser, and his capacity for understatement, make his playing an appropriate contrast to Milt Jackson's technical exuberance and emotional immediacy. Lewis's feelings seem naturally introverted, and I expect it has cost him something in technique and in musical histrionics to learn to project them so quietly yet so firmly. He is a player almost incapable of shouting (but neither incapable of raising his voice nor incapable of making the firmest of musical statements). And he is therefore the kind of player whose music some people almost automatically want to take as a pleasant "background" sound. This quality colored the Quartet's work as a whole, to be sure, and it undoubtedly accounted for some of its borderline following. But the slightest sympathy in attending Lewis's improvising tells another story. Happily for him, Lewis can have it both ways, disappointing neither the casual nor the really attentive listener. Lewis's suggestion to the other members of the Quartet, that they attempt a more cohesive and singular emotional rise and fall in a given piece, may have begun as a piece of self-knowledge. But far from being a matter of audience pandering, it is the most legitimate sort of aesthetic refinement for jazzmen to undertake—and, incidentally, one that Ellington has used for many years.

Milt Jackson is obviously a man of great natural talent, and during his years with the Quartet that talent has been refined and made far more flexible in sound, in dynamics, in range, in expressiveness. I cannot agree that Lewis lacks insight into Jackson's playing, or that the Quartet "inhibits" him. Quite the contrary.

It might be legitimate to say that some of Jackson's most important work was done in 1948 and 1951 when he recorded some classic pieces with Thelonious Monk (and the response

between Jackson and Monk was always a special one), and
that since then, although he has remained a superb player,
he has refined and improved what he could do already. One
aspect of Jackson's work is what seems to me an occasional
sentimentality in slow ballads. It shows in his early contribution to the Quartet's repertory called *Lillie,* and it is laid out
at rather appalling length in the out-of-tempo opening of
How High the Moon. In his accompaniments to Jackson,
John Lewis is usually not as successful in compensating for
this element as Monk has been—compare the two versions
of *Willow, Weep for Me.* But Lewis's accompaniment often
does provide Jackson's solos with decidedly helpful melodic
and emotional shading. Jackson's exuberance is natural, but
it can also be a rather general exuberance which sometimes
overrides his attention to the piece at hand. It seems to me
that very few of the LP recitals that Milt Jackson made under
his own name have been as successful as his work with the
Quartet—the outstanding exception being a date he did with
Percy Heath, Connie Kay, and Horace Silver and which produced *My Funny Valentine* and *I Should Care.* One comparison which makes its point rather succinctly is Lewis vs.
Jackson on *I Remember Clifford*—or for that matter, compare Lewis to any other jazzman on that piece, for it has
tempted many players to excesses. Paradoxically, when Jackson's slow balladry does win out over sentimentality, the vic-
tory is triumphant, as his performances of *Autumn in New
York, Milano, I Should Care,* and *What's New* can bear witness.

Lewis's achievements as a composer include his blues line
Two Degrees East, Three Degrees West and I fear that,
beside it, Milt Jackson's endless permutations on his penta-
tonic *Bags' Groove* theme, under various titles, become almost anonymous. Like some of Monk's best pieces, like
Lewis's earlier *La Ronde,* and some of Lewis's best improvis-

ing, *Two Degrees* reinterprets tradition in a contemporary and personal manner. Its delightful phrasing takes an indigenous blues fragment and uses it with striking insight into its nature and its possibilities.

Another successful Lewis piece is *The Golden Striker,* and, similarly, one might call it a kind of up-to-date version of the *Bugle Call Rag* on a *King Porter Stomp* chord progression. The piece presents a melody, a framework for improvising, and a brief effect of stop-time repeated in a way that gives the ad lib sections both variety and order. It encourages the improviser and helps to order his playing while not inhibiting him.

John Lewis's high achievement as a composer is *Django.* It is a funeral piece in memory of Django Reinhardt, the Belgian-French gypsy guitarist turned jazzman. The main theme seems to imply several things: an elegy as well as French, gypsy, and jazz music. The chord sequence for the improvised section is in effect new material, since it is not entirely derived from the theme. The last eight bars of the theme melody also serve as an interlude separating the soloists. There is still another motif, a simple and traditional blues bass-figure (my earliest acquaintance with it is in the introduction to King Oliver's 1926 piece *Snag It*) which appears and reappears in the improvised section—and in later performances Lewis sometimes counterpoints another traditional riff figure against it. Obviously, in *Django* Lewis also had in mind the tradition of consolation and rejoicing at death that was a part of culture in New Orleans and early jazz.

The subtle movement and range of feeling in a good performance of *Django* make it one of the truly successful and sustained extended works in the jazz repertory. Its melodies and motifs are excellent and excellently juxtaposed. And in performance the act of holding these opposites together cohesively becomes an achievement shared by both composer and players, by the compositional conception and the given performance—and that is the highest achievement of jazz composition.

Outside of his work for the Quartet, Lewis's best piece is a three-part suite called *Three Little Feelings*—I am speaking of the piece as it was originally written for a brass orchestra with Miles Davis as the main soloist. Its melodies are eloquently and deceptively simple, its scoring balances solo and group to the advantage of both, and there is hardly any wasted motion or padding. There are sections of Lewis's score for the movie *Odds Against Tomorrow* that are also impressive, particularly the "prelude," in which John Lewis elucidated a great deal of musical material smoothly, tersely, and interestingly.

By the 1960s some of the Quartet's work had reached a kind of perfection from which there may well have been no place to go, for it is doubtful if these men could have continued to find it challenging to play so well and to play so well together—at least in the same repertory and format. Their two-LP set *"European Concert,"* recorded during public performances in Scandinavia, might stand as a summary of some of the highest achievements of ten years of working together. And their *"Last Concert"* album was a superb, supposedly final, recording.

The European set had a version of *Django*, different from the previous ones, and in its way almost as good, with the structural strength of that piece still forceful and inspirational. Particularly on *Bluesology* (one of the earliest pieces in their repertory) and on *Festival Sketch,* the interplay between Lewis and Jackson is superb. Lewis's solo on *Bags' Groove* is again an unassuming exposition of blues feeling. There are three other twelve-bar blues pieces in the set, and of course Milt Jackson is very good on all of them. There is a nearly sublime performance of *It Don't Mean a Thing (If It Ain't Got That Swing)* on which Lewis again begins his section unaccompanied, then has Jackson behind him, building marvelously suspenseful melodic patterns, until Heath and Kay reenter percussively to relieve the tension. They depart again, leaving Lewis alone. Etc. Brief suspensions of the rhythmic pulse were fairly commonplace by the 'twenties, and it is a delight to find the idea thus reintroduced and extended. There is another attempt at *Vendome;* it is better than the first, and it may even swing more (it at least sounds more jazzy), but it still seems a somewhat specious vehicle, even for such good playing as this. There is *I'll Remember April,* still a good workout and still, I think, too fast for that kind of quasi-impressionist popular song.

Lewis's career, since it risks larger success, also risks larger failure. The future will undoubtedly find him a composer and conductor of his own works for various kinds of ensembles and in various milieus. If his projects lead Lewis into more things like his strange, academic scoring of *God Rest Ye Merry, Gentlemen,* or like his curiously faltering ballet score for the San Francisco company, *Original Sin,* or his mish-mash of a film score, *A Milanese Story,* they may lead him to pretentiousness.

But I am again talking about the shortcomings of something ventured. Lewis's failures are like Ellington's sometimes sentimental ballads, Armstrong's sometimes forced good spirits, Parker's sometimes overripe harmonies, Monk's overpercussiveness—they make successes possible. And John Lewis's successes include, besides musical leadership of perhaps the best small ensemble in jazz history, an important contribution to the synthesis that modern jazz achieved in its second decade; it includes *Django, The Golden Striker,* the *Odds Against Tomorrow* score, *Three Little Feelings, Two Degrees East*—not a small achievement.

15

SONNY ROLLINS

Spontaneous Orchestration

In the late summer of 1959 tenor saxophonist Sonny Rollins stopped taking night club, concert, and record dates. Inevitably there was much gossip. It was said that he had decided to escape a round of work where both public adulation and constant playing were forcing him to repeat himself; that he was preparing some long compositions; that he had been intimidated by critical praise and by the close technical analysis of his recorded work; that he intended to reappear solo, as an unaccompanied improvising saxophonist. The last rumor was perhaps the most provocative. Rollins had frequently appeared without a pianist and—most important—in a sense had taken over the functions of orchestrator and orchestra all to himself.

In mid-1956, Sonny Rollins, formerly the capable, or perhaps the promising, jazz tenor saxophone soloist, had had a musical coming of age. Soon he was winning all the popularity polls, and his records were being reviewed as examples of "uninhibited passion," "inner compulsion," etc. But descriptions of the impact and sureness of his playing tell only part of the story, and the rest of the story makes Rollins a unique hornman in the history of jazz.

By the mid-'fifties, modern jazz was no longer faced with discovering or testing its basic musical language but, as we have said, with establishing some sort of synthesis within the idiom, with the task of ordering its materials which, for earlier styles, had been done by Jelly Roll Morton in the 'twenties and Duke Ellington in the late 'thirties. In the 'fifties, the problem was met, foremost, by Thelonious Monk; by pianist-composer John Lewis with the Modern Jazz Quartet; and by Sonny Rollins as an improvising saxophonist.

In one sense the history of the last thirty years in Jazz might be written in terms of the length of the solos that its horn players have been able to sustain. Certainly one contribution of bebop was that its best players (but only its best) could undertake longer improvisations which offered a flow of musical ideas without falling into honking or growling banalities. I do not mean that the younger players of the 'forties were either the first or the only jazz musicians to be able to do this, only that for some of them a sustained solo was a primary concern. However, a great deal of extended soloing in jazz has had the air of an endurance feat— a player tries to keep going with as little repetition as possible. But when the ideas are original and are imaginatively handled, such playing can have virtues of its own. However, a hornman's best solos are apt to be continuously developing linear inventions. Sonny Rollins has recorded long solos which, in quality and approach, go beyond good soloist's form and amount almost to sustained orchestrations.

Previously, jazz pianists have shown such concern with larger form in improvising. Some examples, a random sampling, are Jelly Roll Morton's solo on *Hyena Stomp,* Willie "the Lion" Smith's *Squeeze Me,* Fats Waller's *Numb Fumblin'.* But of course many pianists have thought formally and orchestrally, even some simple blues men—Jimmy Yancey in *How Long #2* and *State Street Special*—have exceptionally cohesive designs.

Sonny Rollins's early records indicate his later developments only in retrospect. At the time they seemed the work of a talented player, in more or less the style of the time, a style probably best exhibited in Dexter Gordon's work. This style variously combined the robust, extroverted manner of Coleman Hawkins (but without his vibrato) with many of the approaches to melody, rhythm, and asymmetry of phrasing of Lester Young, plus some of Charlie Parker's ideas as well.

One can hear the young Rollins of 1949 with a Bud Powell group on *Bouncin' with Bud, Wail,* etc., and the release of some alternate takes from this session shows that Rollins was really improvising, offering a rather different solo on each performance of each piece. Most of the other players involved had had experience in big bands. Rollins had not; indeed his first job with a regularly working group did not come until he joined Max Roach in late 1955. Big band work can teach lessons of discipline and terseness in short solos, and lessons of group precision and responsiveness. Rollins has learned some of those lessons, but, as I have indicated, he has surmounted not having learned others.

Rollins had his first record date on his own in 1951. *Slow Boat to China* (one of several unexpected pop vehicles to come) and *Shadrack* show a relaxed sureness of phrasing and rhythm, and *This Love of Mine* an increase in saxophone technique. *Mambo Bounce* is (significantly, I think) a twelve-bar blues. It includes four ad lib choruses by Rollins only the second of which uses ordinary ideas. More important, the solo has only one Parker-esque flurry of short notes. Parker himself often used such runs for contrast or variety in his solos; some of his followers might throw them in almost anywhere on impulse. Rollins usually uses such double-time phrases sparsely, and in *Mambo Bounce* the virtuoso run appears in his fourth improvised chorus, where it becomes the climax of his solo. A happy accident? Perhaps. But I wonder, in view of his later work. Perhaps it was conscious and deliberate, but more likely it was the result of personal artistic intuition. It suggests one way that the technical resources of modern jazz improvising might be used structurally. Again, the hint might have come from Hawkins; he was one player of his generation who brought off long solos, and his usual manner was to build in technical complexity.

Sonny Rollins continued to acquire more techniques, learned to use them with more relaxation; as his sound and attack became increasingly personal, his ability to swing reached near-perfection. He also played with Thelonious Monk, and the experience was surely important to his development. And, in mid-1954, he participated in a very good Miles Davis recording session to which he contributed three interesting pieces: *Airegin, Oleo* (probably under the inspiration of such Parker lines as *Scrapple from the Apple,* but again renewing the *I Got Rhythm* chords), and *Doxy,* a modern return to the sixteen-bar patterns of the 'twenties.

A bit later there was *Tenor Madness* on which John Coltrane joined Rollins. Here is relatively early Coltrane, to be sure, but he shows the harmonic searching of the highly sophisticated, vertical player he later became. In the placing and accenting of his short notes, Coltrane is already identifiably Coltrane. Rollins is a confident master of his own materials and he climaxes his own section with a telling moment of technical complexity, just as he had on *Mambo Bounce.*

The two LPs which made Rollins's public reputation were *"Saxophone Colossus"* (done in June 1956) and *"Way Out West"* (March 1957). The latter is a collection, largely of pop "Western" songs in which Rollins plays with remarkable power and ease. Some reviewers heard "anger" or "aggression" in his saxophone sound. There is much humor to be sure; there is parody and even sardonic comedy. And surely Rollins's firm, confident phrasing, his masterful dynamics and excellent use of the range of his horn (from firm, cello-like low notes to bold cries in upper range), surely these things balance the "negative" emotion in his playing. Also on that record there is more than a hint that he was taking a cue from the airy, open phrasing of Lester Young's later work.

Another aspect of the *"Way Out West"* LP is the masterful way that Rollins shows he had absorbed ideas from Monk on how to get inside a theme, abstract it, distill its essence, perceive its implications, and use it as a basis for variations—without merely embellishing it decoratively or abandoning it for improvisation based only on its chords. Besides making public appearances with him, Rollins has several times recorded with Monk. And one might note that, for example, on their version of *Bemsha Swing* Rollins begins his solo with the last idea that Monk had played in his section, and that, as Rollins's line gets more complex, Monk reintroduces orderly reminders and hints of the theme beneath him.

By 1957 Rollins had moved so far along as a kind of one-man orchestra that on the title piece of *"Way Out West"* he returns for his second solo with a spontaneous imitation of Shelly Manne's drum patterns.

Blue 7 from *"Saxophone Colossus"* is a masterpiece, hence it is the kind of performance that one hears anew with each listening and that is difficult to discuss and describe. Its heritage, as Gunther Schuller pointed out in his detailed analysis, includes Monk's *Misterioso* and the Miles Davis-Sonny Rollins *Vierd Blues*. It begins with an almost nonchalant and tranquil bass line by Doug Watkins. Upon this, Rollins states the theme, a simple blues line that has a strong individual character. Yet it is also suspended in an ambiguous bitonality. The piano's entrance behind Rollins assigns it a specific key, and Rollins begins to explore its implied brilliance expertly.

The performance builds from one phrase to the next, yet that structure is so logical and so comprehensive, with its details so subtly in place, that it is as if Rollins had not made it up as he went along, but had conceived it whole from the beginning. Max Roach has said that he and Rollins both had in mind Monk's admonition: Why don't we *use* the melody? Why do we throw it away after the first chorus and use only the chords?

Almost everything that Rollins plays on *Blue 7* is based on his opening theme, but Rollins also structures and builds—he even builds on his elaborations and his brief interpolations, and he is not afraid of an almost direct recapitulation of his theme at one point during the performance. The order and logic of the performance extends also to Roach's solo, based almost entirely on a triplet figure and a roll, while Tommy Flanagan's nonthematic piano solo serves as a kind of effectively contrasting, lyric interlude.

Blue 7 is one of those rare performances which almost anyone can appreciate immediately, I think—anyone, from the novice who wants to know where the melody is, to the sympathetic classicist who can appreciate how highly developed the jazzman's art has become.

Blue 7 is one of the great pleasures of recorded jazz, but its elaborations and distillations of theme do not represent Rollins's only approach to extended improvised form. Another is the one he hinted at in *Mambo Bounce,* but he has never recorded it in the masterful way he has used it in public. In this approach Rollins would first state his theme, then gradually simplify until he was playing only a scant outline. Then he would gradually slip away from it and invent new melodies—at first very simple ones—out of the chord structure of the piece. He would proceed to develop these: his note values getting shorter, his melodic lines longer and their contours more complex. When he had built such a solo over several choruses to a peak of melodic and rhythmic virtuosity, he would gradually reverse himself, return to simpler melodies, to fewer and longer notes. Soon, one would realize, Rollins had begun to resketch his initial theme with certain suggestive notes and phrases, and finally he would restore it completely to a full recapitulation.

My account may make Rollins's performances seem mechanical. Of course his power and sureness alone might prevent such playing from being mechanical, but his spontaneous designs were never so pat as a general description is apt to imply. Long runs of notes are interspersed with short ones and even with short, staccato, humorously delivered single notes. Fragments of the theme are heard in otherwise harmonic variations. Brief virtuoso lines appear in otherwise simple choruses. But these form patterns of prediction and echo in an overall structure, and the way to hear a good Rollins performance is always to try to hear it whole.

There is another Rollins recording which is still differently structured, but which is again based on comparable material, *Blues for Philly Joe*. On it Rollins plays a kind of free, spontaneous blues rondo. Using A to indicate Rollins's main theme, A plus a numeral to indicate thematic variations, and other letters to indicate variations that are not thematic, one might outline the performance roughly this way:

A
A
A-1
A-2
A-3
B

C
A-4
D
D-1
E (A-5?)
Wynton Kelly's piano solo
Exchange of four-bar phrases with drummer Philly Joe
    Jones
A (A-6?)
A

There are several fascinating details which such an outline can't indicate. For example, the new material Rollins
introduces in A-1 appears again in variation in A-2, thus
tying these two choruses together. Subsequently this double-
chorus idea is echoed at D and D-1, at approximately the
middle of the piece, and again at the end of the piece. A-3
is almost, but not quite, a nonthematic chorus; it is as if
Rollins's strong departures from his theme were preparing
our ears for B, which is far enough away to be called non-
thematic. Chorus E has strong reminders of the main theme
toward the end, and is therefore part E and part A-5.
Rollins's four-bar phrases in exchange with Joe Jones are
sometimes melodic and sometimes percussive, as might befit
exchanges with a drummer. The two final saxophone
choruses are thematic, but neither is an absolute restatement
of the A theme, although the final chorus is closer. Again,
let me warn that an outline like this one of a spontaneous
performance is apt to make Rollins's playing seem calculated and mechanical when it is anything but that. However, his sense of order is there—as natural and spontaneous
as any other aspect of his playing—and it is a major part of
his aesthetic achievement.[1]

1. Rollins can be outstanding also at non-thematic, motive-oriented solos: *In
Your Own Sweet Way* with Miles Davis, for example.

The Rollins who returned to public performance in the fall of 1961 was the same Rollins, only more so. One's memory of that Rollins is a memory of performances which nostalgia might exaggerate but which exact memory could obscure. Again there were the long performances, which Rollins seemed to conceive as entities, but which also develop with internal logic, phrase by phrase. There were also extended cadenzas in which Rollins would rapidly execute an entire thirty-two bar theme on a series of two or three chords spontaneously offered him by his pianist, altering only those notes necessary to fit each chord in succession.

I wrote the following account in *Down Beat* of a Rollins concert held in mid-1962: "For Rollins, the promise was fulfilled brilliantly. From his opening choruses on *Three Little Words,* it was apparent that Rollins was going to play with commanding authority, invention, and a deep humor which even included a healthy self-parody. His masterwork of the evening was a cadenza on *Love Letters,* several out of tempo choruses of virtuosity in imagination, execution, and a kind of truly artistic bravura that jazz has not known since the Louis Armstrong of the early 'thirties. The performance included some wild interpolations, several of which Rollins managed to fit in by a last minute and wittily unexpected alteration of a note or two. To my ear, he did not once lose his way, although a couple of times he did lose [guitarist] Jim Hall—and that is nearly impossible to do for Jim Hall has one of the quickest harmonic ears there is. Rollins's final piece was a kind of extemporaneous orchestration on *If Ever I Would Leave You* in which he became brass, reed, and rhythm section, tenor soloist, and Latin percussionist, all at once and always with musical logic."

Again, one is left with the frustration that Rollins's recordings do not show the level of his achievements in clubs and concerts. There is a recording of *If Ever I Would Leave*

You; it is very good indeed, but it is a shadow of the masterful performance described above.

Even the "live" Rollins can be a frustration. *"A Night at the Village Vanguard,"* recorded for Blue Note, is a fine example of generally sustained high-level playing, but it does not have the brilliance of Rollins "live" at his best.

The other side of the frustration is represented on the LP which appeared in 1978 as *"There'll Never Be Another You,"* and offered a June 1965 concert in the Museum of Modern Art's Sculpture Garden. Here is Rollins the passionate, raw, spontaneous, and almost (but not quite) eccentric improviser, ending one solo only to begin another on the same piece, cajoling his sidemen, shifting keys and tempos without warning, walking away from the microphone so that an assertively begun coda is heard almost as a faint echo—and leaving us with some tantalizing unfinished documents, particularly on *There Will Never Be Another You* and *Three Little Words.*

That latter piece was something of a Rollins specialty in the mid-'sixties, and there is a polished studio version from July 1965. But the classic Rollins from that decade is surely his fine set of variations on *Alfie's Theme* (1966) with a sparely used studio orchestra.

I do not find Rollins's (or anyone else's) flirtings with the static rhythms of rock and roll convincing, but the 1970s did see him recording a convincing "modal" improvisation called *Keep Hold of Yourself.* (Rollins's rather high-handed treatment of a chord progression or two on the interesting, and previously underrated, *Freedom Suite* perhaps forecast his ability to handle such a challenge.) And there is *Skylark* from 1971, probably Rollins's masterpiece of sustaining slow balladry, with two fascinating cadenzas (the opening one, more than fascinating). *Skylark* is a kind of spontaneous sonata-etude, if you will, and the kind of performance that makes one wonder again if jazz improvisation has not made possible the highest level of accomplishment in contemporary music.

To return to the earlier Rollins, one of the most instructive comparisons in recorded jazz, and one of the best indications of another aspect of Rollins's position in its history, comes about because several important players have made versions of *Cherokee* and variants thereof.[2] There are records by tenor saxophonist Don Byas, by Charlie Parker (as *Koko*), and by Rollins (as *B. Quick*). At least by the mid-'forties Byas was perhaps as sophisticated harmonically as was Rollins at his peak—witness Byas's version of *I Got Rhythm*. Melodically and rhythmically Byas echoed Hawkins; he was an arpeggio player with a rather deliberate and regular way of phrasing. Accordingly, when Byas plays an up-tempo *Cherokee*, his solo is so filled with notes that it seems a virtuoso display, and in an apparent melodic despair he is soon merely reiterating the theme. Parker of course broke up his phrases and his rhythm with such brilliant variety that he was able to establish a continuous, easy linear invention, avoiding Byas's effect of a cluttered desperation of notes. Rollins's *B. Quick* choruses, however, seem to be filling in again with notes. Of course this is partly because Rollins does not have Parker's rhythmic imagination (what jazzman has?) but, symbolically at least, it means that Rollins's maturity and his major contributions of improvised form came near the end of the great period of jazz which began with Charlie Parker.

2. Among the recordings of the piece are those by Art Tatum, in a smoothly arpeggiated, harmonically imaginative version; by Lester Young with Count Basie; by Lee Konitz (*Marshmallow*); by Sonny Stitt (in several versions, both as *Serenade to a Square* and as *Koko*); by Bud Powell at least twice; etc.

16

HORACE SILVER

The Meaning of Craftsmanship

In April 1954 Miles Davis led an "all-star" recording date which produced *Walkin'* and *Blue 'n' Boogie.* I think that the music on those two classic blues performances could be said to represent the state of modern jazz as it entered its second decade. The pianist involved, however, was a relative newcomer named Horace Silver. Silver's recording activities were then prolific, but his role in jazz was really just beginning, and his work as a pianist, composer, and leader of quintets became pivotal in the jazz of the late 'fifties.

A few years later Silver had produced two LP recitals which seem to me to bring all the elements of his music to a perfection of conception and performance, and even to turn some of the shortcomings of his style into virtues. But at the very moment of such achievement the style he supposedly started was being almost ludicrously popularized. That style was at first called "funky" after an old Anglo-Saxon word for smelly; it was soon turned into a marketable commodity called "soul jazz." When it began, the funky style was supposed to save jazz from the tepid affectations of the "cool" players; it was also meant to restore its rightful heritage and rescue jazz from an affected softness, from what Silver once called a "fagotty" excess. But a borderline jazzman like André Previn was soon playing glib, virtuosic Silver, and much "soul jazz" became a kind of self-satisfied pseudo-rustic posturing made up of a few pat devices derived from Negro gospel music, some conventional rhythm and blues effects, and about thirty saxophone clichés.

Nevertheless, Horace Silver's arrival in the 'fifties *was* important, and the funky style did what it set out to do. If its creativity as a movement was soon spent, Silver's own creativity was not—and his own style seems rather different from the style of his would-be followers.

The words associated with his music were "swing," "groove," "back-home," "low-down," "blow," "wail," "cook," and almost anything else people could think of to imply an earthy, uninhibited emotional expression.

Actually, Silver's is a very carefully designed and carefully rehearsed music, with a deliberate craftsmanship constantly in evidence. There are even built-in protections for the un-inspired soloist in several of his pieces. There is plenty of interest in his music also for the kind of casual listener who asks that his jazz be a fairly lively background that occa-sionally encourages finger-snapping and head-shaking.

In the 'thirties it was just such listeners who formed the core of the jazz audience, of course. It is from the jazz argot of the 'thirties that those terms "swing," "groove," and "blow" were borrowed. If we say that funky jazz was an effort at a return to roots, we should remember these younger modern jazzmen did not return to the music of King Oliver or Blind Lemon Jefferson, but rather to the roots represented in gospel music, contemporary rhythm and blues, the music of Ray Charles, and to the roots as these players knew them in their own youth—to the swing period of the 'thirties.

It has occurred to some commentators to look for a formal synthesis of modern jazz in Horace Silver's work, but Silver has some of his roots set too directly and too firmly in the 'thirties. In his approach to the piano he owes an harmonic sophistication to modern jazz, and he pays an obvious debt to Bud Powell's style (in the sense that Powell played a pianist's version of Parker's alto saxophone, Silver played a pianist's version of tenor saxophone, and he had been a tenor saxophonist) but often his manner of phrasing and some of his ideas of rhythm come very directly from an earlier time. If one says that Horace Silver sounds like a cross between Bud Powell and Pete Johnson, he had better acknowledge that there is an urbanity in several of Johnson's slow blues that Silver, in his determination to cook, may not manifest. Silver's groups sometimes give a similar impression—of a cross between a bebop quintet and a little Southwestern jump-blues band of the 'thirties or early 'forties. But there is more to his music than ingenious hybrid.

Silver's earlier composing shows all this quite readily. *Room 608* has a bebop line, but not an entirely comfortable one. And to balance it, there are pieces like *Stop Time,* which simplifies the bop line of *One Bass Hit;* or *Doodlin',* which is a slightly sophisticated version of a riff figure that was commonplace in the 'thirties; or *Sister Sadie,* which is also based on a durable, traditional riff and which was used in a quasi-spiritual pop tune the Basie band once recorded called *Do You Wanna Jump, Children?*

Silver succeeds in using something of both worlds in *Hippy,* a piece which reveals several aspects of his music. The basic material of *Hippy* is a two-bar riff which I believe comes from Charlie Christian—at least a version of it shows up in the Benny Goodman sextet's *Air Mail Special,* and the old Basie band also used it in later playings of *One O'Clock Jump.* Silver has taken that little phrase intact and, in the manner of bop composing, rather than repeating it over and over, has extended it logically and delightfully into a bouncing melody that covers eight bars. This melody then

becomes the main strain of a thirty-two-bar, AABA jazz
theme. Thus *Hippy* is structurally bop. But rhythmically it
remains rather close to swing.

Hippy also includes a secondary theme based in part on
big band brass figures. Silver's pieces often include such
secondary themes and written interludes, and I think the
one on *Moon Rays* is particularly attractive.

Most of Silver's music makes that kind of direct synthesis
of some elements from the jazz of the 'thirties and some
from the jazz of the 'forties.

Unlike some of his pieces, *Hippy* is harmonized in a fairly
simple way. Several others have the harmonic sophistication
of a rapid and dense texture of written chord changes. When
a soloist begins his "uninhibited" cooking, he has a tight
pattern of chords to run; he handles them according to his
talent or his mood of the moment, either as a challenging
inspiration, as a kind of musical game, or as a neat protection against a lack of ideas. If he runs all the chords cor-
rectly, he will sound as if he is playing something when he
may be playing very little. Silver's accompaniment is simpler
than Bud Powell's, and there are fewer interpolated passing
chords. However, I do find myself in agreement with those
who say that less solo space allotted to his sidemen would
improve some of Silver's performances.

Horace Silver's style does owe a debt to black gospel
music, to be sure, but far less a debt than has been said, and
certainly a less direct debt than one can hear in several of his
followers. I expect that the earlier piece called *The Preacher*
may have been named with irony. It is a leaping, shouting
theme on the outline of the inebriate's favorite *Show Me
the Way to Go Home*—no wonder the Dixieland bands
took it up. And, as I have indicated, *Sister Sadie* could have
got her funkiness at a Count Basie dance as easily as at a
sanctified church.

One striking effect of Silver's career is his special relationship to trumpeters. Silver was in frequent attendance during the early stages of Miles Davis's reemergence in the mid-'fifties. Kenny Dorham matured while he and Silver were both members of the Art Blakey Jazz Messengers. Donald Byrd produced a quite cohesive early recorded solo on *Señor Blues* on a Horace Silver date. I don't think that it was either inevitable or coincidental that Art Farmer settled into being an exceptionally fluent and authoritatively lyric soloist while he was with Silver.[1] Similarly, Blue Mitchell expanded his style while with Silver. It should be obvious that any player would gain rhythmic sureness and dexterity from playing with Horace Silver, but trumpeters seem to gain as melodists, even as Silver bounces, barks, and chops his way around behind them.

The problems inherent in Silver's piano style are obvious, although not all of them of his own making. He does have trouble with slow tempos and the lyricism of jazz ballads. But few of Bud Powell's ballads are successful, and Powell even indulged in a kind of pounded version of Art Tatum's embellishment style on occasion. Thelonious Monk and John Lewis can sustain a ballad meaningfully, but each has a personal and somewhat isolated approach to such material. Other modern pianists who have played ballads well—Al Haig, Duke Jordan, and Joe Albany—have all shown an interesting dependence on Teddy Wilson's brilliance in such moods.

I have indicated that Horace Silver's accompaniments can by rhythmically choppy and melodically static. In solo, the same fault shows itself as a kind of fragmentation; a brief and almost isolated melodic idea is propelled, by each bass chord in succession—bass chord/treble figure/bass chord/

1. Farmer's solo on *Moon Rays* seems a definitive statement of his exceptional talent.

treble figure, in a sort of pianistic ping-pong—sometimes
with little effect of melodic or emotional continuity or pattern. There is also Silver's almost malicious penchant for
interpolation. In the midst of the fine momentum he gets
going in *Blue 'n' Boogie,* for example, he drops an allusion
to the *Hut Sut Song* (!), and in a slow mood piece we may
suddenly be treated to a succession of bugle calls. Such jokes
may be pretty good, but they seem uncalled for.

I began this by saying that I think two of his LPs show
a kind of peak of development for Silver's music. There is
certainly at least one peak performance on each of them.
Cookin' at the Continental (on a set called *"Finger-Poppin"*)
and *Sister Sadie* (on a set called *"Blowin' the Blues Away"*)
are both performed, by soloists and group, with an exceptionally sustained and surging energy and swinging inspiration of a kind seldom captured in a recording studio and
almost as rarely in public performance. The two LPs are
also performed with a rare collective skill and precision.
Cookin', by the way, also has the asset of saxophonist Junior
Cook's occasional willingness to echo Lester Young's style,
an approach which suits Silver's excellently. (I'm sure that
Horace Silver sounded so good the way we first heard him
playing with Stan Getz because Getz also owes much to the
jazz of the 'thirties.)

Among the compositions, *Mellow D* has a very good line
in which the swing and bebop elements are so synthesized
that one cannot really separate them. There is the usual
flirting with "Latin" rhythms on several pieces, which are
sometimes dropped after a chorus or so but which give a
welcome variety to his programs. And there are the continuing efforts to break down thirty-two-bar structures and
their eight-bar patterns in pieces of 16/6/16 etc.

But such things are not so much innovations, it seems to
me, as they are acts of sound conservatism: in them Silver

finds slightly different ways to present the fundamentals of his music.

More important, the writing is usually direct and economical. Some of the secondary themes are remarkably effective, and especially on *Sister Sadie* two horns and piano sound almost exactly like the alternating brass and reed sections of a big band executing call-and-response riffs. One may question why a quintet should want to sound like a big band, but the astonishing results on *Sadie* can only produce a kind of awed admiration, and perhaps the conclusion that on several of his pieces Silver has in effect done some of the best big band writing of the period.

There is even more evidence of an approaching perfection in Silver's piano. The overall impression is one of cohesion and order—the blue notes usually seem to be there for cause rather than effect and the more adventurous intervals seem part of a larger plan (hear *Cookin' at the Continental* especially). In his accompaniments there is still some choppiness, and the rumbling and barking are there, perhaps a little too often. But particularly on *Blowin' the Blues Away* and *Sister Sadie,* Silver uses his piano excellently as a substitute sax or brass section, propelling his soloists along with background riff figures. John Lewis does much the same sort of thing in accompaniment, echoing the same sort of swing period sources, but the effect is different, and a comparison between Silver and Lewis as accompanists can be quite instructive.

A piece called *Saint Vitus Dance* is an exceptional five minutes by a piano trio, and its medium tempo may be just the right one for Silver. The romantic harmonies of *Saint Vitus* will convince you again that Silver can make anything sound naturally earthy, and his improvising has a melodic continuity and design that I don't believe he has shown elsewhere on records.

Perhaps the most remarkable of all is the slow piece called

Sweet Stuff. There Silver's spurting right hand phrases and heavy chords may again seem isolated fragments at first; cumulatively, however, the performance soon takes on the hypnotic effect of a passionately chanted incantation. The right hand phrases on *Sweet Stuff* are rendered with a remarkably sustained emotional directness, and the performer avoids both the sentimentality and callousness which are inherent temptations to lesser players in such a piece. *Sweet Stuff* is a unique, almost unforgettable, performance. And Silver has achieved it not only in terms of his own style, but by taking ingenious advantage of the very things that otherwise seem flaws in his playing. After *Sweet Stuff* the interpolated bugle call that finds its way into *You Happened My Way* seems almost forgivable.

Horace Silver is that kind of talented, determined craftsman that jazz, like any art, must have to sustain itself. Such a craftsman, whether Don Redman, Fletcher Henderson, Count Basie, Roy Eldridge, or Horace Silver, has been there at the right moment to play a crucial role in the development of the music. Certainly jazz would languish without its Armstrongs and its Parkers to renew its language, and without its Mortons, Ellingtons, and Monks to give it compositional synthesis. But without individual, creative craftsmen like Horace Silver among its soloists and its composers, there might be no common language to renew, and no affirmation of what things can be synthesized.

17

MILES DAVIS

A Man Walking

By the early 'fifties, it may have seemed that the productive career of trumpeter and fluegelhornist Miles Davis was just about over. Between 1950 and 1954 his work had become uneven. Obvious aspects of his style had already been siphoned off and popularized by several trumpeters, particularly on the West Coast. And in the East meanwhile there had arrived a young man named Clifford Brown, whose work brought together some of the best aspects of modern trumpet—a sort of synthesis of Davis, Dizzy Gillespie, and most particularly Fats Navarro.

Brown became something of a rallying point for Eastern musicians: in the face of a fad for "cool jazz," it was as if he rose up and shouted to his contemporaries—even to his elders—that jazz should not abandon the other side of its technical and emotional heritage, that it could find a renewed life in a reiteration of some of its first principles.

Most of the first-generation "modernists," at least those who received the earliest praise—Gillespie, Charlie Parker, Bud Powell, Max Roach—were virtuosos in obvious ways. But the musicians who became important in the second decade of the music, almost to a man, were not virtuosos; they became important by virtue of asserting principles aside from obvious technical dexterity. I am thinking of players like Thelonious Monk, John Lewis, and Miles Davis, or players like Horace Silver and Art Blakey. Even Milt Jackson, although he has developed the techniques implicit in his early, bop-influenced style, preferred simpler pieces and contributed a classic blues in *Bags' Groove*. Also, each of these men reflected the immediate past of jazz, specifically the music of the 'thirties and the swing period, some of them—Lewis, Davis, Silver—in a manner that is so direct that it implied a deliberate reaching back.

Miles Davis's earliest records were sometimes able and occasionally faltering, but they showed a very personal approach to the modern jazz idiom. From time to time he did espouse the virtuoso manner of Gillespie, and on occasion he showed a perceptive ability almost to abstract Gillespie's style, as on *A Night in Tunisia* with Charlie Parker. But more often he was involved in a simple, introspective but sophisticated lyricism which seemed to refute the ideas that many people had about modern jazz as a virtuoso music whose simple passages had to alternate with a sustained barrage of sixteenth-notes. And he was sometimes so good a lyricist as to be able to follow, for example, Charlie Parker's superb solo on *Embraceable You* without sounding a hopeless anti-climax.

Davis was an effective foil for Parker's technical and emotional exuberance. But at the same time that Davis offered simplicity and directness, he was preoccupied with particularly lush harmonies, and it sometimes seemed his solos might become a succession of pretty but perhaps bland sound patterns.

Miles Davis's first recordings under his own name were made in 1947 when he was only twenty-one, and the fact that they have a decidedly individual character is even more notable when we remember that he was surrounded by such accomplished players as Charlie Parker (on tenor for the occasion), John Lewis, and Max Roach. The atmosphere of these performances is more relaxed, the themes are more fluent and more legato, and, although Davis has clearly learned from Parker and Dizzy Gillespie, he seemed also to be reaching back to the easy, introverted phrasing of Lester Young. Davis's themes on those records have a built-in harmonic complexity. *Sippin' at Bells,* for example, is a twelve-bar blues, but it is so written that the soloist has to find his way through an obstacle course of some eighteen assigned chord changes in a single chorus. And the shifting structure of *Little Willie Leaps* (borrowed, by the way, but altered from *All God's Chillun Got Rhythm*) almost throws so able a man as John Lewis.

There is an effective tension on these recordings between the surface lyricism of Miles Davis's solo melodic lines and the complexity of their underlying harmonic outline. The wonder is that a man who plays with such apparent simplicity as Miles Davis would have wanted such technical challenges. But he did, and he learned a great deal from the experience. And once he had learned it, he showed an artist's wisdom in forgetting, but still knowing, what he had learned.

Among the most celebrated of Davis's records are the series he recorded with nine-piece groups for Capitol. They have been celebrated for the work of the arrangers involved—Gil Evans, Gerry Mulligan, John Lewis, Johnny Carisi, and Davis—but if they proved nothing else, they would prove that Miles Davis, already an interesting and personal soloist, could produce two great improvisations, each one great in a different way. His blues solo on *Israel* is a beautiful example of classic simplicity of melody and of a personal reassessment of the mood of the blues. His chorus on *Move* is a striking episode of meaningful asymmetry, and it has some phrasing that is so original that one can only say that, rhythmically, it seems to turn back on itself while moving steadily forward.

Many a promising jazzman's career has come to a standstill after such achievements as these two solos, but Miles Davis had more, and still more to offer. Happily, he found ways to offer it all, against personal odds and against the long-enduring public apathy (not to say hostility) toward the very idiom of modern jazz.

Davis once confessed that he was not pleased with many of his own recordings, but he admitted to liking the series he did for Blue Note with trombonist J. J. Johnson. It happens that Davis recorded twice for Blue Note with Johnson. I don't know which is the session he likes, but on each of them he used pieces from Gillespie's early repertory (*Woody 'n' You, Ray's Idea, Chance It* or *Max Is Makin' Wax*), others written along the same lines, and pieces from his own past (*Enigma* for one, is improvised around the framework of Davis's *Deception*). Like Louis Armstrong, Roy Eldridge, and Dizzy Gillespie in their early repertories, Davis in effect reinterpreted in his own terms, the immediate past of jazz—and he did it for much the same reason as the others had, in order to move on.

In early 1954, a key year in the history of modern jazz in several respects, Miles Davis experienced a musical rebirth, a rebirth that brought him maturity as a jazz musician and ultimately led to a widespread popularity and acclaim. The essence of that maturity and, significantly, of that popularity as well, was the discovery of an intense, passionate, sometimes ravishing, highly personal trumpet sound. His style did not otherwise change much, except perhaps that it became simpler, or at least somewhat redistributed, more "open" and less compact. And it is surely important that the first full announcement of the rebirth came on two basic blues performances, *Walkin'* and *Blue 'n' Boogie*.

Dick Katz has written of these performances, "*Walkin'* and its companion piece, *Blue 'n' Boogie* are acknowledged to be classics. To me they represent a sort of summing up of much of what had happened musically to the players involved during the preceding ten years. It is as if they all agreed to get together to discuss on their instruments what they had learned and unlearned, what elements of bop (horrible word) they had retained or discarded. An amazing seminar took place." The "they" also included tenor saxophonist Lucky Thompson, whose ideas of rhythm and phrasing belong to an earlier style; Kenny Clarke, who virtually invented modern jazz drumming; trombonist J. J. Johnson, the first and still most important modernist on his instrument; and pianist Horace Silver, a relative newcomer.

The overtly complex harmonic challenges, the shifting and substitute chords, were behind Davis. He was interested in a direct building up of melodic content, and he had learned to make pause, silence, and space a crucially expressive part of his musical language. Beginning now, one passionate note from Miles Davis seemed to imply a whole complex of expressive sound, and three notes a ravishing melody. Above all, Miles Davis had discovered his trumpet sound.

All of these things had perhaps been implicit from the beginning, but not the renewed emotional intensity of his sound. It frequently found expression in tightly harmonmuted horn, played close to the microphone. But far from being a phenomenon of electronics, it was a triumph of human feeling over its electronic vehicle. And Davis's control of his trumpet, and of the more difficult fluegelhorn, although it is far from obvious, includes a wide range of sounds along with a clear execution of unexpected rhythms.

On the whole, Miles Davis was a lucky man, for apparently he could have it both ways: his records, like those of the Modern Jazz Quartet, seemed to please those who want their music to be a kind of fairly lively background sound issuing from their phonographs. They also pleased those who expect the strongest kind of emotional statements from jazz and who expect the kind of musical and aesthetic interest that the best jazzmen provide. The lightness of his trumpet sound had something to do with his broad acceptance, to be sure, and because of that lightness he has been called "a man walking on eggshells." But Davis the musician walked firmly and sure of foot; if he ever encountered eggshells, his intensity would probably grind them to powder.

A handy introduction to Davis's particular distillation of jazz melody is a comparison in the blues theme he has called variously *Sid's Ahead* or *Weirdo*. In this piece, Davis has abstracted the theme of *Walkin'* and reduced it to an essence of three notes, and he has done it so brilliantly as to make the delightfully original *Walkin'* seem overdecorative. Davis's best improvising has the same evocative economy and hint of mystery.

The *Blue 'n' Boogie* date was no fluke; soon after, Davis produced a lovely solo on *The Man I Love* and an ingenious development of *Bags' Groove*—these also including first-rate Milt Jackson and (on *Bags' Groove*) brilliant Thelonious Monk. At the same time, a culturally lagging public was catching up to modern jazz and each of these soloists was destined for public popularity and success.

Popularity first came to Miles Davis with the quintet he formed in 1955 with tenor saxophonist John Coltrane (a dexterous foil to Davis's lyricism, as Davis had conversely been to Charlie Parker), and a rhythm section that played with apparent smoothness and continuity but that also provided subtly complementary polyrhythms and accents from Philly Joe Jones—a drummer who can roll back on himself while simultaneously moving forward in something of the way that Davis himself had done on *Move*.

The group also frequently played "in two," accenting the second and fourth beats, once the weak beats, in a kind of

reverse Dixieland. In this, in several other aspects of his
style, and in Davis's repertory of the time (*Surrey with the
Fringe on Top, Gal in Calico, I Don't Want To Be Kissed,
Just Squeeze Me, New Rhumba, Ahmad's Blues,* etc.) Miles
Davis was clearly influenced by the trio of pianist Ahmad
Jamal. One can readily understand why, since Jamal is a
sophisticated harmonicist and, like Davis, used space and
openness in his music. Despite the impeccable swing of
Jamal's group, however, his music seems chic and shallow—
all of which is another way of saying that good art, and particularly good American art, can be strongly influenced by
bad. Miles Davis, after all, can undertake such unspeakably
mawkish material as *Some Day My Prince Will Come, Put
Your Little Foot Right In* (which he calls *Fran Dance*), or
Spring Is Here and make them palatable by his intense
involvement as he recomposes their melodies. In repertory,
as in other obvious respects, Miles Davis's music often represents the triumph of an innate artistic sensibility over mid-
dle-brow taste.

Possibly the most miraculous transformation of all is *Bye
Bye Blackbird*: an admittedly light, strutting, but shallow
ditty, which Davis tansmuted into a beautifully pensive
theme, playing one chorus of melodic paraphrase (accompanied "in two") and two choruses of invention (accompanied in an even, four beats with discreet countermovements from Jones's sticks).

With public success came a new alliance of Davis and Gil
Evans on a series of LPs the most celebrated of which is the
first, called *"Miles Ahead."* Evans has frequently provided
a fascinating and effective setting for Davis's improvisations.
On the other hand, it seems to me that Evans did not utilize
the rhythmic idiom of modern jazz. And in his approach
there is the implicit danger that one may end up substituting
a tissue of color-harmonies for music, and as a background

for Davis's horn, a danger which is more fully encountered in some selections on the Davis-Evans LP called *"Quiet Nights."*

The Evans-Davis collaboration called *"Sketches of Spain"* is a truly arresting performance, however. It begins with a reorchestration of the first movement of Joaquin Rodrigo's *Concierto de Aranjuez for Guitar and Orchestra* to feature Davis as the soloist; the recording is something of a curiosity and a failure, as I think a comparison with any good performance of the movement by a classical guitarist would confirm. But Evans provided fanfares for a *Saeta,* a traditional Holy Week vocal lament for the dead Christ, and Miles Davis plays with a stark, deeply felt communal anguish that jazz has not heard since King Oliver.

There was a public Miles Davis during the 1950s therefore, a Davis who performed familiar pieces from his repertory at fast tempos—fast enough to get away from him at times. One found himself asking why. If he is bored with that one then why does he play it? Is he impatient with this one? Why is his opening statement on that one so seemingly lackadaisical? But his playing answers such questions almost as soon as they are asked. When he is successful in such returns to his popular repertory Davis is once again the brilliant sketch artist whose abstractions of standards like *Autumn Leaves* and *All of You* can be as knowingly precise as they are evocative.

Popularity invites artistic complacency, and in our world it particularly invites the complacency of reducing one's successes to a safe formula and repeating it. I cannot say that I believe Miles Davis has always avoided repeating himself. But in 1959 he recorded *"Kind of Blue,"* a remarkable LP recital which took its place as one of the most provocative events in jazz since the mid-'forties.

I have spoken of the surface simplicity of the jazz of the

late 'fifties, of a cutting back, opening up, and airing out of
the density of modern jazz—which involved less emphasis
on complex harmonic background and a greater emphasis
on melody. When such retrenchments of style take place
(an earlier example would be the Count Basie of the late
'thirties), major changes are probably at hand. It is a credit
to Davis that at a moment of public success, his work should
move in the direction of those changes.

Most of the material on *"Kind of Blue"* was new to the
musicians; it was presented to them when they arrived for
the recording session. Most of the pieces were done in a
single take, and most of the improvisation was done using
points of departure that jazzmen had only rarely undertaken
before. *So What,* for example, in a sense restricted as well as
free in its outline, asks the improviser to make his melody
from one assigned Dorian mode for sixteen measures, then
a half-step up for eight measures, then back to the first mode
for a final eight measures. The result was a superb Davis
performance. *Flamenco Sketches* (which was mislabeled *All
Blues,* and vice versa) sets up five different scales and asks
the player to improvise on each of them in turn, moving
from one to the next as he wishes.[1]

1. A brief account of early examples of ostinato improvising might be interesting here. The short ostinato section of Armstrong's *King of the Zulus*
(1926; expanded in his 1957 version), plus perhaps the opening cadenza to
Yes! I'm in the Barrel, is pivotal. *Zulus* was prefigured in Fletcher Henderson's 1924 *The Gourge of Armour Avenue* (and that recording was directly
imitated in Lloyd Scott's 1927 *Symphonic Scronch*). *Armour Avenue* and/or
Zulus became the obvious model for the pedal tone section of Ellington's
Rockin' in Rhythm (1931). *Zulus* or *Rockin' in Rhythm* was also the basis of
the extended ostinato section in Benny Goodman's *Sing, Sing, Sing* (1936). It,
in turn, may have served as a model for Charlie Barnet's *Redskin Rhumba*
(1940). Then there are such swing-era AABA song-form pieces as *Jumpin' at
the Woodside* or *Caravan* or *Air Mail Special* which have little or no required chordal motion in their A themes. There are also eight-bar ostinato
sections for the soloists in Ellington's *Bouncing Buoyancy* (1939). I do not
suggest, however, that these earlier events influenced Davis, John Coltrane,
or Ornette Coleman.

"Kind of Blue" was an influential record both in and of itself and because it paralleled other, independently conceived events in jazz. But for a while it seemed a rather isolated event for Davis himself—one might say that it was more immediately important to John Coltrane's development than to Davis—and for the next few years the repertory of ballads and standards was resumed.

Then, beginning in 1965, Miles Davis returned to the principles he had asserted six years earlier. In association with his tenor saxophonist, Wayne Shorter, and his remarkable young drummer, Tony Williams, Davis began to build up a repertory of original, instrumentally conceived jazz compositions of unusual and generally unhackneyed structures. These placed Davis in the advanced guard of the period.

The pieces, and the LP performances in which they were introduced, inevitably vary in quality, but they form a remarkable series of recordings nevertheless. Perhaps most important, they indicate that Miles Davis had continued to explore and develop his talent for over thirty years. That is unusual, virtually unique, in a music where many instrumentalists have been able only to sustain and refine the achievements of their twenties and early thirties.

However, when one reminds himself that the lyric *Circle*, the "extended" piece *Country Son,* and *Petit Machins,* which are among the high achievements of Miles Davis in the 'sixties, were all written by Davis himself, things appear in a different light. Perhaps, as he entered his forties, the composer in Miles Davis was reborn, and is both sustaining and challenging the instrumentalist in him.

One must acknowledge, if only in passing, the great contribution of drummer Tony Williams to these recordings. The dense, complex, polyrhythmic textures of his best performances are wonders in themselves, yet they are always in motion, always swing, are always responsive to the soloist and

the ensemble, and are never interfering or distracting. And
for his splashing, complex cymbal work alone, Williams belongs among the great drummers in jazz history.

Of Davis's subsequent flirting with rock rhythms and his
avowed determination in the early 1970s to lead the best
jazz-rock fusion group in the world, perhaps the less said the
better. Except perhaps that, aside from moments by Davis
himself, these performances seem failures to me, and failures
partly because of the doggedly static nature of the rhythms,
and consequently the music, involved with them. There is
one remarkable document from the later days of the Davis-
Shorter-Williams group, however, recorded in a Chicago
club, the Plugged Nickel, in December 1965, but first released by Japanese CBS-Sony in the late 1970s. It is, in terms
of musical sound alone, the most advanced statement Davis
has yet made, and, particularly in versions of *So What* and
Walkin', yet another definitive Davis statement in the jazz
that by then was generally called "the New Thing."

Because of its unique, evocative character, Miles Davis's
music has challenged many a reviewer to deal with its emotional content and deal with it in fairly specific terms. One
man says he hears in Davis the defeat and despair of an effete
nihilist. Another hears forceful lyricism. Another ecstasy.
Still another, the whine of a complaining, disgruntled child.

I began by saying that Davis's music, like that of other important contemporaries, echoed the past and particularly
echoed the 'thirties. We hear Gillespie and Parker in him,
but often their ideas are so transmuted that they become
unrecognizable. There is also a deep respect for Lester
Young in him. And sometimes the edge and curve of his
trumpet sound hints that he is reinterpreting the whole
range of the Ellington trumpets of 1939—the textures of the
section, the purer leading voice of Wallace Jones, the growl
of Cootie Williams, and the wail of Rex Stewart's squeezed

half-valves—all on Davis's nearly vibratoless, open, or tightly-muted horn.

But there is one echo of the past that seems to me to be central, and for it Miles Davis had reached back two generations and brought a seminal style up to date. More than any other player, Miles Davis echoes Louis Armstrong; one can hear it, I think, in his reading of almost any standard song. And behind the jaded stance, beneath the complaints, and beneath the sometimes blasé sophistication, Miles Davis's horn also echoes something of Armstrong's exuberantly humorous, forcefully committed, and self-determined joy.

18

SARAH VAUGHAN

The Meaning of Self-Discovery

In the 1950s it was said that Sarah Vaughan made two kinds of recordings. With her trio of piano, bass, and drums, she offered more or less informal and spontaneous treatments of standard American popular songs largely intended for a following that already knew her work and knew what it wanted of her. With large, studio-assembled groups, she did mostly current material in a more subdued manner in search of listeners that she had not yet reached.

Conventional wisdom at the time had it that the trio records were the best records, the records that showed her real talents as a jazz singer. The others were more predictable performances—to some, they were even a kind of commercial sell-out.

I think not, or not exactly. The trio performances did offer adventurous, exploratory treatment of standards. But with the larger groups, she explored her voice, its textures, its range, its dynamics. And on a set from 1956 with the somewhat pompous title *"Great Songs from Hit Shows,"* a collection of standards but this time with a large string-oriented accompaniment, all her resources began to come together and a unique artist emerged.

When Sarah Vaughan first appeared in the 1940s, she was obviously a singer of superior natural vocal equipment. By exploring and developing her voice and her other musical gifts, she has discovered a range of vocal techniques which have by now become a challenge to all singers in all genres of music.

Sarah Vaughan has an exceptional range (roughly of soprano through baritone), exceptional body, volume, a variety of vocal textures, and superb and highly personal vocal control. Her ear and sense of pitch are just about perfect, and there are no "difficult" intervals for Sarah Vaughan. She can make spontaneously the most surprising steps and difficult glides and arrive perfectly. When she first discovered her vibrato, she indulged it. But it has become a discreet ornament, an ornament of uniquely flexible size, shape, and duration. And she uses it, as have some of the great instrumentalists, as an occasional, often terminal, adornment to her phrases. Like that vibrato, her "head tones" are (or should be) the envy of every singer who has heard her. Sarah Vaughan has discovered that she has and can use not one voice or vocal texture, but several. She can take a note at the top or bottom of her range and, risking the impossible, fray it or bend it apparently out of her range.

Sarah Vaughan is an artist with an innate sense of musical structure and musical flow; none of her resources are used as vocal tricks which appear for their own sake. She has developed a sense of phrase that tells her when to sustain, bend, or glide a note, when to hold or cut off a tone, when and how to ally brief or sustained tones—all to discover hidden textures and beauties in the human voice as an instrument of song.

By May 1950, and her second recorded version of *Mean to Me*, Sarah Vaughan had already shown a melodic imagination worthy of the best jazz players, a sensitivity and grace worthy of the great instrumentalists. From the *"Great Songs from Hit Shows"* LP, her reading of *Dancing in the Dark*, particularly in the song's verse and in her concluding few

bars, shows a starkly dramatic side of her talent that was virtually unsuspected. And her reading of *Little Girl Blue*
handles its pathos sympathetically, but with the same sly
rejection of self-pity that we recognize as the substance of
the blues.

The arrangements on that *"Great Songs"* album are skill-
ful, sometimes overblown, and basically in the recording
studio, vocal accompaniment style of the times. Billie Holiday could be the mistress of weak melodies, intuitively revising them by paraphrase. But Sarah Vaughan can revise a
bathetic arrangement, by carefully selecting her notes,
subtly using her range, her dynamics, her harmonic ear—by
alternately dominating and joining her accompaniment:
there are her endings to *Little Girl Blue* or *It Never Entered
My Mind*, or there is virtually all of *Autumn in New York*.
As if Sarah Vaughan regarded the events around her with
the precocious, detached stance of a witty Alice in an adult
wonderland, accepting the conventions, the foibles, the pre-
tense of her elders through the act of questioning and doubt-
ing them.

Sarah Vaughan has had two recorded encounters with the
Count Basie orchestra, and each of them has been special.
From the first in 1958, without the leader present, there is
a version of *Smoke Gets in Your Eyes* which begins with a
ravishing upward vocal glide—and has an ensuing performance that fulfills the promise of that beginning. (And
Smoke Gets in Your Eyes ends, by the way, with a warm allusion to one of the shattering vocal textures of Billie Holiday.) There is also a treatment of *Stardust* which begins with
an angular, wordless rendering of that song's singularly interesting verse, and a lovely, contrasting recomposition of
its chorus that is all curves.

Her second recording with the Basie ensemble, two years
later and this time with the leader's piano, included what

are probably her best versions of the two songs she has somehow shared with Miss Holiday, *I Cried for You* and that
remarkably affecting piece, *Lover Man*—those, plus a version of *You Go to My Head* that is not only exceptional for
her control of a variety of sounds and textures but a dis-
creetly successful handling of the song's somewhat stilted
lyric.

Sarah Vaughan's 1960 *Stormy Weather* is a kind of sublime incantation on that song's simple chord progression, a
fine example of embellishment by simplification and distillation. I should not leave that recording without also remarking on the quietly firm writing for strings which Jimmy
Jones contributed. Jones on piano, along with trumpeter
Harry Edison, also contributed strongly to her 1961 *Ain't
No Use,* an imaginative vocal exploration, intricately integrated with a sustained attitude and mood.

The recorded masterpiece of Sarah Vaughan's career thus
far is surely the "Live in Tokyo" version of that exceptional
Rogers and Hart song *My Funny Valentine,* for its spontaneous but disciplined exploration of the resources of her
voice and of the melody and harmonic structure of that
piece, and for what was obviously a deeply felt experience
for the singer as well as her audience. Indeed, it is on the
basis of such performances that Sarah Vaughan has been
called the great singer of the century, regardless of musical
tradition or genre.

That *Funny Valentine* reflects another aspect of her virtuosity, but one which audio recordings cannot give us fully:
her use of the hand microphone. She has mastered its placement and movement as an aspect of her performances, not
only near her head, her voice box, but in various positions
and placements in or near her body complementing not only
volume but vocal textures, often low and at arm's length
when she is at full volume.

Whatever I say of her here may become incomplete or dated if her future development is anything like her remarkable past. There is a *More Than You Know* from the late 1970s, full of graceful, original phrases and flow of vocal sound that ends with a sustained diminuendo that would surely challenge the control of any other singer. And in a recent performance I saw her execute a similar final tone, beginning at full volume with the hand mike at arm's length but raised gradually, thus increasing its volume as her own diminished, and producing an uncanny effect.

Sarah Vaughan also continues to meet directly two remaining challenges of which she seems fully aware. That of adapting her array of techniques to the subtler demands and nuances of swing. And the challenge of exploring and sustaining the mood and potential drama of each song while not inhibiting herself vocally or musically.

It took several generations of singers in seventeenth- and eighteenth-century Italy to explore the potential of the human voice and arrive at what we call the *bel canto* style. Sarah Vaughan has accomplished the virtual equivalent of such explorations in a contemporary American style, in less than one lifetime, and in a single voice. And like the great jazz instrumentalists, within whose traditions she works, she explores her instrument, her own resources, and her own emotions to their expressive limits and to an expressive perfection. She undertakes such a challenging musical adventure each time she sings, and she can find such an adventure in the most ordinary ditty as well as in the best of our popular songs. And those of us lucky enough to be alive in her time, and to be in her audience, are a part of such a sublime adventure each time we hear her.

19

CHARLIE MINGUS

The Pivotal Instrument

How is one to judge the contributions of Charles Mingus? They are probably sizable, we expect, even before we have thought much about them or decided exactly what they are. And when we do try to decide what they are, the question begins to get complicated. Mingus was, on the face of it, an ensemble leader, but one who seemed to change his ideas of what kind and what size of ensemble he wanted to lead. He was a bass player and evidently an innovative one. And he was a composer.

Mingus's personality seemed to be much a part of his music. But not only his musical personality and attitudes— Mingus's very opinions seemed to be present and to intervene. And there was often enough an odd contradiction between his words and his actions. He admonished his musicians, sometimes in public, to "stop copying" Charlie Parker, and even titled a piece, *Gunslinging Bird* on the saxophonist's supposed revenge on his imitators. Yet his "favorite quintet" of the 'sixties featured Charles McPherson, whose commitment to the idiom of Charlie Parker was self-evident. Mingus spoke out publicly against musicians, particularly Hollywood composers, who used assistants to orchestrate their ideas. But he used such "ghosts" himself, and in his later years he freely credited them.

Probably no jazz musician has ever asked us to take his music so much on his own terms, biographically and psychologically, as Charles Mingus. In this respect, one does think of Jelly Roll Morton. And Morton is a musician to whom some have compared Mingus ("You sound like Jelly Roll," Max Roach once chided him after a long speech). And again there are a couple of recordings, *My Jelly Roll Soul* and the unfortunately condescending *Jelly Roll*. But Morton imposed his life and his ideas between us and his music only late in his career, and often through the encouragement of others. Mingus, through interviews, record liner notes, speeches from the bandstand, the titles of his pieces, and his rather distracted autobiography, *Beneath the Underdog,* seemed to offer us himself as forcefully as he offered his music—perhaps, as I say, as a part of his music.

Probably no leader has taken such advantage of the LP record as Charles Mingus did, yet I think the advantage was probably taken unintentionally. Other leaders and other groups have offered LPs that are memorable because of (let us say) generally good music, some excellent music, and a variety in programming. With Mingus, we remember the cumulative effect of *"Pithecanthropus Erectus"* or *"Tijuana Moods"* or *"Mingus Ah Um"* or *"Mingus Mingus Mingus"* or *"Let My Children Hear Music,"* yet when we re-think or re-hear their individual selections, we find that one portion of this piece works especially well, that portion of another, another part of still another. Rarely do we single out one performance from them for a sustained level of excellence. And we respond to the personal and catalytic energy of the leader and his evident effect on even the least of his musicians and even the least of his compositions. Perhaps Mingus was right to impose himself on us on behalf of his music.

Charles Mingus had the kind of "serious" ambitions to produce "long" works which date back to the ragtime era, evident in the "stride" men—particularly in James P. Johnson—and which became the basis of real accomplishment in Ellington. In Mingus, it seems to me that such efforts did not quite express the man's music. The truest moments in Mingus's *Revelations,* for instance, are not those in which the large ensemble executes the concert-hall-inspired passages (or do I mean Stan Kenton–inspired?) but the turbulent, polyphonic "extended form" passages improvised by the jazzmen. And *Meditations on Integration* seems a quite workable vehicle as re-titled *Praying with Eric* and performed by a sextet. But it was rather over-blown as originally done for large ensemble during the *"Mingus at Monterey"* concert.

Polyphony is a key word in any discussion of Mingus's music, not only in the passages of simultaneous improvising by his players but also in his fine penchant as a composer for the juxtaposition and development of lines, motives, and antiphonal effects. Indeed, it might be difficult to defend Mingus as a melodist, but not at all difficult to praise him for relatively complex musical textures that evolve and build with excellence. *Moanin'* is an exceptional example of the effective juxtaposition of written lines. *E's Flat Ah's Flat Too* introduces a trombone riff over its boogie-like opening line and then, with uncommon timing, builds its textures with new motives and riffs and variants of those already there. *Haitian Fight Song* builds its relentless patterns, from a string bass introduction which becomes a bass-line melody, through a headlong but cumulative pattern of superimposed riffs, call-and-response figures, and counter-riffs. And sometimes Mingus's own shouts and cries become in effect a part of the orchestration.

In his slow ballads, Mingus did not always escape the shadow of his models, and until the end of his career he continued to offer the equivalent of Johnny Hodges vehicles

(Portrait of Jackie, I X-Love, Bemoanable Lady, Sue's Changes, and others) not up to the level of Ellington's and Strayhorn's. But his "Lester Young vehicle," *Goodbye Pork Pie Hat,* is a moving dirge. And *Celia* in its 1963 treatment is exceptional in that it involves one of Mingus's most effective contributions to jazz composition performance, the changes of tempo which he and his players made so intrinsic and executed with such enviable ease. Tempo operates similarly in *Fables of Faubus, Far Wells Mill Valley,* and *Song with an Orange.*

As did John Lewis with the Modern Jazz Quartet, and Horace Silver—and even Thelonious Monk—Mingus conceived much of his music with the accomplishments of the big bands as a guide and approach to small ensemble music. Then in mid-career he began to re-record earlier works with medium and large groups. *Haitian Fight Song,* for one, gains much in clarity of line and precision as re-done for eleven instrumentalists and retitled *II B.S.* But the earlier version has stunning bass work which the latter does not, and on *Haitian Fight Song* the surging, penetrating energy emanating from the leader and his instrument leads some listeners to call *II B.S.* slick by comparison.

Again, the leader's musical energy informs all. As a composer Mingus produced works which seemed to belong only to himself, which seemed to take on their singular life and energy only when he and his groups performed them, and otherwise barely existed at all. On paper, *Pithecanthropus Erectus* (the piece, not the LP) would probably seem only an idea for a performance, and perhaps not a promising one— it might be hard to say. In its recorded version, despite a rather static piano solo, it emerges as one of his most memorable works. And the same sort of thing might be said of such related pieces as *Prayer for Passive Resistance* and *Hobo Ho.* In all of them, the range and variety of musical patterns and musical emotion seem to rise and to fall with a will of their own, yet always under the firm but flexible control of the leader.

Mention of *Pithecanthropus* reminds us of the aforementioned "extended form," Mingus's forerunner of "the new thing," in which a chord or two is spontaneously sustained, to be explored by the player or players at a length of their own choice, with the rest of the ensemble responding intuitively.

I have implied in all of the foregoing that Mingus the bass player is central to all else. And I believe it is Mingus the bassist who has made the most important and durable contribution to jazz. By the mid-1930s, Walter Page had taken the rhythmic lead away from the drums and the other rhythm instruments. And within a few years, Jimmy Blanton had gracefully reminded us how important it was to know and choose the right notes. In Mingus, the bass did not so much maintain the harmonic and time-keeping function established by Blanton and developed so effectively by Ray Brown. In Mingus, the bass ceased to "accompany" and entered directly in the music, a kind of polyphonic participant, but without sacrificing its time-keeping function. It was not simply a matter of his choice of the most interesting notes, but of providing a continuous, inter-playing inspirational part.

Mingus was also a virtuoso bass soloist, outstanding enough to be numbered among the great soloists regardless of instrument. With Mingus the soloist, as with Mingus the ballad maker, the presence of Ellington is still felt, and there are recordings of Ellington standards as bass solos—*Mood Indigo,* let's say, and the medley from *"Mingus at Monterey"* that includes *I Got It Bad, In a Sentimental Mood,* and *Sophisticated Lady.* But for me the standard ballads of others could inspire him more, and the medley on *"My Favorite Quintet"* that includes *She's Funny That Way,*

Embraceable You (a duet with Charles McPherson), *I Can't Get Started* (including a duet with trumpeter Lonnie Hillyer), and *Ghost of a Chance*—these seem imperishable Mingus.

For the crucial quality of Mingus's bass, however, we must return to his own works, for there it is the encouraging presence of Mingus the ensemble musician as well as the soloist who can be heard—on *Cryin' Blues* and on the original *Haitian Fight Song* especially.

And as good as is his work with McPherson and Hillyer, the duet and solo work with Eric Dolphy on *Stormy Weather* makes it a masterpiece recording: a superb bass line (probably one should call it true counterpoint rather than polyphony) and bass solo, juxtaposed with Dolphy's harmonically careful but highly adventurous improvisation.

Haitian Fight Song and *Stormy Weather* seem to me definitive Mingus. In these recordings, Mingus the dazzling, spontaneous presence is contained by the kind of steadiness and durability that only artistic excellence can account for. And with such a bequest to music, Charles Mingus the turbulent, the demanding, the mercurial may rest assured, his contributions secure.

20

JOHN COLTRANE

A Man in the Middle

John Coltrane had his followers, imitators, and popularizers from the time that he was first a member of Miles Davis's quintet in 1955. There were musicians who show the effect of his playing at almost every stage of his career, and that fact reminds us that he was an important jazzman. It also reminds us of how much his playing changed during his lifetime. Or perhaps one should say, how often it changed, because on the surface at least, some of the changes seemed to come abruptly, almost as though some phases of Coltrane's career were not evolutionary exactly, but deliberate.

When he first attracted attention with Miles Davis, Coltrane was sometimes spoken of as another "hard" tenor player—hard as opposed to cool—but even then Coltrane's sound was personal, and it was hard almost to the point of brittleness.

Otherwise, Coltrane was a vertical player, a kind of latter-day Coleman Hawkins. And that means that he moved somewhat counter to the direction that jazz saxophone had been following since the mid-'forties. Dexter Gordon was the leading player of a generation of tenor men who, receiving guidance from Charlie Parker, had made a synthesis of the styles of Coleman Hawkins and Lester Young. They liked Hawkins's big sound, but Young's limited vibrato; they liked Hawkins's harmonic sophistication and exactness, but they preferred Young's linear melodies to Hawkins's arpeggios;

and they favored Young's variety of rhythm and phrase-
length over Hawkins's four-bar, heavy/light/heavy/light
regularity.

However, Coltrane owes more to the Hawkins heritage
and to a brilliant Hawkins follower like Don Byas, than to
Lester Young or any of Young's followers, or to Dexter Gordon or any of *his* followers first or second-hand.[1] And I think
that in Coltrane's early work his rhythmic conception was
a personal adaptation of Byas's, with its heavy accents on the
first and third beats and frequent flurry of notes on the weak
second and fourth beats. If one doubts this, I think he can
find it confirmed in the playing of Coltrane's one-time associate, Benny Golson, for Golson will sometimes slip from a
very much Byas-inspired style into a Coltrane idiom, and
the transition seems logical.

Coltrane's 1955–56 solos with Miles Davis are largely exploratory. He seemed more interested in discovery than in
making finished statements, as though for the time being he
were occupied with turning up a vocabulary with which future sentences, paragraphs, and essays might be built.

There is another aspect of his recorded style, particularly
at this period, which might confirm the view that his approach was tentative. It is a tendency for Coltrane's terminal
phrases to end with an apparent fumble of notes, or to
diminish into a kind of mutter or hesitantly delivered cliché.
Perhaps the exploratory Coltrane swallowed his endings because he found himself suddenly up against a banality which
he saw no way of avoiding, but which he did not really want
to pronounce.

Even Coltrane's most provocative solo from this period,
on the Davis version of Thelonious Monk's *'Round Mid-*

1. Noncommercial tape recordings from Coltrane's younger days exist that
indicate he did go through a brief Gordon period himself.

night (Columbia version), perhaps has a hesitant note here and there, but it was prophetic of the next step in his career. In mid-1957 Coltrane became a member of Monk's quartet. I don't suppose the importance of that event to Coltrane's development could be underestimated, although the importance of the group itself has been assessed here in the chapter on Monk. Coltrane's work remained exploratory, expanding his approach along the lines his previous work had indicated. But with Monk's music (as the truism has it) one has to know the melodies and their harmonies, and understand how they fit together in order to improvise well, and Coltrane understood this. Thus, a solo like Coltrane's on *Trinkle Tinkle,* for all its bursting virtuosity, which runs into elusive corners of Monk's piece and proceeds to build its own structures, is constantly orderly and keeps us constantly oriented because of the nature of Monk's piece and Coltrane's understanding of it.

Leaving Monk, Coltrane rejoined Miles Davis, and his solo with the trumpeter on the Monk blues in F, *Straight No Chaser,* is a powerful and arrestingly full statement of where Coltrane *was* at the time. But several of the harmonically architectonic solos on the Coltrane LP *"Blue Train"* also give indication of where he might be headed and of some of the problems he would encounter.

The title blues, *Blue Train,* has a prophetically eerie and mysterious statement from the leader. The faster *Locomotion* (a 12/12/8/12 blues) gives an exposition of Coltrane's unique melodic-rhythm at perhaps its fullest development. The harmonic étude, *Moment's Notice,* has a rather undistinguished theme but it sets up a series of challenging chord changes for the soloist.

The post-Monk Coltrane, then, was a prodigious saxophonist and a prodigious harmonicist. He had also extended the range of his instrument, the textures of sound he was able to evoke from it, and the human quality of his saxophone voice.

Coltrane could superimpose a complex of passing chords, substitute chords, and harmonic extensions upon a harmonic structure that was perhaps already complex. And at times he seemed prepared to gush out every possible note, find his way step-by-step through every complex chord, careen through every scale, and go even beyond that prolixity by groping for impossible notes and sounds on a tenor saxophone that seemed ready to shatter under the strain.

There were times, also, in the performances with Monk and those with Davis that immediately followed them, when it seemed that, in an effort to get it all in, Coltrane was reaching for a kind of subdivided bop rhythm, into a six-teenth-note accent pattern. Such a thing had to be tried, and was even predictable, but to say so is not to belittle Coltrane for having undertaken the task—particularly not if I am correct that Coltrane's basic rhythmic concept came from Hawkins and Byas, who, in contrast to Armstrong, were almost "European" in their use of heavy and light accents within a 4/4 time context. Such a subdivided rhythm would obviously create problems in both melody and swing—it is difficult to improvise melodically and to swing (at least to swing in the traditional sense) when one is thinking rhythmically in such a rapidity of notes. But Coltrane avoided a direct confrontation with such problems to concentrate on his saxophone sound and technique, and on harmonies.

From one point of view, the post-Monk Coltrane had pushed jazz harmonies as far as they could go. From another, such complex, sophisticated knowledge set its own trap, and Coltrane, still a vertical thinker, careened around like a laboratory hamster trapped in a three-dimensional harmonic maze of his own making. ("You don't have to play *every-thing!*" Miles Davis is reported to have said to him.)

To this Coltrane, a Miles Davis piece like *Milestones,* or pieces like *So What, All Blues,* and some of the others on the Davis recital *"Kind of Blue"* must have come as revelations. Here were "modal" pieces, with harmonic challenges cut to a minimum, and with the soloist allowed to invent on a single chord or scale for sixteen measures, or even for as long as he liked. Coltrane sounded a bit hesitant on *Milestones,* but he met the challenges of *So What* and *All Blues* like a man who saw—or thought he saw—an exit from the maze.

"Kind of Blue" seems to me key evidence of one of the most remarkable events in Western music in this century. Why should a comparable modality suddenly appear—coincidentally and almost simultaneously—in the music of Ornette Coleman, of Miles Davis and John Coltrane, of the Detroit rock and roll groups, of the British rock groups, of the American "folk" ensembles, and even crop up in the music of the more traditional Chicago-based blues bands? In any case, Ornette Coleman is a horizontal melodist of exceptional rhythmic freedom, and his use of modality and microtones is rather different from Coltrane's use of scalar or pedal-point modality. That was true in the beginning (as I think is demonstrated by Coltrane's 1960 versions of some of Coleman's pieces on the LP *"The Avant Garde"*), and it remained true.

Coltrane's first LP as a leader that followed on *"Kind of Blue"* did not immediately build on it. *Giant Steps,* the title piece, echoes *Moment's Notice* in setting up a difficult and ingenious series of chords for the soloist to run through. *Naima* attempts a kind of compromise by suspending a series of sophisticated changes over an *e* flat pedal tone, with a *b* flat in the bridge, and allowing the soloist to take either course. Coltrane's solo on *Countdown,* in which he several times employs a complex double-motive, has been praised for its form. But I think the solo raises fundamental questions about when the reiteration of a motive is a means to order, and when it is a matter of repetitiousness.

At this point in his career Coltrane encountered *My Favorite Things,* and that piece could serve his purposes in almost the same way that *How High the Moon* had served Parker's and Gillespie's. Here was a popular song that had, built-in so to speak, the same sort of things that he had been working on: very little chordal motion, folk-like simplicity, a quasi-Eastern mystery, and incantation. Simple but at the same time sophisticated, the piece could contain Coltrane's prodigiousness as an improviser. In no sense was *My Favorite Things* a compromise—and it should not be a surprise that his first recording of it was a best seller.

As he pursued modality, however, evenings with Coltrane, a vertical player working with minimal harmonic understructures, began to sound to some listeners like long vamps-til-ready, or furious, unattached cadenzas, or lengthy *montunas* introducing rhumbas or *sons* that never got played. As one wag put it at the time, "I went to hear Coltrane last night. He played forty-five minutes of C-minor ninths." And forty-five minutes on C-minor ninth chords, it became increasingly clear, could not lead to musical freedom. Nor could the ultimate absorption of all the material in Nicolas Slonimsky's scale books.

I know that Coltrane's audiences were usually enthralled. I know the sincerity, the powerful and authentic emotion, and the frequent skill involved; I am aware of the truly astonishing contribution of Coltrane's drummer Elvin Jones to his music, and of the innovative importance of his work; and yet—to be entirely subjective about Coltrane's music at this period—I was, and am, repeatedly disengaged. After three or four minutes my attention wanders, and giving the records try after try does not seem to help.

Two extended performances from 1961 represent the turning point, *Impressions* and *Chasin' the Trane*. On each, his improvising had become more horizontal, more linear than previously. *Impressions* uses an opening Debussy-esque melody to revisit, two years later, the same modes and the song form structure that Miles Davis used on *So What*. Before the performance is over, Coltrane is reiterating a little half-scale figure.

Virtually the same figure dominates a portion of *Chasin' the Trane*. *Chasin' the Trane* is the key Coltrane performance from this period and has become a highly influential one among younger musicians. Coltrane's use of reiterated phrases on these pieces seems to me neither sequential nor organizational nor truly developmental. (And in this, he is in direct contrast to Ornette Coleman.) Coltrane's use of such motives seems deliberately repetitive and incantatory. And one man's incantation is another man's monotony. With Elvin Jones laying down a rich and complex pattern beneath him, Coltrane's sing-song lines sound thin, and his occasional saxophone cries and shrieks seem protestations against that very thinness.

I may hear this Coltrane wrongly, but if I do perhaps I can at least put questions to those who hear him better, questions that they may find worth answering. And perhaps the key question is whether so able and knowledgeable a vertical player could still walk upright when setting himself so decidedly horizontal a task.

The Coltrane that I better admire from this period is the deliberately conservative Coltrane. The Coltrane who stated Duke Ellington's *In a Sentimental Mood* so perceptively yet personally and without overembellishment. (Yet with *Take the Coltrane,* on the same LP, we are back with *Chasin' the Trane.*) And there is a similarly conservative Coltrane on the LP called *"Crescent."* There for the moment at least he seemed to have profited by the years of complex harmony and by the years of modality, to return like a hero from a perilous but necessary journey, ready to share the fruits of his experience. Harsh dangers and exotic beauties are related on the title piece, *Crescent,* and the once "impossible" saxophone sounds seem natural and firmly established techniques. Reflections and evaluations of the journey take place on *The Wise One.* And *Bessie's Blues* might be called a joyful celebration of the new insight the hero had provided. Perhaps it was also an element of comparative calm and of reflection that made Coltrane's *"A Love Supreme"* a best seller.

On the other hand, *Ascension* is probably Coltrane's most daring recording. It is a thirty-eight minute performance on which the leader's regular quartet was augmented by two trumpeters, two tenor saxophonists, two altos, and an extra bassist. There is a single, slight thematic idea; there are several turbulent, loose, improvised ensembles; and there are solos by most of the participants. The performance soars and it sings. And it rages, blares, shouts, screams, and shrieks. It is at the same time a contemporary jazz performance and a communal rite.

Ascension is directly indebted to Ornette Coleman's *Free Jazz,* and that fact inevitably invites comparison between the two. For me Coleman's work invokes the contemporary demons as unflinchingly as Coltrane's, but is a thing of beauty and affirmation and hope. *Free Jazz,* to use James Joyce's superb phrase, better sees the darkness shining in the light.

The later *Meditations* was offered as an "extension" of *A Love Supreme.* I would say that it undertakes to lead us through the torments of *Ascension* and into the world of

A Love Supreme, and that the effort is honorable and commendable. The piece seems to state the dichotomy and the
dilemma; it parallels the two moods. But it does not truly
bring them together in resolution. And the final section,
"Serenity," seems both unconvincing and arbitrarily arrived
at—and, perhaps not incidentally, the piano solo that introduces it is a bit pretentious and dubious as jazz.

Thus, some of Coltrane's work from the 'sixties seems brilliant, and some of it repetitious and banal. And there are
times when Coltrane's authentically wild passion seems not
so much a part of the music as a part of the musician, the
reaction of a player who is improvising with a minimum of
built-in protections but who sometimes cries out in frustration against the very limitations that he has set for himself,
limitations that once seemed so necessary. Sometimes my
impression is of having heard musical statements that have
brilliant moments but that become static and remain unresolved, statements that are contained only by a fantastic and
original saxophone technique on one hand, or by a state of
emotional exhaustion on the other. And it is perhaps indicative that several of his later records were faded out by the
engineers rather than ended by the musicians.

I began by saying something about the ways that Coltrane's music changed. And there have been several musics—
Oriental and African, as well as American—that interested
him and directly influenced him during his last twelve years.
The changes in his work may, of course, have been signs of
growth, and if they were, few important jazz improvisers
have grown and developed as much as Coltrane did in so
short a time. But, on the other hand, the changes may have
been naïve. Or they may have been signs of personal indecision or frustration.

Does one, then, with Coltrane take his choice between the
alternatives of a true artistic growth or of mere change? Per-

haps not, or not necessarily. Perhaps a deeper frustration and tormented indecision are part of the unacknowledged truth of the temper of the times which it was Coltrane's destiny simply to articulate rather than interpret. If so, he was a player of primary rank.

I do not intend the foregoing to indicate that I do not consider Coltrane a true artist. I think he was, and I think that like all true artists he spoke of matters of the spirit, not of society and politics. I also think he knew that he did. Indeed, the deeper purpose of the incantatory sections in his music has to be—as with any incantation—to evoke the gods and the demons whose ways are timeless and yet always contemporary. Perhaps, if his music does not quite reach me and satisfy me as it has reached some others, the answer is that the gods he sought to invoke are not my gods.

In any case, Coltrane was bold enough to state his message so that the future must acknowledge that he has been with us.

21

ORNETTE COLEMAN

Innovation from the Source

An American artist will find his own ways of expression, and no one would claim that for him an increase in conventional techniques necessarily has anything to do with an increase in expressiveness. As our comic strip artists become better draftsmen, they may produce more soap opera; as our sound films become more technically resourceful, they may, more important, talk more, say less, and show less.

Jazz, on the other hand, seems to thrive on acquiring new techniques and on periodic change, and, with each legitimate change, to expand its scope and retain its creative life. Change in jazz has involved losses, but so far they have been the inevitable losses of an organic growth—they have been sure signs of life. In describing such changes, one must use the terms he has to describe what he hears—or go to the trouble of inventing and explaining new ones.

It is not enough to say that Ornette Coleman's music will affect jazz profoundly, for it already has so affected it, and not only the jazz of younger men but that of some of his elders as well. His music represents the first fundamental reevaluation of basic materials and basic procedures for jazz since the innovations of Charlie Parker. "Let's play the music and not the background," Coleman has said. And when someone does something with the passion and deep conviction of an Ornette Coleman, I doubt if there could be any turning back; it seems mandatory somehow for others some-how to respond to his work.

In any case, it is surely no longer required, when Coleman writes a fourteen-bar blues, that one remark that he did it deliberately. Or, when, in improvising, he fails to treat a theme as though it automatically set up a series of pre-deter-mined chord changes or a rigid outline of four and eight-bar phrases that must be followed, it is surely no longer required to explain that he does so purposefully and not out of igno-rance. "If I'm going to follow a preset chord sequence, I may as well write out my solo."

Ornette Coleman's first recordings do not so much outline his own music as they juxtapose some of his own ideas with those of his predecessors. The themes are his own. Like all his pieces they are functional vehicles to introduce his improvis-ing—and good, appropriate, sometimes excellent, composed melody seems to flow out of him. But these early vehicles still have the rhythms and forms of bebop clinging to them, and some of them use popular song sequences recognizably: *Jayne* echoes *Out of Nowhere,* and *Angel Voice* is Ornette's *I Got Rhythm.* (It is interesting that the latter seemed to appeal to him as a rhythmic pattern rather than as an har-monic one.) *The Sphinx* and *Chippie,* however, indicate a desire to change the four, eight, and thirty-two bar phrase boxes of song form.

The quest to achieve his own music is clearly stated in his first entrance on the opening bridge to *Invisible,* where Parker-esque accents vie with a loose and highly vocalized phrasing of his own.[1] Throughout the LP, it is clear that Coleman does not want to run chord changes to make his melodies, although he does keep to the phrases of the pieces.

1. I have heard Coleman play an uncannily exact reproduction of Parker's style, by the way, and others attest to having heard him do the same for previ-ous alto styles.

His effort to get his horn to "speak" is also everywhere evident. And it's interesting that his playing is at its most "free" and most personal on a blues (a somewhat tonally ambiguous blues) *The Disguise.*

Coleman's second LP, *"Tomorrow Is the Question"*[2] is a step forward. First, and perhaps most obvious, the chordally anchoring piano has been eliminated, never to return. Coleman's themes and improvisations are freer of bebop accents, and more original rhythmically.

On *Lorraine,* particularly, Coleman's phrasing and melodic rhythm are his own. The piece is the first of a series of exceptional dirges that includes *Lonely Woman* and *Sadness,* and *Lorraine* effectively uses a contrasting fast section both in the writing and the improvising. On the blues with the inspired title *Tears Inside,* Coleman's personally intoned solo is initially unsettling and ultimately self-justifying.

Thus he was becoming an original, interesting, intense, and orderly improviser, if not quite yet a brilliant one.

"The Shape of Jazz To Come," recorded in 1959, is a pivotal record in Coleman's development and in the evolution of the new jazz, and it clarified much about the music.

In the first place, it reassesses the theme-and-variations form for jazz—indeed it ultimately rejects the form, and with good reason. For a theme-and-variations approach the theme is primary and the variations secondary. But in jazz, the improvised variations are often the substance of the music, and variation and interpretation, at least in the form of embellishment and paraphrase, may extend even to an opening theme-statement itself.

In this music, a theme may be freely interpreted even by two horns in an opening and closing "unison" passage. It is

2. I do not like the deliberately futuristic titles of several of his LPs and pieces, and whether they proved to be accurate or not, I expect that at the time they were a tactical error.

obviously difficult to do such a thing without sounding amateurish, but Coleman and Don Cherry do it extremely well.

Further, an opening theme may set a mood, fragments of
melody, an area of pitch, or rhythmic patterns, as points of
departure for the player to explore. It need not set up patterns of chords or patterns of phrasing. Or if it does, these
may be expanded, condensed, used freely—it does not necessarily take eight measures to explore an idea that it took
eight measures to state, and an improvisation initially built
on a melody itself need not also follow a harmonic outline
that melody might suggest. (One remembers Charlie Parker's remark that "You can do *anything* with chords.") Nor
would tempo in improvising have to be constant, but whereas
Coleman (like Monk before him) had at this time used dual-
tempos in his pieces, the question of tempo had to wait for
further development, as we shall see.

But the question of accents and phrasing did not have to
wait, and Coleman's melodic rhythm is freer, more varied,
and more original—without on the surface being necessarily
more "complex." "Rhythmic patterns should be as natural
as breathing patterns," he has commented. And if the past is
a standard, an original development in rhythm is the surest
key to valid innovation in jazz.

Many of Coleman's individual melodic rhythms, and the
responses they inspire in his bass players and drummers, are
quite old-style and simple. But he uses them as parts of a free,
varied, and developing pattern. He does not offer a further
subdivision of the beat, as Armstrong, Lester Young, and
Parker had done, but a greater variety and freedom in rhythm
and phrase. It should go without saying that a free and original use of meters and accents is quite a different matter from
setting up a tricky or difficult time-signature and then (as
happens more often than not in such "experiments") skating
over it with bop phrasing, after making a slight initial adjust-

ment. Melodic rhythm and polyrhythmic juxtapositions are essentials in jazz. And time-signatures, on paper or in performance, are sometimes a fiction or a convenience.

Intonation is a matter of context and expression to Coleman. "You can play sharp in tune and you can play flat in tune," he has said, and a D in a context representing sadness should not sound like a D in a passage of joy. (A modern classicist would say that Coleman uses "microtones.") This is not a matter of "good" intonation, and if there were any doubt about that, there are enough key notes and phrases in Coleman's solos on exact pitch to dispel that doubt. Further, split-tones, harmonics, tense upper register cries, and gutteral low register sounds may be used expressively—not entirely new ideas but techniques which Coleman has developed with taste.

Coleman's improvising is predominantly modal, even diatonic, but under the inspiration of the moment he may move out of key, hence into a momentary atonality. Furthermore, since a chord pattern is not preset to a soloist, or at least may be freely departed from, there is a texture of atonality set up by the juxtaposition of the alto's lines and those of the bass which moves in a kind of interplaying, melodic and dissonant counterpoint rather than accompaniment. There are of course momentary, *passing*, intervalic "clashes" of tones between players in traditional contexts too, between a pianist and his bass player, and among the horns in a New Orleans ensemble. Further, Ornette tends to suspend his lines to leave them airborne, without making customary cadences and tonic resolutions. And he has also functioned with ease in a context of complete "classical" atonality, as his remarkably perceptive improvising in Gunther Schuller's twelve-tone *Abstraction* demonstrates.

Analogies between Coleman's music and procedures in other musics, particularly East Indian music, are obvious.

But I think a better understanding comes when we reflect on how much of what he does is implicit in Coleman's own sources. One thinks of the many "primitive" bluesmen (Clarence Lofton, or vocally, Sonny Terry) to whom the blues is a flexible, not a rigidly twelve-measure form— whether out of ignorance or inspiration may not matter. In the free-handed use of chord changes, one thinks of Lester Young. In the matter of expressive intonation, Coleman has made blue notes and vocally inflected tones into first principles that encompass whole melodies. One thinks also of Charlie Parker's tendency to play slightly sharp. Indeed, one hears all the reed players in jazz history differently for having heard Coleman.

Certainly, Coleman did not contrive any of his procedures, nor force them on the music academically out of a conscious effort to "improve" it. His artistic daemon tells him to do these things. And the procedures show a penetrating, intuitive understanding of the nature of the music and its implications. "It was when I found out I could make mistakes that I knew I was onto something."

Several players preceded Coleman more immediately in undertaking something of the same kind of spontaneity one hears in his music, and to mention some of them is undoubtedly to neglect others. But one thinks of Lennie Tristano's efforts at an unpremeditated group music. One thinks of Charlie Mingus's similar efforts and of his "extended form" in which a soloist may spontaneously extend a piece by turning any of its chords into a pedal-tone for as long as he wishes to explore it—a procedure in which the rhythm section is to follow the soloist. And one thinks of Cecil Taylor's music, particularly in the way that Taylor's piano and his bassists' accompaniments moved in a-harmonic directions. But to mention such efforts is not to raise the question of their "influence" on Coleman, and indeed several of those efforts were largely isolated. It is only to give further evidence that the procedures in his music are not so radical as they may seem, and were probably inevitable.

No one enjoys such theoretical discussion before going to the music, of course, but I can hope that it serves its purpose. In any case, *"The Shape of Jazz To Come"* is a remarkable record in many respects.

Peace is a beautifully conceived piece, and Coleman's improvisation is remarkable for its natural swing. Compositionally it has an opening section of twenty-five measures, a bridge of ten, a return to the opening twenty-five measures, and a closing coda of five. Of course, jazz musicians have been working on the idea of a modification of song form and its measured phrasing at least since Ellington in 1929. But I think Coleman's efforts have a rather different and somewhat more natural quality than some of the others. He does not "break through" or "extend" existing forms so much as he lets each piece take its own form as its own inspiration dictates, with earlier forms as a general source in the background.

Focus on Sanity is an interesting "extended" work. Its two sections, with their separate tempos, do not really make it a "suite," and each ensemble portion truly sets up the impetus for the soloist.

Lonely Woman is remarkable both in plan and in execution, and a strong experience. It opens with bass and drums, each playing a separate but related rhythm, which they continue throughout. The horns enter, unexpectedly, in a third, dirge tempo, and, freely intoned, they interpret the stark theme, with momentary break-aways by the alto. Coleman's solo is in perfect time and tempo, of course, but the freely accented individual phrases and an adroit use of implied double-time give an immeasurable complexity and richness to the performance. "He is the first jazz musician since King

Oliver," a friend has said, "whose playing does not seem
egocentric to me."

I think that the responsive textural richness of the drums
in this piece make one long for more complex, improvised
polyrhythmic textures on other performances here, although
Billy Higgins is an exceptional drummer of exceptional
swing. (It is interesting that from Higgins to Ed Blackwell,
to Charles Moffett, and the single "guest" appearance by
Elvin Jones, Coleman's drummers have played with an increasing variety of textures. But Coleman has not, as I
write, yet found his Tony Williams.)

Congeniality has a much-admired Coleman solo, including
the marvelous "mistake" between bars 127 and 142 in which
Coleman enters "early" and turns the beat around, but
produces a momentary confusion in the rhythm section. He
therefore stretches out a bar to accommodate them. They,
meanwhile, have turned around to him, and Coleman, hearing this, turns his beat around again.

Similarly, there is the moment at the end of *Chronology*
when Coleman is ready for the closing "head" but Don
Cherry does not respond, so the saxophonist uses a few bars
to give him a gutteral saxophone yell and call him in.

Such things are perhaps not "errors" so much as they are
natural parts of a freely improvised music, and they can be
heard on quite another level than a technical one. They are
also complements to the otherwise almost telepathic understanding between Cherry and Coleman on matters of tempo
and length of solo statement, and the responsive inspiration
that Coleman and bassist Charlie Haden provide for each
other.

One central impression that emerged from this recital was
that Ornette Coleman, an obviously impassioned and inventive player, working in a fresh and "free" and even frag-

mented idiom of his own, is also a logical melodist. His music does not invite an a-harmonic chaos, but is decidedly orderly, and orderly along quite traditional lines.

An idea appears, inspired perhaps by the meaning of the theme or by a single note or accent. It is phrased, and re-phrased, offered from every conceivable angle, developed sequentially until it yields another idea. Or it appears and reappears periodically in various guises within an otherwise contrasting context as a kind of point of reference. Patterns of tension and release are thus set up by the introduction and ultimate development of brief motives, or by their appearance and reappearance. Ornette Coleman has extended fundamental principles of orderly jazz improvisation that have been around at least since King Oliver. And it seems to me, that he took these matters up just where Thelonious Monk left them with his *Bags' Groove* solo.

If such continuity does not immediately occur to a listener from a performance like *Congeniality,* he might try one of Coleman's few solos on a piece by another man, Gunther Schuller's *Variants on a Theme by Thelonious Monk,* from Monk's *Criss Cross.* Coleman's entrance virtually dictates to the rhythm section the quality of the beat he wants. Melodically, he is clearly interested in Monk's theme and the ideas it suggests to him as his point of departure.

I have said above that a modality comparable to Coleman's had appeared almost simultaneously and apparently independently in the work of other jazzmen. This, plus the fact that Coleman unquestionably influenced him later, invites a comparison between Coleman and John Coltrane. Coleman's use of key motives is developmental and sequential. Coltrane's seemed to me repetitious and incantatory. Further, it seems to me that his modality *cum* atonality released Coleman melodically and rhythmically. But Coltrane undertook "drone" modality out of a desire to cut back and limit a sizable harmonically oriented technique.

Coleman's best statements seem to me complete. He may avoid conventional resolutions, but his solos are entities because of their rhythmic and motivic continuity and development. And one is much less aware of the drone in his playing, I think, than in that of other modal improvisers.

Coleman's *"Change of the Century"* was recorded at about the same time as *"The Shape of Jazz To Come,"* and, if it does not expand on any of that album's ideas, it still has some good music. *Ramblin',* for example, is a sort of light, blues impression of a Southwestern hoe-down. And *Free* has Ornette using some striking accents in his opening solo and an interesting moment when the fast tempo stops and then resumes with the exchange of soloists.

On *Beauty Is a Rare Thing,* from mid-1960, we hear a collective improvisation by all four members of the quartet. That idea led to the remarkably conceived and remarkably influential *Free Jazz* (1960), a flawed but brilliant work. A double quartet—two trumpets, two reeds, two basses, and two drummers—in a collective improvisation that lasted thirty-six minutes plus. There are solos, or rather there are exchanges of a lead voice with comments, encouragements, and countermelodies from the other players as they feel inspired. And there are written themes that introduce each section—these, plus the order of solos being the only premeditated aspects of the performance in the turbulent, purposeful, harrowing, and joyous textures. Here is a realization of the polyphonic possibilities that were implicit in Coleman's music since its beginnings.

There is effective contrast between the more traditional phrasing of Freddy Hubbard's trumpet and Eric Dolphy's bass clarinet, and the accents of Cherry and Coleman. On bass, Scott La Faro's virtuosity and Charlie Haden's almost lyric directness work beautifully together—indeed, the sections by the bassists and drummers (Billy Higgins and Ed Blackwell) are extraordinary. Coleman's section, which is roughly twice as long as the others, is both inspired and inspiring to the ensemble, although one wishes that the shuffle beat that gets set up behind him might have been tempered. Jazz is a music full of the stuff of life, and *Free Jazz* has the stuff of life in it as no other recorded performance I know of.

C. & D., from 1961, returns Coleman to a quartet, here with La Faro and Blackwell. Its theme has been praised for its melodic logic; its originality is equally evident. Similarly, Ornette's solo is almost traditional in its materials but not in his use of them.

R.P.D.D., from the same session, has a much praised solo. It benefits, I think, from the richly textured virtuosity of La Faro's bass, which is less sympathetically complementary than Haden's, but in its way no less inspiring to Coleman.

One thing that was eminently clear at this point was Coleman's mastery of the alto saxophone. But when he chose to make a subsequent recording on tenor sax (the instrument he had played for several years in rhythm and blues bands), he sounded entirely comfortable on that instrument. *Cross Breeding* has an admired tenor solo, and on *Mapa* he returned to the proposition of simultaneous improvising by the members of the quartet in a performance that moves back and forth from almost antiphonal textures to polyphony.

The trio recordings Coleman made in 1965 in Sweden show a striking renewal in his music. I do not admire his violin or trumpet playing as such, but on *Snowflakes and Sunshine* they are functionally effective parts of a singular, and even sophisticated, musical performance, to which David Izensohon's bass also makes an important contribution.

Dawn, truly an ensemble creation, is a beautiful piece, full of fear, expectation, and splendid, shining beauty.

The Riddle is a wonder: an extension of the traditional idea of double-timing perhaps, a radical attack on the idea of fixed tempo, and a real contribution to the jazz language. Under the inspiration of the moment, the soloist and group collectively and almost telepathically move in and out of several tempos with such ease, naturalness, and musical logic that one may barely notice what is happening, or recognize its significance.

Also on *Antiques* from the Swedish performances, a deliberately meandering, fragmented piece, there are casual changes of tempo. But the idea gets a further development on Coleman's later *Garden of Souls,* where tempo changes are, again, clearly an integral part of a musical development. But on *Broadway Blues* (built on the reevaluation of an old riff), the tempo changes seem to be extensions of the retards built into the theme itself. *Round Trip* takes up the idea of polyphony again, but I think the most significant work in that idiom since *Free Jazz* is a piece called *Trouble in the East* from a 1969 concert.

Trouble in the East, played by Cherry, Coleman, Dewey Redman on tenor saxophone, Charlie Haden on bass, and Coleman's son, Denardo, on drums, is unlike any other collective improvisation ever undertaken in this idiom or any other idiom. It seems spontaneously ordered in all its aspects, due it would seem (I am guessing at this) to the assignment of certain recurring motives to be freely used, particularly by Redman.[3] I wrote of its first performance that it "had the timeless joy and melancholy of the blues running through it. It had its feet planted on the earth and it spoke to the

3. On the LP of this concert, however, Redman is lamentably underrecorded.

gods. It was one of the most exciting, beautiful, and satisfying musical performances I have ever heard."

I have said little in the foregoing about the development
of Don Cherry, who began as an adroit "modernist" on
Coleman's first LP in whom one hears a synthesis of the work
of so many trumpeters of the 'forties and 'fifties. But I will
here mention his piece *Complete Communion,* for it seems
to me the most interesting effort at an extended work in the
new jazz. Cherry has used counterpoint, both written and
improvised; he has used both his bass and drums as melodic
voices; Cherry's themes and improvised sections change
tempo and flow one to the next; little ideas and riffs from
each section echo through the rest of it. The solos are frequent, usually brief, and although I think a couple of them
do rush to their climaxes a bit too soon, both the written
passages and improvisation are related parts of a commendable overall compositional plan.

A music like Coleman's, which depends so much on reflex,
and has so few built-in protections, risks much and demands
inspired players. Coleman is inspired. And there is not in
his music the sizable element of throw-away expendability
one hears in the music of some of his younger followers,
wherein one waits through twenty minutes of effort for three
minutes of excellence.

Coleman is an orderly player, but I do feel that, particularly since about 1962, his solos and his use of recurring
motives may sometimes extend past the point of inspiration
to the point of ingenuity and, beyond it, to the point of
repetition—and I think that is true of some initially brilliant
solos. But his example means that jazzmen may improvise
with less premeditation and with fewer protections in harmony and phrase—and this is the element of his music that
has received wide acceptance among older and younger

players alike. Like all the great innovators, Coleman has brought fresh and varied ideas of phrasing and melodic rhythm to the music, and he has affirmed the idea of variations in tempo. Finally, there are his ideas of emotional pitch and of individual and group tonality.

Such things represent major insights into the nature of jazz and into its source of growth. How future musicians will use those elements and insights is of course a matter for musicians—and perhaps the genius of the music itself—to decide. Meanwhile, for Coleman they have been a means by which he has brought us an authentic and impressive body of jazz.

22

THE MEANING OF A MUSIC

An Art for the Century

The arts in our time have been perhaps unduly subjected to the quest for meaning. And that quest, often when it is called "social" and sometimes even when it has been called psychological, has been basically political either in its motives or its consequences. Indeed, one suspects that some contemporaries tend to treat a political situation or system as a "given," an absolute, and not as an expression of man's psyche.

The question of meaning in so abstract an art as music is one of the most difficult and tenuous that one can undertake. And particularly so for jazz which, although it has had a direct emotional appeal to a relatively broad audience, also has standards of its own to which traditional aesthetic categories in music (or in the music of the Western world)—such as those categories are—should be applied only with the greatest care.

Jazz is a music evolved by black men in the United States. It has been in general best played by American black men, and its development has been dependent on their artistic leadership. But at the same time, it is a music which men of other races, and men in other countries, can play and sometimes play excellently. And it is a music which obviously has a deep meaning for extraordinary numbers of men all over the world.

My book has had little to say about that deeper meaning, that content, to which men have responded so deeply. I have saved that question for the conjectures which follow.[1]

Traditionally, there have been two approaches to the question of the content of jazz; we might call them "impressionist" and Marxist. In the first, a commentator offers his emotional response to the work at hand, describes the feeling he gets from Miles Davis or Billie Holiday or whoever. Often he is convinced that what he is describing is in Billie Holiday's singing. But inevitably, he must be describing the response he discovers in himself to her singing.

Such comments can be enlightening and valuable. We may feel they give us insight into our own responses to the music, responses which would otherwise remain vague, unformed, unconscious, unexpressed. But such descriptions tend to be self-limiting and tend to set up self-contained categories labeled "Billie Holiday" or "Miles Davis." And like descriptions in impressionist criticism of all kinds, they may tend to become substitutes for the experience of the music itself.

Marxist critics have of course taken an apparently broader view, and they find in jazz a confirmation (not to say an affirmation) of their views of society and man. To the more fundamental Marxists, jazz is musical "social protest." (When one tries to tie down such a concept, he will find precious little confirmation in the lyrics to traditional blues, incidentally, which deal far more often with the problems of courtship, personal morality, and natural forces—storms, floods—than with society.) I find Marxist interpretations unsatisfactory for it seems to me that they see the complexi-

---

1. I do not, and would not, presume to say what jazz means at its origins and in the immediate context of the lives of Negro Americans. But for a superb discourse on that meaning and its implications, I recommend Albert Murray's *Stomping the Blues* (McGraw-Hill).

ties of man and his art as merely the transient tools of "social forces." It seems to me that even most perceptive and receptive Marxists—certainly the narrow and doctrinaire ones—turn art into a reductive "nothing but" proposition, robbed of its complexities and its humanity.

Perhaps, then, we might try a somewhat different approach, one which may be based more directly on the "knowable" aspects of music, and on those ways in which jazz differs from other musics—or at any rate other Western musics.

First, jazz knows of no absolutes: there is no one "best" way of performing a piece. Each day, each moment has its way, and hence its own meaning. Tomorrow's way is not today's; today's is not yesterday's.

That does not mean that there are no standards. Yesterday's way may have been better than today's, or not as good. Tomorrow's may be better still, or less good. And I may be perfectly clear and specific about where the inferiority or superiority lies. But I accept such differences as inevitable and natural, and I take each day's way of performing for its own meaning. At the same time, my standards themselves change with my own growth and change. And I accept these changes too.

Thus, in several respects, the dimension of time is acknowledged in the nature of the music. And, again, there are no absolutes.

Philosophically, then, jazz is a twentieth-century music. Through *doing,* jazz musicians have arrived at, and have lived, a fundamental insight of contemporary philosophy.[2]

Jazz is philosophically contemporary in another sense.

2. Thus phonograph records are in a sense a contradiction of the meaning of the music. That is, they tend to make permanent and absolute music that is created for the moment, to express the meaning of the moment. On the other hand, records attest that what is made up for the moment *can* survive that moment aesthetically.

The Greeks, as José Ortega y Gasset has pointed out, made
the mistake of assuming that since man is the unique thinking animal (or so they concluded him to be), his thinking
function is his superior function. Man is at his best when
he thinks. And traditionally, Western man has accepted this
view of himself. But to a jazz musician, thought and feeling,
reflection and emotion, come together uniquely, and resolve
in the act of doing.

No music depends so much on the individual as jazz. Indeed, jazz requires not only an individual interpretation of
melody, it demands spontaneous individual invention of
new melody, individual articulation of emotion, and individual interpretation of musical sound.

No jazz player is supposed to sound like any other player.
A musician's instrumental voice should be as uniquely personal as is his speaking voice, but obviously its quality must
be more a matter of deliberate, conscious development than
that of his speaking voice. One could probably tell the history of jazz in terms of the way in which this concept of
individual sound has been developed, modified, and en-
larged over the years.

But at the same time that jazz depends on the individual,
it also depends on group co-operation. In all its styles, jazz
involves some degree of collective ensemble improvisation,
and in this it differs from Western music even at those times
in its history when improvisation was required. The high
degree of individuality, together with the mutual respect
and co-operation required in a jazz ensemble carry with
them philosophical implications that are so exciting and
far-reaching that one almost hesitates to contemplate them.
It is as if jazz were saying to us that not only is far greater
individuality possible to man than he has so far allowed
himself, but that such individuality, far from being a threat

to a co-operative social structure, can actually enhance society.

Art does not reflect society and environment and consciousness so much as it tells us what environment and society and consciousness do not know. It compensates for conscious attitudes; it reveals to us that there are other, perhaps opposite, but still tenable ways of looking at things, of feeling about things. Art tells us what we do not know or do not realize. And it prepares the way for change. If it is superior art, it may also resolve at a deeper level the conscious and unconscious attitudes through paradox.[3]

In the 1930s, in the midst of the Great Depression, when no people were harder hit than American black men, the Count Basie orchestra played with a surging, joyous momentum and a new rhythmic flexibility. Such qualities not only characterized the Basie orchestra itself, they fundamentally and permanently affected the most basic jazz idiom—the twelve-bar blues. Such musical-aesthetic facts (and one might cite many more of them) involve, it seems to me, a strong criticism of narrowly Marxist or "social" interpretations of the art.

Now it is true that many listeners hear only the "happy" side of Basie's music—or Fats Waller's or Louis Armstrong's music—and they interpret jazz only in such terms. They miss the paradoxical melancholy and pain in Basie's music. They hear the joy in King Oliver but miss his anguish— or at least their consciousness misses it. And this may be particularly true of white listeners.

3. In passing, I might add that I think that many native American arts and artists have functioned best with a mask, a valid artistic persona, of light-heartedness. And whoever receives that light-heartedness as mere lightness or superficiality will probably not understand our artists, nor appreciate the size and depth of the comments on the human condition which the best of them have made.

The joy in the music is of course not a simple, facile effort to cheer oneself up in the face of hard times—a sort of "have a drink and forget about it" attitude toward something which cannot be forgotten and needs to be faced. At the same time, the paradoxical pain and melancholy in the music are never self-indulgent, and they go deeper than any outer circumstances of poverty or rejection.

Indeed, jazz is a music of the most profound paradox, capable of balancing joy and pain, capable of being at once banal, or even grotesque, and grandiose (the essence of Armstrong's art). It can be collective, even "primitive" if you will, and yet personal and individual quite beyond standards so far acknowledged by Western man.[4]

In general, as I say, white Americans recognize the "happy" side of jazz. Historically we have scorned the music, pushed it into the most despised and unrecognized areas of our lives. In righteous, high-minded, middle-class America jazz has taken its place in the barroom, in the whorehouse, in burlesque houses, in tawdry night clubs, and on the soundtracks of crime films—areas with an inevitable and still persistent association with big-time crime. And yet, in some form it captivates us.

It would surely take a lot of research, thought, and exposition to dig deeply into the social meanings of the musics of the black American, but if one were going to undertake such a task, I think he might start with the hypothesis that, for whites at least, the music represents important aspects of our lives, but aspects that are associated with all our unresolved problems, with our unrecognized lack of self-knowl-

4. Paradox is a part of the inherently contrapuntal nature of the music, to be sure. It is obvious in the New Orleans style, in the simultaneous improvising of the horns. But even for a soloist with rhythm accompaniment there is at least a counterrhythmic juxtaposition. However, I here refer to the dual emotional nature even of a single improvising hornman.

edge, with all the truths about ourselves which we refuse to admit to or face up to—things, some of which James Baldwin wrote of so perceptively in *Notes of a Native Son*. Those things, however, are positive as well as negative in that they involve a fundamental redemption if we could acknowledge them.

Jazz, then, has to do with vital and crucial things about Americans that are not a part of the comfortably benign, self-righteous, innocent side of ourselves we like to present both to the world and to ourselves. Those unadmitted things are sometimes joyful as they are sometimes painful. They are potentially tragic, which does not mean that they are defeatist but that they may be ennobling.

I offer here a remarkable statement on the meaning of the music by one of its earliest artists, Sidney Bechet, in his autobiography, *Treat It Gentle*:

> After emancipation . . . all those people who had been slaves, they needed the music more than ever now; it was like they were trying to find out in this music what they were supposed to do with this freedom: playing the music and listening to it—waiting for it to express what they needed to learn once they had learned it wasn't just white people the music had to reach to, nor even to their own people, but straight out to life, and to what a man does with his life when it finally *is* his.

Now, if I may be allowed to interpret him a bit, it seems to me that Bechet acknowledges here that the music reaches beyond its immediate circumstances, even beyond its ethnic origins, and tells all men something about themselves which they do not know and have never heard before.

We are living in a time of the rebirth of the gods, as a contemporary psychologist has put it, that is, a rebirth of the fundamental principles and symbols by which men live

and by which the spirit of man survives.[5] And there can be
no doubt that much contemporary art has as its purpose the
breakdown of the old principles and the old symbols. But
at the same time as it destroys, some contemporary art perhaps also rebuilds, and perhaps jazz rebuilds in ways that
are unique.

Jazz not only exalts the individual finding his own way,
it also places him in a fundamental, dynamic, and necessary
co-operation with his fellows. It handles paradox—the paradox of emotion but also the paradox of thinking and doing
—in ways that perhaps no other music has. It does not deal
in absolutes, and it does not deny the relative function of
time.

Why is it the music of so many people? It was made by
American blacks, and they have provided its leadership, still
do, and I have no doubt will continue to. But as I say, all
sorts and conditions of men the world over respond to it
deeply. It is easy enough to say that the conflicts with the
outer world experienced by Negroes gave the music its birth
and have kept it alive. But I believe that if those outer conflicts were somehow resolved, the conflicts that are fundamental within each human being would then keep jazz alive
and developing, for jazz has been deeply in touch with those
fundamental conflicts all along. And it is from these inner
conflicts that comes the true impetus of art.

Jazz is the music of a people who have been told by their
circumstances that they are unworthy. And in jazz, these
people discover their own worthiness. They discover it in
terms that mankind has not experienced before. I have
deliberately borrowed a theological term in saying "unworthy." I think it is an apt one because the experience of
feeling unworthy is fundamental to the twentieth-century

5. See C. G. Jung, *The Undiscovered Self.*

man who, whether he admits it or not, is in danger of losing his old gods or has lost them already. But the music involves discovery of one's worthiness from within. And it is thus an experience that men of many races and many circumstances have responded to.

Perhaps through jazz, then, the gods, in some small way, prepare for their metamorphosis.

DISCOGRAPHICAL NOTES

What follows is my effort to list the most recently available releases (usually, if not always, domestic American releases) of the recordings mentioned in the text. Admittedly it includes some LPs that were out of print as I compiled this listing. And on a small few occasions I was dealing with records so long out of print that I have simply omitted them.

My listings may be out of date by the time this reaches print of course, but they may at least help identify which version of a given title the text discusses where more than one exists. Recordings go in and out of availability rapidly and with an apparent casualness unknown in other fields. And the rights to recordings change hands frequently as well.

I have included (and suggested) some *import* LP issues. These imports are frequently available in big city shops, although they may go unlisted in the standard monthly guide, and often at the equivalent of domestic prices. Overseas issues, particularly common market RCA and CBS, and now also Japanese issues, should always therefore be consulted.

The "private" (and outright illegal) reissue of classic recordings, and the issue of broadcast material, has become widespread in recent years, here and abroad. I have tried to avoid listing all such issues except for a few releases that were otherwise out-of-print, or where the sound quality of the tape transfers on the "private" labels seemed to me outstanding.

I will have further suggestions at the end of these listings.

2. KING OLIVER

Milestone M-47017 collected all of the King Oliver recordings made for Gennett, including *Snake Rag, Alligator Hop, Krooked Blues, Canal Street Blues, Mandy Lee Blues, Chimes Blues, Weather Bird Rag,* and *Dippermouth Blues,* and for Paramount, including the two "takes" of *Mabel's Dream* and *Southern Stomps,* and a version of *Riverside Blues.*

Smithsonian Collection album 2001 collects all of the Oliver Creole Jazz Band's Okeh and Columbia selections including the other *Snake Rag,* the Okeh *Dippermouth Blues,* the other *Riverside Blues,* the faster *Mabel's Dream,* plus *Where Did You Stay Last Night?, New Orleans Stomp, Chattanooga Stomp,* and *Jazzin' Babies Blues.* That album also offers *Morning Dove Blues.*

The Oliver Savannah Syncopators recordings ("Dixie Syncopators" on some early record labels) including *Snag It, Wa Wa Wa,* and *Deep Henderson* are collected on MCA 1309. The Oliver Victor recordings collected on Vintage LPV-529 included *You're Just My Type, Too Late,* and *New Orleans Shout.*

The "collector's" issue Herwin 106 collected all of Oliver's Gennett recordings. The distribution was understandably limited but the tape transfers of *Canal Street Blues, Mandy Lee Blues, Chimes Blues, Weatherbird Rag, Dippermouth Blues, Snake Rag, Alligator Hop,* and *Krooked Blues* and the rest were excellent.

3. JELLY ROLL MORTON

Milestone M-47018 collected Morton's early (1923–24) piano solos from Gennett, Paramount, and the smaller Chicago-based labels, including *King Porter Stomp, New Orleans Joys, Grandpa's Spells, Kansas City Stomps, Wolverine Blues, The Pearls, Frog-i-More Rag, Mamanita,* etc. The set also had *Muddy Water Blues* and *Big Fat Ham* by the septet.

The best recent source of Morton's Victor records was a series of French RCA "Black and White" issues, unfortunately not done chronologically, but the LP transfers were well done except on the first volume numbered 730.599. All but completists may want to forego Volumes 7 and 8 of the series, and perhaps Volume 6 (numbered 741-070), which, however, does have *New Orleans Bump.* Volume 2 is numbered RCA 730.605, Volume 3 is RCA 731.059, Volume 4 is RCA 741.040, and Volume 5 RCA 741.054.

Commodore AM 14942 is the best LP issue of the *"New Orleans Memories"* piano and vocal album with a fine *King Porter Stomp,* plus *The Crave, Mister Joe* (earlier *Buffalo Blues*), and a version of *Perfect Rag* titled *Sporting House Rag.*

The most recent appearances of the Morton Library of Congress recordings were on a series of Classic Jazz Masters LPs made in Sweden, and on the Testament label. The problems of speed and musical pitch (inherent in the source materials apparently) were corrected on the Swedish issues, but the transfers were otherwise not distinguished.

The "collectors" issue, Fountain FJ-104, collected nineteen of the 1923–24 piano solos in excellent transfers.

4. SIDNEY BECHET

Smithsonian Collection, two-LP set, 2026 offers Bechet's *Kansas City Man, Old Fashioned Love,* and the earlier collaborations with Louis Armstrong including both versions of *Cake Walkin' Babies.*

What a Dream and *Just One of Those Things* were on Columbia CL 836. The Bluebird set AXM2-5516 collected *Shag, Blues of Bechet, Blues in Thirds, Nobody Knows the Way I Feel This Morning, When It's Sleepy Time Down South,* and most of the other Victor recordings except, unfortunately, *What Is This Thing Called Love?* (which might still be found on a French RCA issue, however).

Summertime and *Blue Horizon* are included in Blue Note 81201/2E. And Inner City Jazz Classic 7008 collected the Bechet–Martial Solal performances, *It Don't Mean a Thing, Rose Room, The Man I Love,* and the rest.

Bechet's collaborations with Muggsy Spanier, long out of print, were issued on Atlantic 1206 and Riverside RLP 138.

5. LOUIS ARMSTRONG

King Oliver's *Dippermouth Blues* solo can be heard on Milestone M-47017 (and on the "collectors" issue Herwin 106) along with *Chimes Blues.* An alternate version of *Dippermouth* is in Smithsonian Collection 2001.

Smithsonian Collection 2026 includes the Blue Five version of *Everybody Loves My Baby.* Ma Rainey's *Countin' the Blues* was last issued on Milestone M-47021.

The Columbia Armstrong series, now over twenty-five years in print, is still basic; Volume 1, CL 851, has *Hotter Than That;* CL 852 has *Potato Head Blues, Gully Low, S. O. L. Blues, Wild-Man Blues,* and *Twelfth Street Rag;* CL 853 has *Muggles, West End Blues, Weather Bird,* and *Skip the Gutter;* CL 854 had *I Can't Give You Anything But Love* and the two takes of *Stardust.* The Columbia anthology G 30416 duplicates several of the above selections and also has *Beau Koo Jack* and *I'm a Ding Dong Daddy.*

Bluebird set AXM-2-5519 had *That's My Home, When It's Sleepy Time Down South,* the second *Basin Street Blues, I Gotta Right To Sing* the Blues, and I've Got the World on a String. The Armstrong Between the Devil and the Deep Blue Sea (take "3") was last on Columbia CSP JEE 22019. The superb Sweethearts on Parade has had several LP releases in Europe including Odeon XOC 176 or 0-83-262.

French MCA 1301, "Young Louis the Sideman," includes a Wild Man Blues, an interesting alternate version to that on Columbia.

The 'thirties were represented on Decca DL 8327 with Jeepers Creepers, I Can't Give You Anything But Love, and others. Decca DL 9233 had Jubilee, The Skeleton in the Closet, Ev'n Tide, and Lyin' to Myself.

My more recent examples (Struttin' with Some Barbecue, Basin Street, Lazy River, Georgia on My Mind, King of the Zulus) are drawn from the singularly uneven Decca set called "Satchmo, a Musical Autobiography," (French MCA 2-20006). The collection also includes a new I Can't Give You Anything But Love with an arrangement based on the 1929 version. The separate LPs of the "Autobiography" album are beginning to appear singly, and the two LPs in "The Best of Louis Armstrong" (MCA 2-4035) also use some of the "Autobiography" material.

The 1948–52 Armstrong-Hines alliance is also represented on "A Monday Date" on Decca 8284 and on other Decca sets.

6. BIX BEIDERBECKE

Milestone M-47019 collected all of the Wolverines' recordings including Jazz Me Blues, Riverboat Shuffle, Royal Garden Blues, Tiger Rag, and Big Boy.

There is a series of three Beiderbecke volumes on Columbia, the first (CL 844) by a small group under Bix's name, the second (CL 845) with Trumbauer's usually larger groups and including Singin' the Blues, Way Down Yonder in New Orleans, For No Reason at All in C, I'm Comin' Virginia, and Riverboat Shuffle. The final volume (CL 846) is largely devoted to solos with the Whitman orchestra, including Sweet Sue.

An RCA Victor set (LPM 2323) includes the rediscovered I Didn't Know, two takes of Lonely Melody, and Dardanella.

7. COLEMAN HAWKINS

As this is written, many of the Coleman Hawkins titles cited are out of print in the United States. A "Complete Coleman Hawkins" series on

French RCA should be helpful for all titles originally recorded for Victor records: *Hokus Pokus; Sweet Music; I Wanna Count Sheep; Body and Soul; Wherever There's a Will, Baby; One Hour; Hello Lola; Dinah; The Sheik of Araby.*

The other Henderson titles, *T.N.T., The Stampede, King Porter Stomp, Blazin', New King Porter Stomp,* and *Honeysuckle Rose,* are included in Smithsonian Collection 2006.

Sweet Music and *I Wanna Count Sheep,* along with *Hokus Pokus,* were in the Henderson set on Bluebird AX M25507.

Hokus Pokus was in RCA Victor's Coleman Hawkins set, *"Body and Soul: A Jazz Autobiography"* (LPV-501), which also has the first *Body and Soul, Wherever There's a Will, Baby, One Hour, Dinah,* and *The Sheik of Araby.* (Incidentally, the tenor soloist on the Lionel Hampton *Early Session Hop* included in this album is not Hawkins but Ben Webster.) An alternate take of *Hokus Pokus* was used in Victor's Red Allen album (LPV-556). *Hello Lola* was on Camden CAL 339. The European *Honeysuckle Rose* and *Crazy Rhythm* are on Prestige 7633. *It's the Talk of the Town* last appeared in the United States on Prestige 7645.

Hawkins's second version of *Body and Soul* was last on Grand Award 33-316. The Hawkins-Eldridge-Wilson *I'm in the Mood for Love* was on Emarcy 26011, which reappeared as Trip 5515E. The Hawkins-Eldridge *I Surrender Dear* (1940), on Commodore XFL 14936, is another exceptional performance from the great period.

The session which produced *The Man I Love, Sweet Lorraine,* and *Crazy Rhythm* was last available on Flying Dutchman FD 10146, *"Classic Tenors."*

My choice for relatively recent Hawkins, on the Shelly Manne LP, was on Impulse A-20.

8. BILLIE HOLIDAY

Verve VE2-2503 contains the 1956 Carnegie Hall concert, with *Yesterdays, I Cried for You, What a Little Moonlight Can Do,* and *Fine and Mellow.* The earlier *Yesterdays* is a part of Commodore XFL 14428, which also contains *I Got a Right To Sing the Blues,* the first *Fine and Mellow,* and *I Cover the Waterfront.*

Many of the early Billie Holiday and Teddy Wilson selections which I have mentioned are included in Columbia's three-LP set, C3L21: *Your Mother's Son-in-Law, Riffin' the Scotch, These Foolish Things, A Fine Romance, Easy To Love, The Way You Look Tonight, Pennies*

*from Heaven, I Can't Give You Anything But Love, Why Was I Born?,
The Mood That I'm In, I'll Never Be the Same, Without Your Love,
Swing, Brother, Swing!, They Can't Take That Away from Me, Getting
Some Fun Out of Life, Trav'lin' All Alone, When You're Smiling, If
Dreams Come True, I Can't Get Started, Back in Your Own Backyard,
On the Sentimental Side, The Very Thought of You, All of Me, I Cover
the Waterfront, The Man I Love, Body and Soul, Love Me or Leave
Me, Gloomy Sunday.*

Columbia's second omnibus volume, C3L40, offers *Painting the Town
Red, You Let Me Down, Let's Call the Whole Thing Off, Moanin' Low,
Mean to Me, I'll Get By, He's Funny That Way, I Can't Believe That
You're in Love with Me,* and *More Than You Know.* (I prefer an earlier
released take of the last piece over the one included here.)

Columbia's series of two-LP sets on *"The Lester Young Story"* has all
of the Holiday-Young collaborations, some of them with alternate
"takes," including *Me, Myself and I* and *A Sailboat in the Moonlight*
(Vol. 1 CG33502); *When You're Smiling* and *He's Funny That Way*
(Vol. 2 CG34837); and *The Man I Love* (Vol. 4 JC34843).

Lover Man is on MCA M006E. The April 1946 concert is on Verve
VE2-2503, which also offers a good cross-section of post-1952 work, including the later *These Foolish Things.*

9. ART TATUM

Tatum's 1933 *Tea for Two* and *Tiger Rag* are included in Columbia
CS-9655-E.

MCA 4019 was drawn from Tatum's 1934–40 Decca recordings and
included the 1940 *Get Happy* and the earliest *Sweet Lorraine.*

Tatum's *Mop Mop* solo, a feature of an "all-star" recording date, was
recorded for Commodore and was included in Commodore XFX14936.
My reference is to the originally released "take" of this version.

The Tatum Capitol collection with the classic treatments of *Willow
Weep for Me* and *Aunt Hager's Blues* is M-11028, and also has versions
of *Someone To Watch Over Me, Sweet Lorraine, I Gotta Right To Sing
the Blues,* and *Dancing in the Dark.*

The 1953–55 Tatum sessions, first released on Clef and Verve, were
collected in a boxed set of thirteen discs as Pablo 2625 703. In addition
to the cited *Jitterbug Waltz, Have You Met Miss Jones,* and *Tenderly,*
there are exceptional versions of *Love for Sale, Just a' Settin' and a'
Rockin', This Can't Be Love, There'll Never Be Another You, Ill Wind,
That Old Feeling, What's New, Blue Moon, Stars Fell on Alabama, I've*

Got a Crush on You, You're Blasé, Dancing in the Dark, In a Senti-mental Mood, She's Funny That Way, Sweet Lorraine, Everything I Have Is Yours, I Didn't Know What Time It Was, Tea for Two, Come Rain or Come Shine, I Only Have Eyes for You, I Gotta Right To Sing the Blues, S'posin, Someone To Watch Over Me, Out of Nowhere, Over the Rainbow, Somebody Loves Me, Wrap Your Troubles in Dreams, Isn't It Romantic, and *Caravan.* More recently, the Pablo discs have begun to appear singly and as this is written, the issues are up to record number 9.

The "discoveries" sessions with *Too Marvelous for Words* appeared on the 20th Century Fox two-record set TCF 102-2, which also included versions of *Tenderly, Someone To Watch Over Me, Yesterdays, My Heart Stood Still, In a Sentimental Mood,* and *Sweet Lorraine.* Some of these (including *Too Marvelous for Words*) were included in Movie-tone 72021.

10. DUKE ELLINGTON

Main Stem was last available in the United States on RCA Victor LPM-1364. Ellington's early *Rainy Nights, L'il Farina, Choo-Choo, I'm Gonna Hang Around My Sugar,* and *If You Can't Hold Your Man* were last issued on Riverside 12-129.

The Smithsonian Collection's Ellington series will provide in *"Duke Ellington 1938"* (2003), *The Prologue* and the *New Black and Tan Fantasy, Braggin' in Brass, A Gypsy Without a Song, Blue Light* (two takes); in *"Duke Ellington 1939"* (2010), *Subtle Lament* (two takes), *Bouncing Buoyancy, The Sergeant Was Shy;* and in *"Duke Ellington 1940"* (2015) *Jack the Bear, Ko-Ko* (two takes), *Concerto for Cootie, Cotton Tail, Never No Lament, Dusk, Harlem Air Shaft, Rumpus in Richmond, Sepia Panorama* (two takes), *In a Mellotone, Warm Valley, The Flaming Sword,* and *Across the Track Blues.* All of the above are collected in the boxed set *"Duke Ellington: An Explosion of Genius"* (Smithsonian 2018). And *"Duke Ellington 1941"* (Smithsonian 2027) offers *Take the "A" Train* (two versions), *Blue Serge* (two versions), *After All* (two versions), *The Giddy Bug Gallop, Chelsea Bridge* (two versions), *Rain Check, Moon Mist,* and a version of *Cotton Tail.*

Vintage LPV-506 included *Daybreak Express* and *Echoes of the Jungle.* And Vintage LPV-568 included 1927's *Black and Tan Fantasy, Creole Love Call, Black and Tan Fantasy,* and *Black Beauty.*

The Columbia set C3L 27 can fill in *It Don't Mean a Thing, Lightin', Bundle of Blues, Echoes of Harlem,* and the *Diminuendo and Cres-*

cendo in Blue. And Columbia C3L 39 the later *Creole Love Call, Reminiscin' in Tempo, Azure,* etc.

The fine 1950 extended version of *Mood Indigo* is on Columbia CSP JCL-825. And Columbia CSP JCS-8015 includes *Black, Brown and Beige* but the later version restricted to the piece's first movement. Prestige P-34004 includes the complete piece, indeed the premier performance recorded at Carnegie Hall, plus the rest of that evening's altogether remarkable concert of January 1943.

Columbia CSP JCL-1033 offers *"Such Sweet Thunder,"* and CSP P-14359 has *Suite Thursday.* Atlantic SD 2-304 has another performance of *Suite Thursday* from a remarkable 1963 Paris concert, which also had the *Asphalt Jungle Music.* And Columbia KG 33341 has *The Clothed Woman.* And *The Queen's Suite* is on Pablo 2310-762.

Main Stem is also included in the Complete Duke Ellington series on French RCA, which covers all of the Ellington material originally recorded for Victor records, including *East St. Louis Toodle-oo, Black Beauty, The Mystery Song, Jungle Nights in Harlem, Daybreak Express, Shout 'Em Aunt Tilly, Misty Morning, Black and Tan Fantasy,* the original *Old Man Blues, The Flaming Sword, The Giddy Bug Gallop, Dude, Conga Brava, Ko-Ko, Concerto for Cootie, Sepia Panorama, Blue Serge, Moon Mist, Dusk, Cotton Tail, The Flaming Sword, Never No Lament, Harlem Air Shaft, Across the Track Blues, Sherman Shuffle.*

French CBS has a similar series which will provide versions of *East St. Louis Toodle-oo, Black and Tan Fantasy, Old Man Blues, Creole Love Call, New Black and Tan Fantasy* and its *Prologue, New East St. Louis Toodle-oo, It Don't Mean a Thing, Braggin' in Brass, Azure, Slap Happy, Blue Light, A Gypsy Without a Song, The Sergeant Was Shy, Subtle Lament, Bundle of Blues, Echoes of Harlem, Lazy Rhapsody,* and *The Clothed Woman.*

11. COUNT BASIE AND LESTER YOUNG

The most recent United States issue of Basie with the Benny Moten band was on RCA Vintage LPV-514, which had *Moten Swing, Toby,* etc., and the *Jones Law Blues* from 1929.

The 1937–39 Basie classics including *Honeysuckle Rose, Swinging the Blues, Texas Shuffle, Jumpin' at the Woodside, Jive at Five, Blues in the Dark, Doggin' Around, You Can Depend on Me, Sent for You Yesterday, Roseland Shuffle, One O'Clock Jump, Topsy,* etc., are on MCA 4050E.

Columbia's *Lester Young Story* begins in Volume 1 (CG 33502) with the *Lady Be Good, Shoe Shine Boy* small group session, and includes *Me, Myself and I* and *A Sailboat in the Moonlight*. Volume 2 (CG 34837) has *When You're Smiling* in two "takes." Volume 3 (CG 34840) includes *Taxi War Dance* in two "takes," and *Twelfth Street Rag*. And Volume 4 has *Song of the Islands, Tickle Toe, Dickie's Dream* in three "takes," and *Lester Leaps In* in two "takes." Missing is *Nobody Knows*, last available on Columbia Encore P14355, "*The Count.*"

Count Basie and the Benny Goodman Sextet on *Gone with "What" Wind* are included in Columbia G 30779 "*The Charlie Christian Story.*"

The small group, piano-less Kansas City Six sessions with *Way Down Yonder in New Orleans, I Want a Little Girl, Them There Eyes,* etc., each with alternate "takes," are collected on Commodore XFL 14937.

Blues for Helen is a part of Vanguard's album "*Spirituals to Swing: The Legendary Carnegie Hall Concerts of 1938–39*" (VRS 8523-4); also included in that set, incidentally, is *Mortgage Stomp*, a sketch for the masterpiece, *Lester Leaps In*.

Classic post-1950 Basie (beautifully played but not well balanced for the recording) are the "live" performances originally on Verve MGV 8199, "*Basie in London,*" which has the best *Shiny Stockings.*

Again, French CBS is involved in issuing a "complete" Basie, all the selections recorded for the American Columbia labels in the 1930s and early 1940s.

The post-Basie *These Foolish Things* last appeared on Blue Note LA456-H2, and the broadcast version with Nat Cole on the "collector's" label Spotlite SPJ 119. The 1949 *Ding Dong* session is on Savoy SJL 2202.

12. CHARLIE PARKER

Charlie Parker's *Lady Be Good* solo was included in the album "*The Charlie Parker Story*" (Verve MG-V 8100-3). That set was a cross-section of Parker's work belonging to Verve and has the *Just Friends* with strings, and the *What Is This Thing Called Love?* with strings. The set consequently duplicated some (but not all) of the selections listed below in the Verve Parker "Genius" series. The Norvo *Hallelujah* was last on Parker Record PLP 408.

The Parker Dial selections last appeared in the United States in a limited edition boxed set on the Warner Brothers label. The Dial selections in "*Very Best of Bird*" on Warners 2WB 3198 are not necessarily

the best selections nor the best "takes." The British Spotlite series of
Parker Dials was widely distributed in the United States and may still
be found. Spotlite 101 had *Moose the Mooche, Ornithology,* and *Night
in Tunisia;* Spotlite 103, *Relaxin' at Camarillo;* Spotlite 104, *Bird of
Paradise, Embraceable You, Dexterity;* Spotlite 105, *Klactoveedsedsteen, Scrapple from the Apple;* Spotlite 106, *Drifting on a Reed, Crazeology, Quasimodo*—in each case with alternate takes.

The historic Gillespie-Parker quintets and sextets are on Prestige
24030, and the Dizzy and Bird Carnegie Hall concert, including *A Night
in Tunisia* and *Confirmation,* was last on Roost 2234.

Savoy album 5500 collects all of the titles recorded for that label,
record date by record date, *Koko, Billie's Bounce, Now's the Time,
Parker's Mood, Bluebird,* and the rest, again with alternate takes. And
Savoy SJL-2210 collects the originally released takes of each piece.

In general the Savoy series has Miles Davis, Tommy Potter, and Max
Roach, but the pianist will be Duke Jordan, John Lewis, or Bud Powell,
depending on the date.

From the *"Genius of Charlie Parker"* series on Verve, Volume 2 (8004)
is the with strings set with *Just Friends.* Volume 3 is a collection of
quartets, and includes a version of *Confirmation* (Verve 8005). Volume 4
(8006) is the "reunion" with Gillespie, with Monk on piano, including
Bloomdido, Mohawk, Melancholy Baby. Volume 7 (8009) has *Card-
board, Visa, Passport.* Volume 8 (8010) has *Swedish Schnapps, Lover
Man, She Rote.* The Verve material was also collected on VE 2501, 2512,
and 2523.

13. THELONIOUS MONK

Blue Note set LA 579-HZ includes the 1948–50 classics *Evidence, Criss
Cross, Eronel,* and *Four in One.*

Smoke Gets in Your Eyes and *Let's Call This* were on Prestige 7508,
"The Golden Monk." Monk's solo on *Bag's Groove* with the Miles
Davis group is on Prestige 7650E. Riverside 6068, *"The Unique Monk,"*
includes *Tea for Two* and *Just You, Just Me.* Monk's best recording of
'Round Midnight, plus the blues *Functional* (the first take is prefer-
able), and the solos on *I Should Care, All Alone,* and *You Took the
Words Right Out of My Heart* are in *"Pure Monk,"* Milestone 47004.
Trinkle Tinkle and other performances with John Coltrane are on
Milestone M-47011. And the best *Blue Monk* was on Prestige 7363E.
Prestige 24006E is a two-LP set from that label's Monk.

Monk as a member of Coleman Hawkins's quartet was issued on

Prestige 7805, and Monk as a participant in the Minton's jam sessions was on Everest 5233. *Gallop's Gallop,* a far from ideal version of a superior piece, was on Savoy 12137. Monk with the Art Blakey Jazz Messengers was on Atlantic 1278.

"*Monk's Dream,*" Columbia CL 1965, had second versions of *Bolivar Blues, Just a Gigolo, Sweet and Lovely, Body and Soul,* and *Five Spot Blues.* And the big band versions of *Evidence* and *Epistrophy* were last included in Columbia KG 32892.

14. JOHN LEWIS AND THE MODERN JAZZ QUARTET

The suite called *Fontessa* which was on Atlantic 1231 formed the concluding sections of *The Comedy.* The themes called "Harlequin," "Pierrot," and "Colombine" were originally a part of Lewis's Atlantic 1272.

Most of the several recorded versions of *Bag's Groove* by the Quartet would bear out my point about John Lewis and the blues, beginning with his solo on the version which appeared on Atlantic 1265. The John Lewis version of *I Remember Clifford* was on Atlantic 1375, as is the best version of *Two Degrees East, Three Degrees West.*

The four titles from 1948 by Milt Jackson, Lewis, Clarke, Al Jackson, and Chano Pozo have been issued on Galaxy 204. Savoy SJL-1106 collects the Quartet's 1951 work, including the first *Softly, as in a Morning Sunrise,* but mechanical distortion crept into some of the tracks in transfer to a twelve-inch LP. The later *Morning Sunrise* is in the Prestige two-LP set 24005 as are *Concorde* and *Ralph's New Blues,* the 1954 version of *Django, Vendome,* and *Autumn in New York.*

The Quartet's version of *God Rest Ye Merry, Gentlemen* was on Atlantic 1247.

Lillie is on Blue Note LA590-H2, as is *What's New* and Jackson's version of *Willow, Weep for Me* with Thelonious Monk is on Blue Note LA579-H2. The session with Horace Silver that included *I Should Care* and *My Funny Valentine* is on Prestige 24084.

The later *Willow, Weep* by the Quartet was on Atlantic 1231. *How High the Moon* was included in Atlantic 1325, along with a version of *Django* and *It Don't Mean a Thing (If It Ain't Got That Swing). The Golden Striker* and the triple-fugue *Three Windows* were on Atlantic 1284.

Three Little Feelings was reissued on Columbia PG 33402. The sound track for *Odds Against Tomorrow* appeared on United Artists 4061.

The "*European Concert*" set by the Modern Jazz Quartet, with versions of *Django, I Remember Clifford, It Don't Mean a Thing, Festival Sketch, Bluesology, Bag's Groove,* etc., is Atlantic 2-603. Also recommended is the Quartet's *"Last Concert"* on Atlantic SD2-909.

Among the many exceptional Milt Jackson blues solos, there is *Opus Pokus* on Savoy SJL-1116, which reinterprets some traditional blues ideas with new insights.

15. SONNY ROLLINS

Rollins's earliest recordings, with Bud Powell's groups, are collected on Blue Note 81503E and 81504E. And his own first record date is, including *Mambo Bounce,* on Prestige 7856E. Prestige 7847E includes the Miles Davis collaborations, *Airegin, Oleo,* and *Doxy.* *"Tenor Madness"* is Prestige 7821E, and *"Saxophone Colossus"* with *Blue 7* can be found as Prestige 7326 and in the two-LP set on Prestige 24050.

"Way Out West" is Contemporary 7530. A version of *Misterioso* with Monk and Rollins is on Blue Note 81558E. And *Vierd Blues* is on Prestige 24012, along with *In Your Own Sweet Way. Blues for Philly Joe* is in *"Newk's Time"* on Blue Note 84001. A version of *If Ever I Would Leave You* was included in *"What's New?"* in RCA ANLI-2809.

"A Night at the Village Vanguard" is Blue Note 81581E. The "unauthorized" *There'll Never Be Another You* and *Three Little Words* are in Impulse 1A-9349. And the studio *Three Little Words* and *Alfie's Theme* are in AS-9236-2. *Freedom Suite* is Milestone MSP 9042. Rollins's *B. Quick* is in Prestige 24082. And the Don Byas *I Got Rhythm* is on Commodore XFL 14938.

16. HORACE SILVER

The Miles Davis "all-star" *Walkin'* and *Blue 'n' Boogie* are on Prestige 7608E. On Blue Note 81518E are pieces by Silver, Kenny Dorham, and the Art Blakey Jazz Messengers, including *The Preacher, Room 608, Hippy, Stop Time,* and *Doodlin'. Señor Blues* is on Blue Note 84017. Blue Note 1589 with Art Farmer as a member of the Silver quintet included *Moon Rays* but as of this writing it is long out of print in the United States. *Sweet Stuff, Cookin' at the Continental, You Happened My Way,* and *Mellow D* are on Blue Note 84008. *The Saint Vitus Dance, Sister Sadie,* and *Blowin' the Blues Away* are on Blue Note 84017.

17. MILES DAVIS

The early Miles Davis session which included *Skippin' at Bells* and *Little Willie Leaps* is included in Savoy SJL 2201.

Capitol T 1974, "*The Birth of the Cool*," offered *Israel, Jeru, Godchild, Move,* and the rest of the Davis nonet performances. The sessions for Blue Note with J. J. Johnson which included *Ray's Idea, Chance It, Woody 'n' You, I Waited for You, Enigma,* and *Weirdo* are on Blue Note 81501 and 81502.

Prestige 7608E had *Walkin'* and *Blue 'n' Boogie;* Prestige 7650E collected the all-star session on *Bag's Groove, The Man I Love,* etc. *Sid's Ahead* was on Columbia PC 9428E. Of the several LPs by the Davis quintet that featured John Coltrane, "*'Round About Midnight*" (Columbia PC 8649E) is perhaps the best; it includes *Bye Bye Blackbird.* The later *Bye Bye Blackbird,* along with *Neo, Well You Needn't,* and *No Blues,* were on "*In Person*," Columbia C2L 20. The concert performances of *Autumn Leaves* and *All of You* are on Columbia PC 1682E.

"*Miles Ahead*" is Columbia PC 8633E and "*Porgy and Bess*" was CL 1274. "*Sketches of Spain*" with *Saeta* was on Columbia 1480.

"*Kind of Blue*," with *Flamenco Sketches* and *So What,* was on Columbia CS 8163.

Petits Machins was on "*Filles de Kilimanjaro*" (Columbia PC 9750); the same LP has a good "drone" piece by Davis called *Frelon Brun. Country Son* is a part of "*Miles in the Sky*" (Columbia PC 9628). And *Circle* can be heard on "*Miles Smiles*" (Columbia PC 9401). Indeed, the general level of composition and performance on "*Miles Smiles*" is very high. "*Sorcerer*" (Columbia PC 9532) is also representative of Miles Davis's better work in the 'sixties (one brief vocal track by Bob Dorough excepted), and has outstanding work by drummer Tony Williams in several selections.

Twelve of Davis's Columbia LPs have been collected in C6X-3697. "*Miles Davis at the Plugged Nickel, Chicago*" is CBS Sony 25AP.1.

18. SARA VAUGHAN

"*Great Songs from Hit Shows*" is a somewhat abbreviated version, but including *Little Girl Blue, Dancing in the Dark, It Never Entered My Mind,* and *Autumn in New York,* was last available on Trip Jazz TLP-5589. *Mean to Me* is on Columbia CSP P-13084, "*Sarah Vaughan in Hi-Fi.*"

Vaughan's *"No Count Sarah,"* with *Smoke Gets in Your Eyes* and *Stardust,* was last on Trip Jazz TLP-5562. And *"Sarah Vaughan and Count Basie,"* with *Lover Man, You Go to My Head,* and *I Cried for You,* was last on Emus ES-12010.

Stormy Weather was included in Emus ES-12007. And *"The Divine Sarah,"* with *Ain't No Use,* originally Roulette 52060, also briefly appeared on Emus.

The *"Live in Japan"* set, with the remarkable *Funny Valentine,* was Mainstream 2401. And *More Than You Know* is on Pablo 2310-821.

19. CHARLIE MINGUS

"Pithecanthropus Erectus" was last issued on Atlantic SD 8809. *"Tijuana Moods"* with *Los Mariachis* has several times appeared on RCA labels, most recently on RCA APLI-0939. *"Mingus Ah Um,"* with *Goodbye, Pork Pie Hat,* is on Columbia CS-8171. *"Let My Children Hear Music"* with *Hobo Ho* is on Columbia KC 31039. *Mingus, Mingus, Mingus* with *II B.S.,* the second version of *Celia* and a version of *Mood Indigo* were on Impulse AS-54. *Revelations* was a part of Columbia WL 127.

Song with an Orange and a version of *Mood Indigo* are on Columbia CS-1440, *"Mingus Dynasty."* I do not recommend the posthumous re-editing of several of Mingus's recordings, represented on Columbia CG-30628; they seem to me to confirm the wisdom of their original versions.

Atlantic 1260, *"The Clown,"* had *Haitian Fight Song.* And Atlantic 1305 had *Cryin' Blues, Moanin',* and *E's Flat, Ah's Flat Too.* (Some of Mingus's Atlantic selections have also been anthologized.) *"Mingus at Monterey,"* with the Ellington medley, and *Meditations on Integration* appeared on Fantasy JWS-1/2. As *So Long, Eve,* the latter piece was on Fantasy JWS-9, *"Mingus at Town Hall."* Limelight LS 86015, *"Mingus Revisited,"* had *Prayer for Passive Resistance,* and that LP was reissued on Trip TLP 5513. *"My Favorite Quintet,"* with *She's Funny That Way, Embraceable You, I Can't Get Started,* and *Ghost of a Chance,* last appeared on Fantasy JWS 5.

The superb *Stormy Weather* was last included in Barnaby album 2BR 6015, along with the Mingus-Dolphy "new thing" performances *What Love, All the Things You Could Be by Now,* etc.

20. JOHN COLTRANE

Miles Davis's '*Round Midnight* last appeared on Columbia PC 8649E. Coltrane and Monk can be heard on Milestone 47011, which includes *Trinkle Tinkle*.

Miles Davis's version of *Straight No Chaser* was on Columbia PC 9428E, as was *Milestones*. *Blue Train, Locomotion,* and *Moment's Notice* were on Blue Note 81517. The Davis *"Kind of Blue"* set was Columbia CS 8163.

Giant Steps, Naima, and *Countdown* were on Atlantic 1311; *My Favorite Things* on Atlantic 1361.

Chasin' the Trane is on Impulse A-10; *Impressions* on Impulse A-42. *In a Sentimental Mood* and *Take the Coltrane* are on Impulse A-30; the *"Crescent"* LP is Impulse A-66. *A Love Supreme* is on Impulse A-77. Coltrane's *Ascension* is on Impulse A-95. And *Meditations* is on Impulse A-9110.

One addition: *Three Little Words,* which was on the LP *"Bags and Trane"* (Atlantic 1368), for the pacing of Coltrane's adventurous solo.

Atlantic's *"The Art of John Coltrane"* (SD2-313) included *My Favorite Things* and *Giant Steps.*

21. ORNETTE COLEMAN

Basic Ornette Coleman:

Peace, Focus on Sanity, Lonely Woman, Congeniality, and *Chronology,* were on *"The Shape of Jazz To Come"* on Atlantic 1317.

Free Jazz is on Atlantic 1376.

The Stockholm recordings are Blue Note 84224, with *Dawn;* and Blue Note 84225, with *Snowflakes and Sunshine, The Riddle,* and *Antiques.*

Trouble in the East was Impulse AAS-9187, a two-record set not available singly.

Supplementary Coleman:

Jayne, Angel Voice, Chippie, The Sphinx, and *Invisible* are on *"Something Else!"* (Contemporary 7551).

"Tomorrow Is the Question," with *Lorraine* and *Tears Inside* is Contemporary 7569.

Ramblin' and *Free* are on *"Changes of a Century"* (Atlantic 1327). *Beauty Is a Rare Thing* is on Atlantic 1353.

C. & D. and *R. P. D. D.* are on Atlantic 1378. And Coleman on tenor, with *Cross Breeding* and *Mapa,* can be heard on Atlantic 1394.

Coleman's performance on *Abstraction,* and his interpretation of Thelonious Monk's *Criss Cross,* were on Atlantic 1365.

"Ornette Coleman, Town Hall, 1962" on ESP Disc 1006 had a version of *Sadness,* and a piece called *Doughnut* in which (as far as I know) the idea of spontaneous, collective changes of tempo first appears. I am told that Coleman likes his playing on *The Ark* from the same LP. Another version of *Sadness* and also of *Doughnut* can be heard on *"An Evening with Ornette Coleman"* released in England on a two-record set on International Polydor 623 246/247. (These two albums also include works by Coleman for string quartet and woodwind quartet—both of which are outside the limits of this discussion.)

"New York Is Now!" (Blue Note 84287) has *Round Trip, Broadway Blues,* and *The Garden of Souls* (plus a rather boyish joke that doesn't come off called *We Now Interrupt for a Commercial).*

Don Cherry's *Complete Communion* is Blue Note 84226.

Smithsonian Collection releases are available through Smithsonian Recordings, P.O. Box 10230, Des Moines, Iowa 50336.

In the search for individual selections and titles, well-stocked shops will usually make the standard, loose-leaf reference volumes (which list the contents of LPs by individual selection) available to customers. Or a sympathetic, knowledgeable clerk will help.

The following North American shops specialize in jazz and will usually have both rare items and imports available:

The Jazz Man Record Shop, 3323 Pico Blvd., Santa Monica, CA 91205.

Ray Avery, Rare Records; 417 E. Broadway; P.O. Box 10518, Glendale, CA 91205.

Jazz Record Mart, 11 West Grand Avenue, Chicago, IL 60610.

Jeff Forsythe, 14 Jason Lane, Mamaroneck, NY 10543.

Coda Publications, P.O. Box 87, Station J, Toronto, Ontario M4J 4X8, Canada.

These two specialize in direct imports that are not otherwise available, frequently Japanese imports:

Daybreak Express, P.O. Box 250, Van Brunt Station, Brooklyn, NY 11215.
Dan Sevro, 165 William Street, New York, NY 10038.

And here is a partial list of British and Continental shops which specialize in jazz for the reader who may want to deal directly:

Dave Carey, The Swing Shop, 1-B Mitchum Lane, Streatham, London SW16, England.
James Asman's Record Centre, Mail Order Dept., 63 Cannon St., London EC4, England.
Jazz Bazaar, P.O. Box 1126, 5466 Neustadt, Germany.
Pierre Voran, Pan Musique, 35 rue de France, o6 Nice, France.

Discographical references include:

Jazz Records, 1897–1942 (in two vols.) by Brian Rust (Arlington House)
Jazz Records 1942–1967 (in several vols.) by Jorgen Grunnet Jepsen (Karl Emil Knudsen).

Discographies and other jazz books are available from:

Oak Lawn Books, Box 2563, Providence, RI 02907.
Walter C. Allen of Canada, Box 929, Adelaide Station, Toronto, Ontario M5C 2K3, Canada.

INDEX